Donkey's Years

Aidan Higgins was born in 1927. His books include the novels *Langrishe, Go Down* (1966), which won the James Tait Black Memorial Prize and the Irish Academy of Letters Award, and was filmed for television with a screenplay by Harold Pinter. *Balcony of Europe* was shortlisted for the 1972 Booker Prize. His selected shorter fiction, *Helsingør Station & Other Departures*, and travel writing, *Ronda Gorge & Other Precipices*, were published in 1989. The novel *Lions of the Grunewald* appeared in 1993 to great acclaim.

AIDAN HIGGINS

Donkey's Years

Memories of a Life
as Story Told

HIGGINS

Nil desperandum

Minerva

A Minerva Paperback
DONKEY'S YEARS

First published in Great Britain 1995
by Martin Secker & Warburg Ltd
This Minerva edition published 1996
by Mandarin Paperbacks
an imprint of Reed International Books Ltd
Michelin House, 81 Fulham Road, London SW3 6RB
and Auckland, Melbourne, Singapore and Toronto

A CIP catalogue record for this title
is available from the British Library
ISBN 0 7493 9694 6

Printed and bound in Great Britain
by Cox & Wyman Ltd, Reading, Berkshire

In Loving Memory

Bartholomew Joseph Higgins
1892–1969

Lillian Ann (née Boyd)
1892–1966

Josef Gustave Moorkens
b. Herentals, Belgium
1897–1952

Niet mijn will, o Heer,
maar de uwe geschiede
Luc. XXII, 42

Genadige Jesus, geef zijne
ziel de eeuwige rust

In the County Kildare the circumstances and appearance of the population located on the bogs, or in their immediate vicinity, are very unfavourable. On each side of those parts of the canal that pass through the bog, the land is let in small lots to turf-cutters who take up their residence on the spot, however dreary and uncomfortable. Their first care is to excavate a site fit for habitation on the driest bank that can be selected, which is sunk so deep that little more than the roof is visible; this is covered with scanty thatch, or more frequently with turf pared from the bog, laid down with the herbage upward, which is superficially assimilated with the aspect of the surrounding scenery that the eye would pass it over unnoticed, were it not undeceived by the appearance of the children and domestic animals sallying from a hole in one side, and by the occasional gush of smoke from the numerous chinks in the roof. The English language is everywhere spoken.

Samuel Lewis Esquire
A Topographical Dictionary of Ireland,
1837

I do not long for the world as it was when I was a child. I do not long for the person I was in that world. I do not want to be the person I am now in that world then.

Alan Bennett

The stench of sensation is like anaesthetic made visible.

Eudora Welty

Contents

Preface

In the Civil Survey 1654–56 the lands of Ballymakealy, Tirow and Sealstown are described as merging 'on the East with the lands of Kildrought, on the West with the lands of Griffenrath, on the North with the lands of Castletown and the lands of Mooretown, and on the South with the lands of Ardresse' (Ardrass).

According to the same survey Possockstown (Roselawn) was west of the lands of Ballymakealy. Griffenrath had for long periods been farmed by the Dongans of Possockstown and possibly for that reason came to be so described. In 1643–44 during the wars there were references to Thomas Dongan of Griffenrath, Balligorne and Possockstown receiving special protection.

Richard Talbot, Duke of Tyrconnell who acquired Allen's interest in Ballymakealy, Tirow and Sealstown was brother of Mary, wife of Sir John Dongan of Castletown and Possockstown, and thus had a special interest in acquiring the adjoining lands of Ballymakealy.

Richard Talbot's estates were confiscated following the defeat of the Jacobites and his death during the Siege of Limerick, but his widow Frances Countess Dowager of Tyrconnell succeeded in establishing her claim to the lands of Ballymakealy, Sealstown, Tirow and Oldtown as those lands were part of her jointure.

Bartholomew Van Homrigh purchased Ballymakealy and Oldtown and had to be content with allowing the Duchess to retain the lands for her lifetime.

xi

The Duchess was to outlive all the Van Homrighs and
died in 1730 aged ninety-two.

The house called Springfield must have been built by
John Clarke who in 1763 granted to John Franklin, then of
Springfield, 'All parts of the lands of Ballymakealy, Saltstown
and Tirow containing 70A-3R-7P Irish Plantation Measure
in which is included the part lately occupied by Richard
Hawkshaw Esquire and also that part which John Clarke
lately had in his own hands and the whole equals that
granted by William and Katherine Conolly to John Clarke
except 40A-3R-3P which is on lease to Denis Tilbury (now
T. Tyrrell's) together with the dwellinghouse and all other
edifices and buildings on the said lands'.

John Franklin sold his interest to Richard Phillips of the
2nd Regiment of Foot for the sum of £284–3–3. In 1780
Richard Phillips married Dorcas Sheperd daughter of Rev.
Samuel Sheperd Vicar of Kildrough and two years later
leased it to Richard Baldwin Thomas of Dublin; Ballymakealy, Saltstown and Tirow, then known as Springfield, and
held under lease of 15th September 1763 for three lives in
Perpetual Renewal at a yearly rent of £80.

The property was then described as 'All that part known
as Springfield with the dwellinghouse edifices and buildings
thereon and containing 70A-3R-7P'.

From 1780 onwards, Springfield had a succession of
owners. Nicholas Archdall Esq. was succeeded by Thomas
Long, a member of the Dublin family of coach-builders,
who in 1801 leased to James Langrishe and to his heirs 'all
that part of the lands of Springfield containing 47 acres
with the dwelling-house and outoffices in as ample a manner
as held by Thomas Long, for the lives of Christina Clarke
née Finey daughter of George Finey and wife of John
Clarke, Williamina Baillie wife of Arthur Baillie and Miss
Catherine Clarke only daughter of John Clarke survivor of
them'.

Catherine Clarke later married Richard Nelson and their

interest in Springfield continued until it was acquired by the Earl of Leitrim.

In 1806 Revd James Langrishe, Archdeacon of Glendalough, leased to Francis Walker of Elm Hall, Celbridge. In Pigotts Directory of 1824, Capt. John Bradshaw of Springfield is named as one of the Gentry of the Celbridge area. He leased the dwelling-house and outoffices with 33 acres to James Williams in 1833. Williams was succeeded by John Thomas Haughton, son of the late Jeremiah Haughton of the Celbridge Woollen Mills. He occupied from 1845 and was in possession of the house, outoffices and two gate-lodges with 52 acres of land. Jeremiah Haughton was succeeded by John J. Langrishe who died before 1889, when, according to the Valuation Books, his widow Maria Langrishe occupied.

Mrs Langrishe died in August 1898, the last of the family to live at Springfield as the contents of her house were sold by public auction in October 1898.

Subsequent occupiers were Major Hamilton, Captain Mitchell, Captain Richard Warren and Mr Bart ('Batty') Higgins from whom Matthew Dempsey purchased in 1940.

'Springfield in the Townland of Ballymakealy'
by Lena Boylan. *The Celbridge Charter.*

Acknowledgements

I am indebted to the following kind persons for the data that made possible this memoir of lost times; of which a sequel (*Dog's Dinner?*) follows, if the writer is spared:

Mrs Fiona Adamczewski of De Crepigny Park, London; Mr Luke Baxter of the Longford Historical Society; Mrs Lena Boylan of Celbridge; Mr Matt Dempsey Jnr of Griffenrath, Celbridge; Mrs Teasie Connolly Fagan of The Manse, Co. Westmeath; Fr Roland Burke-Savage, SJ, of Clongowes Wood College; Mr and Mrs Charlie Clements of Killadoon; Professor Cormac Ó Gráda of University College, Dublin; Mr Geoffrey Rowe of Greystones; Mrs Camilla Smyth of Carrick-on-Shannon; Mr Tom Newman of Melview, Longford; Mrs Margaret Moorkens of Terenure, Dublin; Mrs Lyndie Wright of Islington, London; Mr Alistair Campbell of Bath; Mr Syl Higgins of the Battery Road, Longford; Mr Stefan Bailis of Wichita Falls, Texas; his mother Mrs Moira Bailis of New Jersey; Dr Niall (Paddy) MacAllister of Baltimore, Maryland; Mrs J.D. Higgins of Muswell Hill Broadway; Mr John Gibson, librarian of *Irish Times*; Mr Stephen Higgins of Bloomington, Minnesota.

PART I

Kildare

The Great Flood

I am consumed by memories and they form the life of me; stories that make up my life and lend it whatever veracity and purpose it may have. I suspect that even before I saw the light of day on 3rd March 1927 I was already being consumed by memories in Mumu's womb and by her memories prior to mine and by her granny's prior to her, bypassing my mother, stretching as far back as accommodating memory could reach into the past.

My first conscious memory is of our village being flooded, which would have been 1933 when I was but six years old. Our nanny, Nurse O'Reilly – a longshanked rawboned buck-toothed Cavanwoman of indeterminate age who took no nonsense from anybody but her superiors, who knew her place – would have been unable to push the pram much beyond the Abbey on the outskirts of Celbridge, through the water lapping against the wall of Flynn's bicycle shop and flooding Darlington's forge.

I was a year older when the Woolfs drove into Celbridge in style and inquired the way to Marlay Abbey, the home of Swift's devoted Vanessa, country seat of the Dutchman Vanhomrigh, Quartermaster for General Ginkel on the winning side at the Boyne, a bad battle to lose.

The posh London diarist looked about with some disdain ('Grafton Street is not on the level of Sloane Street,' she noted sniffily), noticed the grey sham-Gothic Abbey weathered to look ancient (even Time was deceitful in Ireland) with its sham-Gothic windows blocked up. It was a brief courtesy visit and they missed Vanessa's Bower.

Mumu read, recited, chanted to us (the Dote and I), rarely sang. Where Have You Been, Billy Boy? Billy Boy? Abdul the Bulbul Amir. James, James, Morrison, Morrison, Wetherby George Dupree took great care of his mother, though he was only three. Mumu held my elbows and bounced me up and down on her lap, laughing in my face, bringing my hands together, chanting Clap hands, clap hands till Daddy comes home! Pies in his pocket for baby alone!
    'Dead easy,' brother Bun said, strolling about in his CWC blazer, hands in pockets. 'Buck privates.'
    Mumu spoke feelingly of 'hard' and 'soft' water for washing and drinking purposes; very conscious of how the wind blew and the changing quality of wind; the soft winds of summer, the cold east wind of spring, the north wind of winter.

Dado held me in his arms at the nursery window, pointing to the wonders of the world without. A goat in a tree, flying fish over a meadow, sailing boats disappearing into clouds. I fidget in his arms, turning like a top spinning, always missing the sailing boat hidden in the clouds, the goat hidden in the leaves, the flying fish hidden in the meadow. All I see are clouds passing over Springfield, cowslip dancing in the meadow, a tree quivering where something living has just flown out of it.
    'Ah Da! ah Da!' I cry, twisting and turning in his arms. 'Lemme see!'
    Dado holds back his head and laughs at me. He smells of hair-oil, linseed oil, his quiff is parted in the centre like

Mandrake the Magician, he wears pointy patent-leather shoes. 'Look A.,' he says, torturing me. 'Can you see it?'

I draw stick-men with straight lines for arms and legs and a circle for the face, with broomhandle hair sprouting as on the gollywog on the jamjar, with vacant expressions stamped on their moony faces.

'Can you do pooley?' Nurse O'Reilly asks us.

For lost things Mumu advises a prayer to Saint Anthony; and the lost things turn up in the strangest places; the half-solid ball behind the hotpress door, the pencil-sharpener behind the mangle, the Yo-Yo in the knitting basket, the cricket bat under the bed, *Ballygullion* under the bath.

A coalfire burns in the kitchen range, the Dote cries because his hands are frozen after riding back from eight o'clock mass. Old Mrs. Henry roasts a rabbit in the oven. At Christmas at the back of the church by the confessional (PP Revd. Fr. Hickey), in the holy crib among the straw, the Holy Family appear to be dead. Saint Joseph crouches forward, staring with a dead man's vacant stare at the dead mannikin in the straw. A coffin is mounted on trestles by the curate's confessional

'The days are drawing out,' Dado announces.

'Where are the snows of yester-year?' asks Mumu.

Out for a spin towards Clane we run over a cat at Barberstown Cross. I look back and see its guts stuck to the road across which a patriotic hand had chalked 'UP DEV!' and beyond it from ditch to ditch another hand has scrawled 'O'DUFFY IS THE MAN!'

'Don't look back,' my father advises, his gloved hand on the steering wheel. 'Never look back.' We drive grandly on.

Lizzy had put his best suit in the oven, to air; the sick

black kitten crept in, the oven door was closed and next morning the kitten is removed stiff as a board.

'Got any tickles?'
  No.
  'No tickles for Aunt Cissy?'
  No.
  'I just can't believe that!' cries the hearty aunt. 'Cissy will soon find out.'
  Now practical fingers probe and dig into me, her strong hands hold me, begin to torture. I am alive with tickles. It's a Chinese torture.
  I wet myself, howling with laughter, tumble off the sofa, squirm like a snake on the carpet, wet myself some more, mortified with shame. The hearty aunt is all over me, tickling, laughing, spluttering. I lie dead with embarrassment on the carpet. An amused strange face regards me fondly. My aunty is the famous horsewoman who rode champions, won cups, laid into lazy mounts with a switch, mucked-out stables at cockcrow, could drink Lough Erne dry.

'Who wants a piggyback ride?' asks Dado, down on his hands and knees on the carpet.
  I ride on his back. He is an elephant. We are in India, in the Punjab, I hold on to his huge elephant ears. He trumpets at the young Raja in a turban on the veranda. His back shakes, he bucks me off behind the sofa. Now he is a bucking bronco in Texas. I am a cowboy. Rita Phelan sings:

> I'm a rambler, I'm a gambler,
> I'm a long way from home.
> But if you don't like me
> Just leave me alone!

Our cat has a mouse in its mouth. The cat takes it into a corner and plays with it. Tired of play, curving its paw, pushing, kitty bites the mouse's head off, begins to eat it. I hear the crunch of little bones; the tail sticks out and is swallowed last.

'Did you ever see a crow flying and a cat sitting on its tail?' Dado asks.

No.

'Then I'll show you. Watch this now.'

It's a riddle.

On a blank page of my sketchbook he draws a crow on the wing, a black bird on the wing that Dado calls Crow, and, below, spells out C R O W. He turns over a page and draws a smiling cat with whiskers and spells beneath it C A T, sitting on its own tail. My father shows me the crow flying and then on the next page the cat sitting on its own tail. It's a trick question.

'There,' says Dado.

I am sick.

If I take the medicine and stay in bed and do as the doctor says, Dado promises to give me a surprise present.

'What?'

'I can't tell you what. It's a surprise.'

'Well, tell me what it's *like*. What does it look like?'

'It looks like nothing.'

'It can't.'

My father thinks.

'It's something with whiskers that you keep in a glass cage.'

On the verge of sleep I heard the intruder climb the paling below and jump heavily onto the scuffled gravel, and heavy dragging footsteps slowly cross the gravel and climb the steps and pass through the open front door. Crossing the hall the slow dragging steps came on, ascending the stairs, turning in on our landing, passing the hot-cupboard and now I heard the harsh rasping breath outside the nursery door, which slowly opened, gave inwards. Rigid with fright I sank slowly under the bedclothes, but not soon enough, for the horror had already entered, its huge shadow crowding over the ceiling lit by the wavering blue night-light before Gina Greene's altar. The apparition filled the nursery – the rasping breath, the sound of nailed boots; the puttees and tin helmet, the heavy service revolver in its holster, the baggy cavalry twill worn as if on a scarecrow or a dead man. I heard the glass case being roughly opened and the sound of rummaging as the intruder did what he had come to do. The gloved hands were fumbling at the toys, the breath rasping. He left, making no attempt at secrecy, the slow footsteps dragging themselves along, retreating down the landing, dragging the sack behind, onto the carpeted stairs, then limping across the hallway, out the front door, across the gravel, over the paling.

I heard him scale the far paling and enter the plantation and came up from under the bedclothes to find the glass case hanging open and all our toys and books gone, a note stuck to the glass. Someone was having a good laugh at our expense down in the plantation, dressed as an officer of the British Army in the Great War.

A note in a sprawling slapdash rascally hand was sellotaped to the glass: 'I take, therefore I am.' And below that:

> 'Danger – Stranger!
> H E   W H O   I S
> (signed)   The Evictor.'

If Dado was not exactly our Arts Master he liked to watch us when we were drawing and colouring with pencils and sometimes invited himself into the circle and then would be asked to draw.

He always sketched the same profile of this long-nosed man with elephant ears and centre parting in his oily quiff (himself) always facing left. Then out of the nostrils some-thing was expelled like vertical strokes of rain, a sudden rainfall out of clouds. What could it be?

'Snot!' we screeched. 'It's snot!!'

Mumu would have considered this the very essence of vulgarity but he only smiled a knowing smile. To his cronies and equals he was Batty but to his employees and social inferiors he was M'striggins.

'Wait here,' Mumu would say to unexpected visitors who were always unwelcome, 'just wait here and I'll see if I can get him.'

He smelt of Brylcreem and whiskey and scent, sharpening the point of an incredible pencil and turning a page. He would write us a poem.

'Wait now lads,' he said, narrowing his eyes, touching his nose, thinking it over.

'Wait now,' he said, preparing to expel some scurrilous stuff.

He wrote:

> Miss Hart let out a fart,
> She tied it on a string . . .

But here, alas, inspiration died.

'Whaa din, Da?'

He deliberated afresh; then completed the clinching couplet:

> She kept it in Miss Coyle's house,
> Then let it go again!

Miss Hart, who cut our hair, lived in the village with a sick old mother who wheezed like a Pekinese. She asked awkward questions ('Would you fight your match?'). Miss Coyle was most ladylike and owned 'One Down' the piebald mare, groomed and ridden at steeplechases by Grogan with his cruel hands; but 'One Down' never won anything, not a sausage.

The pencil-sharpener is within a little blue and white globe

of the world that revolves in my hand as I turn it carefully
and there is the pleasant smell of lead and wood shavings as
the pencil is sharpened to a point and the wood shavings
curl from the globe. Gina Greene does not know how to
spell Pompeii but Mumu does and I spell it out to her
dictation.

I write out: 'The giant had a tiny hand and he passed
me.' And: 'The giant heard the boy laughing in the mountain.' And: 'Some of the Romans in Pompeii started poking
spears into the lava balls.'

'Where did you get that, my pet?' Mumu asks.

'I don't know.'

'Spelling improving,' Mumu says, laying her hand on my
head. 'Hot head.'

In the drawing-books that Dado buys for us at Woolworth's
in Grafton Street in Dublin the Dodo has drawn a menagerie
of jungle beasts; these were drawn and painted in when he
was our age. They are kept under lock and key in the
Lamproom which presently will become the Dodo's reference library with *Picture Post* and *Lilliput* and *Tatler & Sketch*
and *Illustrated London News* neatly piled and tabulated.

The Dodo had a careful and all-too-selective hand, those
white hands he was forever washing and scrubbing and
manicuring. He had drawn lions and little hunters in a
jungle and coloured them in watercolours to make them
come to life with lolling red tongues and dark manes caught
in mid-leap over the jungle path at the small hunters armed
with rifles, dwarfed by huge trees, all creepers and lianas
and pythons wreathed about high branches and monkeys
looking down at the little mannikins in khaki shorts, pith
helmets, bush-boots and puttees who fired at point blank
range at the lion whose head and outstretched claws disappear into the puffs of smoke from the rifle barrels.

With coloured plasticine and a nail file and his endless
patience the Dodo made a perfect little Robinson Crusoe
with a parrot on his shoulder and a fowling piece by his lap,

a dog by his foot, his face burnt terracotta by the implacable island sun scorching the sand, scorching Crusoe in his furs.

Grogan mucked out the stables, watered the horses, tipped a bucket into the tank full of tadpoles and frogspawn, swirled it about until he got a fill of bad-smelling water, whipped it out, rolled up his sleeves and washed his hands, forearms and neck in axle-grease. He asked us whether we wanted to 'see Dublin'. We said yes; it was a trick he played. He stood behind me with his stubby fingers pressed to my temples and lifted me up so that with slitty coolie eyes I 'saw' Dublin (i.e. nothing). 'Me now! Me next!' Now it was my brother's turn; Dublin was twelve miles to the west of us. All the horses were chomping hay in their loose boxes and Tommy Flynn was taking his melodeon off the big nail in the harness room and the bell was ringing from beyond Killadoon wood, so Clements's workers were knocking off for the day.

The poor and their mongrel dogs were clustering at the front door, stinking up the porch, asking for apples, begging for food and old clothes or anything that was being thrown out, and with implacably lofty bearing Mumu was mounting the stairs to find the Master in the study going over the rent-books and payments for field-hands and kitchen staff, and the good news was that he would be down presently.

'God bless you, Ma'am!'

Mumu recited:

> Beware and take care
> Of the Bight of Berin.
> Of the one that comes out
> There are forty go in . . .

Gina Greene recites:

> Little Polly Flinders
> Sat upon the cinders,
> Warming her pretty little toes;

> Her mother came and caught her
> And spanked her little daughter
> For spoiling her nice new clothes.

But who is this Polly Flinders? And who is Gina Greene?
Gina lives in the village with all the other Greenes in a dark
narrow hovel full of bicycles and dogs and sometimes helps
out at Springfield and Rita Phelan (the cat) says that I am
'soft' on Gina, who has long auburn hair done in plaits and
a lovely sweet smell and a lovely sweet smile so why wouldn't
I be soft on her?

Nurse O'Reilly, chomping with her great buck teeth, recites:

> There was a little man
> And he had a little gun;
> Up to the mountains he did run . . .

No, pipes up the Dote, that's wrong, and recites:

> There was a little man
> And he had a little gun;
> And his bullets were made of lead, lead, lead;
> He went to the brook and shot a little duck
> Right through the middle of the head, head, head.

In the kitchen Lizzy Bolger recites:

> There was a little man
> And he had a little gun,
> Up to the mountains he did run,
> With a bellyful of fat and an old Tom cat,
> And a pancake stuck to his bum, bum, bum.

Having made a disgusting stink my brother rises from his
pot, one arm upraised, to cry 'Mafeking is relieved! Hurrah!
Stinky, stinky parley voo!'

'That's not nice,' Nurse O'Reilly says.

The gramophone plays 'Hold Your Hand Out, You Naughty Boy', dust rises and is pierced by spears of sunlight, the heavy record revolves and music smelling of musty herbs issues from the slatted side of the box as a jolly male voice sings in a rollicking sort of a way:

> As you walk along the Bois de Boulogne
> You can hear the girls declare,
> 'He must be a millionaire! He must be a millionaire!'

I try to imagine Europe. Joss Moorkens stands with arms folded outside his dugout, waiting for the gas-attack; a train is about to leave a French station, on the side of the carriage is painted HOMMES-CHEVAUX, while a beery voice sings in German. It's the music of Franz Lehar. I try to imagine Vienna. Gay Vienna, city of a thousand melodies.

People are dancing, a carriage is drawn up before a lighted ballroom, Richard Tauber alights in top hat and silk scarf to sing 'Girls were made to love and kiss'. Georges Gautier sings in English, entering the chorus of 'O Bella Marguerita!' like a Riley running downhill without brakes. 'Picking Grapes With You!' 'Betty Co-Ed' follows, then 'The Man Who Broke the Bank at Monte Carlo'. The high strange male voices are all jolly but music makes me feel sad.

A ship under full sail with flags flying from the mizzen waits in the bay as Errol Flynn, smiling gallantly, grinning away under his moustache springs onto a rock and sheathes his sword, leaving Basil Rathbone to expire in a pool. Ronald Colman fights Douglas Fairbanks again, up and down winding narrow stairs in a castle, as I wade upstream and the wind blows in my long hair, I feel the secure weight of my sword by my side. I hear my brother calling. He is cutting quarter-staves in the plantation. I hear black slaves singing. The moon rises over the bay and the ship claps on full sail as a horn sounds in the forest.

I press down hard on my 2B pencil and the lead breaks.

A trapdoor opens at my feet and harsh voice exclaims, 'Villain!'

'On guard!' I cry out in a thin voice not my own.

Then 'The Stein Song' sung by beery weepy German voices. A little boy is flung from high battlemented walls, Rome burns. My father enters, poking into his ear with the end of a match.

'What's going on here?'

'Nothing.'

In the long steam-driven trains of the Great Southern & Western Railways, the first-class carriage into which we were ushered by Mr. Dooley with a formality that stopped just short of obsequiousness, smelled of stale cigarette smoke, trapped biscuity air, dusty upholstery, hair-oil; framed sepia photographs like aquatints were set above the plush, showing hardy souls in long loose bathing-drawers wading in the surf at Lahinch and Parknasilla and gents in baggy plus-fours struck poses on the golflinks at Greystones and Delgany. An advertisement for Fury's Coach Tours was phrased with old fashioned restraint: '*We Lead. Others May Follow*'.

Waggling its wings, a monoplane passed low over Springfield, circled about, and then came in again for a low pass over the front meadow. The daredevil airman Captain Shern, a friend of Dado's, waved gallantly, and flew straight through the telegraph wires, shearing them as if with secateurs. The wings wobbled, the engine coughed a few times, the pilot struggled with the controls. My father leaped off the front step and ran across the gravel, calling back, 'By Christ, I think he's down!'

But he wasn't, for the engine picked up again and the little plane flew out over the plantation, the pilot waving back, crazy in his goggles, heading off for Baldonnel Aerodrome. Dado said he was a gas card.

My three brothers and I, Desmond, Brendan, Colman and

myself, well-spaced out gallant walkers, none on speaking
terms, arrived at Hazelhatch Station in 'good time', following our long hike through the village. Dado liked to arrive
an hour before the train was due. He and the station master,
Mr. Dooley, paraded up and down the departure platform,
gossiping and sucking Zubes. The tall horse-faced man had
a lugubrious manner and stopped when Dado halted to
make a point. We watched them both in sullen silence,
hating this parade.

So the months passed agreeably enough.

Oh I knew my place all right; was I not that thinshanked
Papist brat? Timid, anaemic, diffident, else why permanently
unwell (whooping cough after infancy, adolescent cuts and
abrasions became sores that instantly went septic), always
difficult to feed (meals were eaten back to front, starting
with jelly and ending with soup), always faddy and averse to
any change, strange food, timid with strangers (the gent at
the garden gate who rattled small change in his trouser
pocket and asked, 'Is your daddy about, sonny?'), fearful of
nuns and priests (who were scarcely human), fearful of the
crumpled little nun who prepared us for First Holy Communion. Fearful ('I do be a-feared,' the Keegans said) of
the old deaf Bishop who confirmed us, gave us a stroke
upon the cheek, made us 'strong and perfect Christians'
(*moryaw*), fearful of big strong Gardai Siochana in blue
uniforms on big strong pushbikes with pumps under the
crossbar and truncheon at hip, afraid of the 'pinch-dark'
cellar.

Hidden behind the old cook's skirt smelling of flour or in
the currant bushes, that was my place.

'Me fawdur's out but me mudder's a-din,' I lied brazenly.
    'Do you want to grow up like your father?'
    'No.'
The visitor jingled the coins in his pocket and with a

strange lopsided smile twisting his lips handed me a half-crown through the bars of the gate.

But Dado had always told us to say that he was out but not expected back and no one knew where he was; when in fact he was sunbathing in the long grass and him covered in olive oil with nothing on but the handkerchief about his neck and another on his head, knotted at the four corners, himself soaked in olive oil and scalded by the sun.

The visitor went off whistling down the front avenue.

Mumu said that the Keegan boys were just hobbledehoys who had come up from the bogs. But the Dote and I went to school with John Joe and liked Patsy and we wore hobnail boots like them, sucked Bull's Eyes, amazed that John Joe ate his own wet snot; we spoke as they did (dey did) and had inherited their fears and prejudices. We said dis ting an' dat ting, dis, dat an' de udder ting, me brudder, me fawdur, me mudder. We were as they, felt as they, our pals, and Patsy Keegan was my best pal and I felt proud of his strained face and flared nostrils, of the superhuman effort he put into sailing over the hedge and ditch of water beyond, that sneery Neddy had dared him to jump. He was a true champion.

When did you last see a woman wringing her hands or an old fellow wearing vulcanite bicycle clips or nervous black greyhounds on the leash or the inextinguishable fires of wayside itinerants and their washing draped on hedges and bushes and they themselves (The Great Unwashed) none too clean?

I recall: Aladdin paraffin lamps and anthracite and coke and Bird's Custard and sago and tadpoles (pollywoggles) wriggling in the pond at the edge of the Crooked Meadow and cruel hare-coursing and blooding of hounds and the baying of the pack after foxes and twists of hardboiled sweeties in paper bags, a pennyworth and tuppenceworth, and Findlater's men carrying in a week's supplies and being checked by the cook and Wild Woodbines in open packets of five for tuppence halfpenny old currency with farthings in the change and the mad dog frothing at the mouth running in mad circles in humpy commonage near Oakley Park one lovely summer's day returning from the village with fags and brother Bun and I feeling sick and giddy from the first tobacco and the PP's alarming *Diktat* from the pulpit on Sunday and pea-picking for Mumu in the garden and the Bogey Man lurking in the cellar with the arrowheads and the mouldy masks and looking for mushrooms in Mangan's long field with Mumu and the Dodo early one morning in summer and the stink of ammonia in the convent class and the damp poor clothes in the hanging cupboard and the musty smell of nuns and the rustle of their habits and the small turf fire dying in the narrow grate when Sister Rumold prepared us for First Holy Communion and told us, 'You must prepare yourself to receive Our Lord' and the hot smell of the big girls and the provenance of sin – a writhing serpent impaled on the Patriarch's crozier and St Brigid the patroness blushing scarlet up on her pedestal and St Patrick watching with his curly beard – and the purple-shrouded statues at Passion Week and the whispering in the dim confessional and Crunchies in golden foil wrappings and chocolate whirls with whipped cream centres that the Dote and I called Dev's Snots and then Bull's Eyes and Peggy's Leg and liquorice twists and fizzy sherbets and stirabout with cream and brown sugar in the dark after early Mass and servants churning in the chilly dairy and butter pats in the tub and bluebottles buzzing against the larder screen and a snipe rotting on a hook and the cat-stink behind the mangle and the sheets airing on the stiffened hillocks of the frozen bleach-green and the tracks of the hare in the snow and lowing cows calving and calves on spindle legs suckling their mothers and mares foaling and stallions mounting with flared nostrils and sows farrowing and ewes lambing and the baldy priest in the awful brown wig saying mass below us at Straffan and the polychrome Christ bleeding with one

arm missing at the scourging in the Stations of the Cross
that stuck out in little polychrome grottos from the nave
and the nun with pinched bloodless lips genuflecting and
extinguishing candles with a long snuffer and the lovely byroad by the Liffey to Odlums' and the May procession
between the cypress trees along the convent avenue and the
gravel biting into my bare knees and I thinking only of
the cold roast with lots of salt and the ruffled nun walking
against the wind and ruddyfaced Sister Rumold nodding
her wimple – like the scuffed lining of a shallow Jacob's
biscuit tin or glacé fruit packings – and leaning forward
from her highbacked chair in the Holy Faith Convent wait-
ingroom and genteely offering Mumu a Zube from a little
oval box sprung open in her white speckled hand and my
mother in her blandest grandest way (with fur coat thrown
open so that the nun could get an eyeful of her expensive
Switzer's dress) saying how important education was and the
wimple nodding like mad for Sister Rumold couldn't agree
more, for the youngest (aged four) and myself (aged six)
the middle child were to be taken under her wing the
following Monday in the class of Second Infants and Lizzy
Bolger had painted her mouth with the reddest lipstick and
seemed to be bleeding from the mouth and was coaxing,
'Gizzakiss, ah g'wan!' and the big girls were tittering in the
playground and the men were playing Pitch & Toss after
Mass above Killadoon front gate and the hay-bogies were
grinding along the Naas-Celbridge road and the steamroller
belching smoke and stinking of tar and twenty Collegiate
College girls in slate-gray uniforms were rounding Brady's
corner and two teachers with long forbidding Protestant
horse-faces pacing along in front and their shadows flitting
along the wall and myself in great embarrassment cycling
rapidly by and Satan dining at Castletown (narrated dramatically by the Keegans as if they had been present, carrying
in steaming dishes) and the PP sweating and called in after
the Vicar couldn't shift His Nibs who sat there sneering and
then the PP showed him the crucifix and told him to go

about his business and the PP himself sweated seven shirts and died but Satan had gone straight through the floor in a puff of black smoke, leaving a cracked mirror behind as a memento as you can see to this day; all that I recall of those grand times that can never return.

I recall: the bridles and winkers and saddles and stitching and teasers and the stoked furnace going full blast with coal and Josey Darlington beating up sparks in the forge and the farriers and harness-makers of those days and the poor rabbit choking itself to death in the snare and the Bogey Man having breakfast with Dado in the Grand Hotel in Greystones when we were on holiday and the pair of them shaking out their napkins and telling dirty jokes and spooning prune juice into themselves and the suicide old Jem Brady lifted stiff out of the quarry (reputed to be depthless) in grappling irons pulled by the Guards and Nurse O'Reilly lifting up the Dote to view the corpse in its brown shroud in the coffin on trestles at the back of the church by the confessional and the soldiers firing patriotic volleys over the open grave of the patriot about to be interred.

Now read on.

2

The Keegan Boys

The Keegan boys had us constantly amazed.

They had a mysterious hieroglyphic language, peculiarly their own, utilising their own turds; as my young brother and I were to discover when we became friendly with the youngest brother John Joe, walking a mile to the Holy Faith Convent in the village near the site of an old brewery.

The brothers fought like cats and dogs among themselves; it was their nature, something the poor did. When our favourite, Patsy, the middle brother, was not torturing and tormenting John Joe, he in turn was being unmercifully set upon and bullied out of his wits by Neddy the eldest, a sadist in a cloth cap who smoked fags and played the mouth-organ.

Patsy was held head-down flush to the ground, one arm locked behind his back, Neddy grunting and tittering and Patsy pleading, 'Ah give over!' But the long cruel stringy arms held him as in a vice and Neddy gave off a sour smell of manly sweat, forcing the arm out of its socket.

'Ah Janey,' groaned Patsy, one with the earth. 'Ah be Janey Mack, give over!'

They knew nothing of '*Pax*!' nor any remission of unremitting chores from morning to night, chopping wood, hauling turf, running messages, doing chores about the cottage, each fighting for his own survival. They came out with great cuts of Boland's bread in their fists, chewing, taking gulps of strong tea, masticating the pap. They rolled up their sleeves and made a muscle, the blue veins swelling, throbbing. Neddy made catapults from forked branches and car tyres, set snares, killed what he caught, trapping the rabbit's head under his boot and yanking upwards or dispatching it with the heel of his fist in the nape of the neck. The rabbit made a sound like a sigh. The Keegans were great ones for riding bicycles, mending punctures, performing acrobatics. They went to bed early, for they were up betimes; saying the Family Rosary in the gloaming, all kneeling on the tiles of the kitchen floor, the old man giving out the invocation.

The brothers crouched at sudden stools as if about to burst, used the ditches and fields as open-air latrines, wiping themselves with leaves and grass. Their cottage had an outhouse earth-closet used by the parents and red Mona herself, the sister, but the three brothers 'went' in the woods and fields.

They were always promising to show us something unusual and one day right enough Patsy bade us follow him to see a marvel, and my brother and I followed him across the paddock, over the gate, and there on the slope of the bank by the hedge were steaming turds shat out as curlicues in the manner of stop-start cartoon animation or the stylish effects achieved with marzipan and icing by forcing-bags in Mrs Beeton cookery hints.

'Wha's dat? whaa's dis?' we asked, amazed.

'Bedad tis a furry fuhball match.'

A fairy football match!

Since they owned neither bathroom nor toilet nor pyjamas they stood at the door in their long-johns and pissed in great joyful parabolas of ascending and descending arcs into the yard, bouncing it off the outhouse door and upsetting the hens. Their powerful pee curved out like rainbows under clouds, John Joe's under Patsy's and Neddy's above, and the three pissers smiling to themselves, each holding his mickey with the utmost care and tenderness and delicacy, before they retreated and closed the door and knelt down for the Holy Rosary as they did every evening when the day's chores were done. My brother and I crouched on the roof of their outhouse with two Rhode Island Reds and marvelled at this. Communal crapping sessions in the plantation were to cement a fast bond of friendship between us and the three Keegans, all of us crouching and groaning manfully at stool. It was a token of trust and equality. We covered up and hid our craps with dead leaves, neat and clean as cats.

Casual labouring men passing through left their calling-cards in the form of gigantic stools in the bottoms of ditches, in the plantation and even close to the house in the side shrubbery where one was liable to tread in a Finn MacCool-ish evacuation left there as territorial claim or territorial insult, gradually acquiring a top-knot of fluff (unless dev-oured by crows) akin to the grassy mounds that are all that remain to us of the Norman motte-and-bailey defences. Great turds were also left balancing on a crumlech of stones, as a tribal threat, to indicate where those passing through had relieved themselves mightily.

In freezing weather the Keegan boys came out at dusk with jugs and basins of cold water which they threw down on the already icy road between the two lodges, to let it freeze solid overnight, and next morning they had a slide a good hundred yards long and were already using it in their hob-nail boots reinforced with brads at the toes.

In those days few cars went by, cyclists kept to the footpath and the turf carts remained at home as Neddy took a long run, jumped onto the slide and went sailing down, calling out, 'Wheeeeee!'

He had a splendid repertoire of styles invented on the spot, which Patsy attempted to elaborate on: arms out-stretched as if crucified, arms akimbo, hands in pockets or turning to face the way he came, gliding down backwards, twirling or hands clasped behind the back as if figure-

skating, crouched down on his hunkers and then slowly
rising up again, and then down again – this was 'The Postman's Knock'.

My young brother and I took many tosses, cutting hands
and knees but it was great gas all the same. The Keegans
spent as much time as they could between chores. Neddy
had to saw wood, pile some of it and bring some of it in,
Patsy had to cycle to Celbridge on messages for his ma (half
a stone of flour, a Boland's loaf, a dozen rashers), and John
Joe, bleeding like a stuck pig, had homework.

Otherwise we crept through the plantation, did our business, and had fine times in a yew tree with John Joe who
never blew his nose, never had a handkerchief, but always
had crusty nostrils or runny snot which he licked up, or
rather in, blowing his nose between thumb and first finger
like his da, old Ned.

Neddy was a fearless tree-climber and thought nothing of
ascending any of the tall pines until he was out of sight and
we had to run into the meadow to see him; we saw only his
cap come twirling down and heard the harmonica play
'Mairzy Doates' with all the glottal stops out. And there he
was eighty feet up, a fore-topman in the shrouds, swaying
and hallooing.

The big wooden door of the Abbey stableyard had a lich-
gate let into it, but both were closed and rarely opened and
the outer frame of the big door closely aligned to the wall,
flush with it, so that the inquisitive (i.e., myself) could not
see in. Such a fortress-like granite bulk with its sham-Gothic
windows permanently sealed up just below the battlemented
skyline that looked so hostile and forbidding in the setting
sun was suggestive of Rafael Sabatini or Baroness Orczy
castle-keep-and-moat costume-drama and Ronald Colman
and Douglas Fairbanks in acrobatic swordfights along the
lines of *The Prisoner of Zenda*, which we had seen at the Metro-
pole, or *Captain Blood* with Errol Flynn and Basil Rathbone,
who was wickedness personified, at swordplay on the sands.

Swordplay would take place on these battlements and

punitive acts be carried out secretly within the keep and hanged men with tongues lolling out be suspended from windows as dire warnings, like the dead rats I had seen strung up on palings by a farmer, and shrivelled away to skin and bone.

Dado had told me some such story involving a Judge Lynch of Galway town and how he had come to sentence his own son to death and stayed up with him all night preparing his (the son's) immortal soul for the hereafter following breakfast and the noose next morning; how the father hung the son 'with his own hands' from one of the windows overlooking the meandering main street that changed its name three times before it finished, ran out of names; topping him at daybreak. But there again I may have got the details all wrong and all that stayed with me was a dead man suspended from an arched window, swinging in the breeze, gaped at by passers-by.

The small barred Judas set high up in the narrow arched front door of the Abbey suggested a deterrent against importunate charity-seekers. I had seen one such desperate and very determined shawled beggarwoman with babe hidden in smelly folds of the shawl, persistently begging charity as her right; revealing just the crown of the babe's head, she asked charity only for the child. And then waiting by the closed door until it opened again, just wide enough for the nun's hands to reach out with the stale bread and the high meat and the closed door receive the most profuse and insistent thanks of Godblessandkeepyou and invocations to the Holy Mother and all the saints.

And sure enough, by 1952, some years after we had quit Springfield for pastures new, the Abbey and grounds had again reverted to Church hands and the charitable-minded Hospitaller Brothers of St John of God were using it as a community house for the overflow of mentally retarded and physically handicapped inmates from Oakley Park, renamed again and now St Raphael's; later again I scaled the battlements and dropped down to walk by a recently scuffled path, going on the edge, leaving no footprints. Shovels and rakes were as they had been thrown down at the summons of the bell or the whistle for teabreak and the Brother and his mentally defective charges had hurried off for scoff, and were out of sight in the stableyard with a half-wit scullion pouring out generous dollops of strong tea from an outsize taypot before handing around thick wedges of bread and butter.

My first troubling memory is of my younger brother (hereinafter The Dote, for whose sake I would be permanently two years behind at school and indeed would never catch up) grinding his teeth ferociously in sleep. This was dismissed by Mumu as worms but as nothing was ever done about it, the grimly determined teeth-grinding went on, as though my unconscious brother was turning something over in his mind; his embryonic nature expressing itself annoyingly as lead pencil screeching mindlessly across slate.

Dado owned (*owndid* had a more downright positive ring to it, as roundly pronounced by the Keegan boys, *I owndid it, it's mine!*) two gate-lodges and third lodge *forninst* Killadoon, all occupied by poor tenants who paid a nominal rent when they could, or no rent at all when they couldn't. The gate-lodges with rent-dodgers intact were situated at either end of the avenue, protected by brakes of timber. The front gate-lodge or East Lodge was occupied by the Keegans, the oldish couple Ned and Una, the three boys, Neddy, Patsy and John Joe and their sister Mona, the redheaded hot-tempered girl junior to Neddy but senior to Patsy, our pal.

The back or West Lodge was occupied since time immemorial by a genteel single Protestant lady, Miss Coyle, who *owndid* the race-horse called 'One Down', famous for never having won a race. 'One Down' was fed, watered and groomed by Burke, her bailiff, butler and general factotum, in our back stableyard, before Cooney took over the running of the stables. Mr Cooney had left his wife and run off with his pretty secretary, got into the London tabloids, become famous; a story that must not be told.

A wheezing tubercular tenant by the name of Collins occupied the third lodge opposite Killadoon back gate; a bachelor not in the best of health. He paid no rent, contesting that the place was alive with rats and had the Health Board condemn it as being unfit for human habitation, causing the roof to be removed; whereupon he retired in good order into Peamount Sanatorium in the foothills of the Dublin mountains where he passed away soon after, having wheezed his guts out.

All I recall of him was the constant terrible effort to catch his breath. He chainsmoked Wild Woodbines in open packets of five, racked with painful fits of coughing.

The Keegans were responsible for the opening and closing of the heavy wrought-iron gates by the front lodge, responding to the blare of the klaxon halfway down the avenue. Miss Coyle could not be expected to open the smaller and lighter gates by the back lodge, although she might do it as a favour, for she was a lady.

A masterly possessive squeeze of the right hand in its pigskin glove on the black rubber bulb clamped outside the driver's door would be sufficient to bring two or three Keegans running to force open the heavy gates with their shoulders and then stand aside, grinning and saluting as a guard of honour, to calls of 'Av'nin M'striggins!', one of them (generally Neddy) going out to direct the Overland into a clear road. The Guards were already bribed with loads of firewood to stay out of the way, his spies would be on the bridge, and a straight run through the village guaranteed to Hazelhatch Station and a long chat with Mr Dooley before the Dublin train arrived.

Molly Cushen in a gym-slip too small for her is forbidden to play with her skipping rope.

'Molly can give it a few twirls,' the old nun says, groaning. 'But there is to be no skipping or jumping.'

'Listen to what the priest tells you,' says the old nun.

'Do not play with yourself,' whispers the priest behind his cage at Confession.

'What's *adultry*?' I ask.

The old nun's redrimmed eyes stare at me from within her coif as if she can't believe her ears. She gives the desk a brisk rap with her knuckles and comes down off the little wooden rostrum to stand behind me.

'Don't ask such a question!' she cries, pushing me roughly in the small of the back. 'Don't you dare ask that! Adultery's a crime!'

The big girls are taught in the schoolroom at the bottom of the playground. I walk in procession behind the big girls who sing with ineffable sadness:

> Deep in Thy wounds, Lord,
> Hide and shelter me.
> So shall I never,
> Never part from Thee!

My brother and I leave our bikes behind the spare counter in King's shop where we buy the evening papers for Dado and the *Dandy* and *Beano* and *Hotspur* with the pennies we are given, or we buy three-tier buns.

'Do you mane to tell me you never herd tell of the celly brated outlaw Robin Hood?' Mr King, hands in trouser pockets, asks a customer who gapes at him in astonishment.

It was in the days before bicycles were chained. More than half the parish owned bikes and these were laid or flung indiscriminately by latecomers against the church walls or on either side of the great free-standing bell which could be heard ringing for Mass as far away as Killadoon when the wind was in the right direction, namely from the north-east.

Wielding cricket stumps as broad-swords with cricket pads

buckled to our arms as bucklers we clank in heavy armour
into a clearing in the shrubbery to fight a duel of honour,
while a girl with long brown hair who resembles cousin
Honor waits for the outcome, weeping and wringing her
hands, in a long conical headpiece like an elongated dunce's
cap and a thin off-the-shoulder dress, locked in a high battlemented tower, waving a small handkerchief.

I hear the girls' cries in the shrubbery and the bamboos
disturbed and a high excited voice (my cousin Maeve) calls
out, 'He's over here!' While the bamboos are being buffeted
I am hidden in a place where no one can find me; I can
move like a fox and no one can ever find me. I slip back
into the house. Maeve Healy is now coming downstairs in
shorts. Mumu says she is a minx, a slithery article, Miss
Notice Box. Mumu strongly disapproved of those who 'put
on airs,' drawing attention to themselves by showing off;
only 'consequential little articles' put on airs.

Lizzy strikes the dinner gong with the padded drumstick
and calls out, 'Are yiz all ready yit?' and the Dote comes in
his heavy armour through the front door, calling '*Pax*!'

I slip out of my pyjamas and hide behind the nursery door,
hearing Dado coming upstairs to say good-night to us. I
spring out and bending down open my behind like the
little black monkey in the Dublin Zoo, looking backwards
through my legs I see Dado's pointed shiny brown shoes
approaching and my brother runs upstairs without a stitch
but a duster on his head, disappearing into the schoolroom.

'That's not nice,' Dado says. 'Put your pyjamas back on.'

'He's just over-excited,' Mumu says.

'We were only being Fuzziwuzzies,' I say lamely, knowing
I have gone too far.

My brother, stark naked with boot-blacked face, is clashing
zinc chamber-pots together in the shrubbery.

'Get your brother in,' Dado says in a resigned voice.

'If you didn't know you were doing wrong, then you did
nothing wrong, pets,' Mumu said, tucking us in.

'We were being Fuzziwuzzies.'
'Of course you were.'

Embroidered like battle standards the banners of Passion Week glisten in royal purple and violent emerald above pews in the packed church in Celbridge and the heavy bell tolls in the yard outside and I smell incense and wood polish and the dense pong of the congregation coughing and shuffling their boots as the officiating priest in gorgeous vestments seems to wade about the altar and sings out in a phenomenally high voice, '*Credo in unum Deum!*' To which the mens' choir responds, '*Et in terra lux perpetua!*' in a deep collective drone. As incense ascends to the roof St Patrick and St Brigid are shrouded in purple with St Joseph and IHS, IHS, IHS trembles on the banners as they shift and I taste metal in my mouth. The rising incense and the deep drone makes me dizzy, the old priest moves in a dream of sanctity, his heavy vestments held up by two serving novices.

Flowers from Springfield garden adorn the high altar, brought by Mumu in the Overland and kept fresh in buckets of water and then arranged by her and the nuns where hundreds of wax candles burn. I read my prayer-book, feel holy, selected, pure as the driven snow.

Panis Angelicus!

a tenor solo sings out. The tabernacle door is open, the tabernacle empty, a breeze from the habits of the slowly passing veiled nuns touches my face, but my eyes are closed for Perpetual Adoration.

The carbide light makes a tunnel in the dark and I free-wheel down the hill past Muldowney's cottage and soon I feel the Holy Eucharist dissolve in my mouth and putting the tips of my fingers together I cross my thumbs and lower my head until my nose touches the index finger and feeling a vague holy love stirring I rise slowly and move backwards from a kneeling position at the altar where I have received

Holy Communion, and still with closed eyes, still entranced,
I move back to my place.

My brother comes clanking towards me in cricket pads worn
as breast-plates, an enamel chamber-pot strapped to his
head.

'On guard, villain!' he cries in a choked voice. 'I'll make
mincemeat of thee, varlet! On guard!'

We fight to the death.

We parley; he retreats wounded. We come together,
weapons clash.

'*Pax!*'

We refresh ourselves with Mi-Wadi. Wearing a loose woollen jersey knitted by Mumu in candy stripes but now with
the stitching run here and there along the arms, the tops
of his wellington boots turned down, the Dote approaches
resolutely for a bout of single combat with cricket stumps
as broad-swords. Receiving a mortal death-stroke he falls
backwards in slow motion into the clump of bamboos, both
hands clapped to his right eye from which blood spurts – a
death-blow! He opens a mailed fist to show me his pierced
eyeball gushing blood.

'*Pax!*'

Dado strolls past in his cut-down shorts, a handkerchief
on his head, tied at four corners, wearing nothing else.

'Be careful with those stumps. You could put your
brother's eye out.'

'Oh we will.'

Pulling back the skin of his mickey, Cox directs a thin jet of
piss through the high slit-window of the Convent jax and as
it splashes outside we hear the big girls scream. With his
shirt rolled up and his pointed bum out for business, Coffey
crouches like a monkey above the jax and, groaning deeply,
lets No. 1 go between his legs. It splatters on the drain and
the stench of ammonia and beasts rises up strong as the
wild reek of the Lion House in the Dublin Zoo.

The Dote and I read unsystematically through old Mrs Warren's library, shelf by shelf. We read A. E. W. Mason, Clarence E. Mulford, P. C. Wren, P. G. Wodehouse, Sapper, Rafael Sabatini, Baroness Orczy.

Mumu's heroes were Walt Disney, Noel Coward, Beverley Nichols, Anthony Eden, who was a 'thorough gentleman', and the Emperor Haile Selassie of Abyssinia, who was as black as your boot. Her peerless diplomacy in the nursery:

> Let bygones be bygones . . .
> It never rains but it pours . . .
> Every cloud has a silver lining . . .
> It's as broad as it's long.

She was a member of the County Council lending library wherever she lived. Brother Bun cycled to Celbridge when we lived in Springfield and to Delgany when we lived in Greystones, to borrow more books and hand back the books that Mumu had read or put aside as not worth reading. She could get through four or five books in a week, no bother.

She got through Kate O'Brien, Negley Farson, Rose Macaulay, Norah Hoult, Philip Gibbs, Stefan Zweig, George Moore, Oliver St John Gogarty, Hall Cain, Frank O'Connor, Brinsley MacNamara, Aldous Huxley, Somerset Maugham, John Dos Passos, John Steinbeck, Sherwood Anderson (*Winesburg, Ohio* was indeed a discovery for me), Willa Cather. Of course all were not from the lending library; she read whatever she could lay her hands on, including banned books lent by Helen O'Connor, the doctor's daughter.

With unruffled patience she read Patience Strong, Maura Laverty, Olivia Manning (*The Dreaming Shore*), L. A. G. Strong (*Dewer Rides*), Maurice Walsh (*The Road to Nowhere*).

She had a regular repertoire of sayings, *bons mots* and catchphrases, among which prominently featured: 'A land', or 'a bit of a land', meant an unexpected disappointment, a let-down. 'Donkey's years' meant aeons of Time (presumably

Irish, meaning unreliable Time). 'A cock and bull story'
meant a tissue of lies. 'Thick as thieves': intense complicity.
'Gas' ('a gas article') meant a merry grig, an amusing
person. A 'rip' (or 'right rip'): a bad egg, a scoundrel.

Shooting at missel thrushes in the front field with my new
Daisy rifle, the sash window falls on my hand. My father,
standing over me, pulls the window up, crushing the top
joint of my fingers as he releases it. I am given hot Bovril
and bread and the tears dry on my face. My young brother
strikes me with a cricket stump and terrified of reprisals
runs weeping into the house; staggering in I am punished
for making him cry.

I hide under the long table in the diningroom. The linen
cloth reaches to the floor, and my patience with my elder
brother is exhausted. I wait until the family have taken their
places and then growling like a mad dog sink my teeth into
the white calf of brother Dodo's leg and hang on as he rises
straight up with a high-pitched scream. I taste pure venom
in my mouth as he staggers from the room.

'Come out of there,' Dado commands. 'This time you
have gone too far. You will pay for this.'

My mother holds a napkin to her face. I crawl out, still
unrepentant.

Droll old saws and venerable maxims rolled off the lips
of brother Bun with the tired precision of a mechanically
recorded message, RAF slang parroted out with a line from
Shakespeare, from Conan Doyle, from here and there: Press
on regardless, steady the Buffs and let the Rangers pass,
Mafeking is relieved (heard at a News Cinema), do you use
Long Melford (can you box?), skedaddle, buckshee, good
show, bad show, bit of a bind, when beggars die no comets
fall, a bit dicey, what's the gen?, hunky-dory, not half, jolly
good show, dead easy, haven't a clue, mollies, softies, tinkers'
gets. Blokes were 'bods'.

He wore heavy army boots and leather puttees, a baggy mossy-green Local Defence Force uniform with forage cap worn at a gallant angle, carried a heavy Lee-Enfield rifle but no bullets, cycling off down the back avenue to training sessions at Straffan Town Hall, prepared to defend his country against Nazi parachutists to the last drop of his blood, for he was one of the lads.

Get him!

In smart mustard-yellow suiting of Irish tweed Oliver St John Gogarty walked into the garden with Mumu and was taken through the rockery to see her rock flowers. He had arrived in great style in a yellow Mercedes wearing yellow pigskin gloves and yellow calfskin handmade boots. He laughed getting out of the car, saying that yellow was a colour pleasing to God.

Now he walked with his chest thrown out and hands behind his back, one gloved and one bare, smiling at Lizzy who was setting the tea-things outside the summerhouse, the cucumber sandwiches cut very thin and the best china out for the guest.

The yellow Mercedes that stood leaking oil on the front driveway fairly breathed opulence, with leather straps on the bonnet. Of the painter Orpen, whose obituaries he had attended, he said wittily: 'He never got under the surface, Lil, until he got under the ground,' and gave a rich chuckle to which Mumu added her high unhinged laugh, Dado taking his cue from her and laughing too.

Gogarty was a surgeon with his own practice. He told Mumu that he intended to move to America, he was tired of the Celtic chloroform and had no use for Dev: 'A cross between a corpse and a cormorant'. The nineteen Dublin hospitals were lazar houses and the whole country rotten with TB.

From Mumu's bedroom window, opening a slat of the venetian blinds, I watched the great surgeon and wit depart in his yellow Mercedes. A gloved hand out the window waved adieu.

Mumu had told me of his escape from the IRA execution squad led by a Clonskeagh tram driver; how he had escaped their clutches and leaped from the parapet into the freezing Liffey, escaping into the dark, vowing to donate two black swans to the river into whose tender mercies he had entrusted his life.

Despite the lubricious promise of their titles (*Tumbling in the Hay*) I was to find his books disappointing, mere social tittle-tattle in brother Bun's opinion, promising more than they delivered. The debonair specialist would later remove Bun's adenoids, as he had removed W. B. Yeats's tonsils, but cannot have made a very good job of it, for he was to be adenoidal all his life, snoring like a foghorn.

Mumu may have inherited some of old Mrs Warren's taste in reading matter along with her very miscellaneous library. Whose was the much-read volume of Beverley Nicols' *Down the Garden Path* with hand-drawn and end-papers?

She had known Brinsley (*The Valley of the Squinting Windows*) MacNamara through her brother Aubrey, and she knew Crosby Garstin and Percy French and Oliver St John Gogarty, who had an interest in gardens and sent her inscribed copies of his books. She had watched Kate O'Brien taking tea with another lady in the Shelbourne and had brazenly introduced herself to Noel Coward in the same lounge when she discovered him at tea with a handsome young man whom Noel Coward introduced as his secretary. Mumu referred thereafter to dear Noel and dear dear Beverley.

With us who lacked nothing in the way of home comforts, 'want' was a dirty word; servants and nannies were always there, dancing attendance. We lived, as Mumu put it, in the very lap of luxury, and servants attentive to our every wish were at the end of every bell-pull, five or six of which were situated strategically about the house, in the upper rooms set into the wall by the fireplaces of white marble, the roaring coal fires.

Our cook, old Mrs Henry from the back road, was one of the old breed of servants – that hardy tribe that accepted lifelong servitude as a bond and contract never to be reneged or broken. If she was too bent and arthritic to be expected to drag herself upstairs at the peal of the bell, Lizzy was there and before the bell pealed twice she would be on her way, adjusting her mob-cap, straightening her black stockings in the long hall mirror below the officers' crossed swords; already clearing her throat for the formal interrogative, 'Yessum?'

Old Mrs Henry was too uncouth and humble. When introduced to 'new Gintry' her formal obeisance was more than a courtesy, profound and reverential as a genuflexion – the courtesy ossified. The smear of blacking on the wizened servile features or across the iron-grey hair, where a hasty hand had smeared it, lending a barbaric touch, the very badge and seal of servility. The smell that attended her entrances and exits were ineradicable.

Of course every effortful trip upward had to be countered by the fretful return downward; indeed twice there and twice back. For after the preliminary foray to ascertain what was required, came the return to base-camp to collect whatever condiments were lacking, then the triumphant return to Mistress with the missing items arranged artfully on the heavy tray, the comb of honey, the gooseberry jam, the jug of cream, the boiling water, the cubes of sugar, the tongs; then the return to kitchen until the meal upstairs was ended, when another peremptory peal of the bell sent Lizzy flying upwards again, scurrying over the damp flagstones past the cellar where we believed the Bogey Man lived in permanent darkness and on via the servants' quarters – under the iron bedstead with its threadbare coverings an outsize chamber was full to overflowing with sulphurous yellow piss – to the warm study or library where meals were taken in winter.

Or up another flight of stairs to diningroom or livingroom on either side of the hall; up three more angular flights to either of the two master bedrooms where meals were sometimes taken in summer, in Mumu's big bedroom overlooking cattle grazing in Mangan's field and the hazy blue of the Dublin hills in the distance.

Of course the poor, whom by divine decree we would always have with us, were suffering permanently from a chronic lack of everything, for ever begging and being ingratiating, hands reaching out and always dirty.

'Others won't have your advantages,' Mumu told us. 'Always remember that. You should consider yourselves lucky. Now would one of you give that bell a good pull?'

3

The Goat in the Tree

'**Q**uite honestly, Sir,' pipes up the Dote in an affected fluting English accent, 'really and truly, I'd feel much better after a jolly good hiding. Ten of the best.'

'Is that so now,' I purr, doing the heavy Moderator, the hard Beak. 'Is that so, my lad. Then it shall be done. Down with your trousers this instant!'

My brother raises his eyes to me as if beseeching, beginning to slowly undo his braces. He is the errant son, the lax pupil; I the morally inflexible Pater of Teddy Lester.

'No slackers in this dorm!' I cry.

'But, Sir . . .' blurts the Dote.

'No blubbing, Higgins Minor, *if* you please. We only want plucky lads in this school. Now be a man, bend down and grit your teeth.'

'A jolly good licking,' whispers the Dote, beginning to lower his shorts. He bends, holding his knees, exposing a pale helpless bum.

'Ready now, Sir – lay into it! I need a good birching. I'll take my gruel like a man,' squeaks he.

The whippy bamboo cane cut that very morning smashes down again and again on the desk and splinters into pieces as my brother hops about the schoolroom, rubbing his bum. '*Yarooo!*'

The Beak, grinding his teeth in a fury, has administered
the very father and mother of a caning to Higgins Minor,
lamed him for the big match. The morning of the big
match had dawned fine and clear and the entire school was
converging on the rugger field, a Slapton XV versus their
arch-rivals.

'Yaroooo!' bawls the Dote, hopping.

The honour of the school is upheld.

I stand on a pile of books, like the boy on the forestool
before the drumhead court of Roundheads in the painting
'And When Did You Last See Your Father?' For now it is my
turn for punishment. I am honest Arthur Digby owning up
to a feast in the dorm. Before me stands the implacable
Beak, my brother with a new upraised cane.

He thunders at me: 'Well, Digby, what is it this time?'

'Insub-b-ordin-nation, Sir. Quite honestly, I deserve a jolly
good tra-tra-tra-trashing.'

I am afflicted with a painful stutter. The beating-block is
rearranged: I step forward, plucky.

'Your old pal,' Mumu says smilingly laying her hand on my
head, 'and what does *he* say?'

Bowsy says Da Munts, Da Yeers, Da Lurry, Da Dunky, Da
Flure, Da Wurrild, smelling of shag tobacco and the blood
of slaughtered beasts and old clothes, and makes all seem
both near and far away at the same time, both perfectly
formed and twisted, both exact and forlorn, and with him I
feel at peace and protected.

Dado told him that the PP had been at him to take my
pipa away from me, that I am too young for it, it was 'causing
a scandal in the parish'. It had to go.

'Now hadn't he a hell of a neck to go and say a thing like
that?' Dado asked Mumu who purses up her mouth as if
tasting something bitter.

The vapoury blue eyes look askance at me under twitching
sandy-coloured eyebrows and always he has something wet
in his nostril hairs. He sets me on his knee, offers me a fill

of shag tobacco, paring it carefully towards his thumb. I smell an old man who lives alone, who never changes out of his clothes, who never changes.

'Whaa dodey tach yew in skule?'

'Summs,' I whisper.

'I nivver heerd.'

'Dey do tach me summs, Bowsy.'

'*Doon an durris mawsh aye doh hulla,*' Sister Rumold says.

I march to the door and close it.

'*Uskle an fwinnoge!*'

I close the window.

'*Cunnus taw tu?*'

'*Taw may gu mah,*' I answer.

'You may sit down,' Sister Rumold says quietly. The girls are afraid to whisper. The storm has blown over. The strap lies hidden again in the shallow drawer of her desk on the rostrum where she punishes us. Dicky Hart cleans the Irish off the blackboard without making a sound. We go about our business quiet as mice, counting the hours and minutes until we will be set free.

'Ned Colfer you have me heartscalded,' declared Sister Rumold, coaxily. Ned smiles a thin sickly yellow smile. She coaxes Colfer: 'You great lug you.'

Ned throws a wild bemused look about the classroom.

'*Gradigy suss a hain-a-do! Gradigy suss, gradigy suss, a hain-a-do!*'. Sister Rumold prompts, clapping her hands softly together as we stamp around the classroom, raising the dust, chanting, '*A hain-a-do!*' An aquatint of a large forlorn collie dog sitting on a quayside watches us marching around the classroom until at a sign one of teacher's pets throws open the door and we can run shouting and screaming between the walls.

'*Gradigy, gradigy, gradigy!*' intones Sister Rumold beside the open door of the classroom, beating time with her hands, looking amiable now, having told us that we are without exception the laziest and stupidest class she has ever encountered, and that she would prefer to dig drains or be tarring the roads, something like that, rather than waste her time trying to beat some sense into numbskulls.

Breaking ranks and cheering wildly the class runs out into the village. Over the humpbacked bridge huge brilliantly lit clouds tower up and up, vasty cloud cathedrals; white castles loom.

Eating a Granny Smith (2d.) on my way home I try to imagine Sister Rumold baldheaded with wimple off and black taffeta skirts furled up, tarring a road for the County Council or lifting a pick in an irrigation drain.

I cannot.

'The Bowsy stinks.'

'You must never say that of a poor working man.'

'But he does. He *stinks*!'

I thought I was being bright, but I was only being smart. Mumu threw me a very dismissive look.

The desks were scored and gouged and crisscrossed with penknife stabs. We dip our penny pens in inkwells that smell of smelling-salts and ether. The big ink jar is kept in the closet and Sister's pets fetch it for her when required.

Loaded with ink my pen follows the stippled line and writes 'Empty Vessels Make Most Noise' and then 'Necessity is the Mother of Invention.'

The nun who has a red face comes from West Cork and her voice goes up and down. She has a rough temper to match the red face, but when in a good mood she tells us stories of Michael Collins and of her own youth in West Cork. She sucks lozenges to keep her breath sweet but I can tell you that her temper is not too sweet.

The strap is kept in a shallow drawer of her desk, the desk itself mounted on a wooden rostrum a foot from the wooden floor. When her dander rises Sister Rumold slowly stands up and pulls open the shallow drawer where she keeps the strap and without looking takes out the heavy leather strap with lead in it. When we do not know our times-tables or Catechism or Irish, all drummed into us by chanting and rote, she stands behind us and pulls at our ears.

She drags at Colfer's ears as if she intends to wrench them off, lifting Colfer up. He makes a grimace but as though he were in league with her, agreeing to the punishment.

'Will I take the strap to you? Will I now?' she demands of Ned Colfer; her dander and her colour rising.

The angry nun stands behind Colfer and drags grimly at his ears until all the blood drains out of Ned's face.

'Ah be Janey,' Ned Colfer groans, his face now pulled close to the scratched desk, 'ah ah ah!'

'Oh you great numbskull Colfer, open those big waxy ears of yours!' the nun cries, leaning over with the strap in her free hand. She beats Colfer as if beating a carpet, Colfer flinching at every blow.

'Now Aidan Higgins, let me hear you.'

I stand up.

On cold days we sit around the small turf fire and Sister's pets huddle close to her and she tells us again how Michael Collins walked into Dublin Castle with a briefcase marked OHMS under his arm, bold as brass.

A basin of blood stands on a table in the middle of the girls' cloakroom and those who have had teeth pulled are allowed to go home early. Molly Cushen is deathly pale, her face framed by coal-black hair; she holds a bloodsoaked handkerchief to her mouth as she goes slowly over the bridge and the wind blows hair into her face.

Being poor at Irish I am not one of Sister Rumold's particular pets. She has changed from the gracious nun who spoke so deferentially to Mumu in the Convent waiting room. I see her now as a pallid nun with a short temper who has it in for Colfer. I feel her standing close to me, her patience growing short, sucking a spearmint. Two desks in front,

Colfer holds his hands under his arms; the whole row is getting it, the nun has twice taken the strap to Colfer. His ears are blazing red.

At break the big girls come screaming like snipe into the playground. The days pass. I walk to school.

Three great processions passed through Celbridge. In 1690 the only son of Dongan, killed at the Battle of the Boyne, was carried from the field to the family mansion at Castletown and interred in the parish church by the front gate. The Dongans, Earls of Limerick, were one of the few Catholic families in the Pale to be restored to their estates.

Thomas Dongan was obliged to sell 1,730 acres to Speaker Conolly who had already acquired ten thousand acres of forfeited lands in forced acquisitions in Meath, Westmeath, Roscommon, Wexford, Waterford, Fermanagh, Dublin, Kildare, Donegal and Wales.

Conolly died issueless of a heart attack in his grand mansion in Capel Street, the remains carried in great pomp in the state coach with mourning outriders to the family vault in Tea Lane. An immense concourse of mourners walked behind the hearse, and heard a panegyric to a great man gone.

In 1878 Lord Leitrim's murdered remains – dispatched in Donegal by some of his tenants – were carried via Killadoon with ostentatious display to the ancestral vaults in St Michan's in one of Dublin's poorest districts. Hearing whose funeral it was the people mobbed the hearse, uttering 'fearful execrations', tipped the corpse onto the roadway, vilified the dead man. In this shameful manner he was set upon twice, murdered twice. In Donegal, standing erect in the side-car, he had fought for his life, pulling out handfuls of red hair from the man who killed him.

4

The Bogey Man

A narrow freshwater stream flows out into the sea by the Kilcool end of the South Beach at Greystones and after breakfast my young brother (the Dote) and I went down there with buckets and spades, Gina Greene trailing after us.

Blocks of rough-cast boulders the size of removal crates had been dumped higgledy-piggledy below the railway line as storm-breaks. The line – with which I would in later life become so familiar – ran from Rosslare to Dublin, following the coastline from Bray to Dun Laoghaire. In summer the larks sang above a hilly wheatfield. The iodiney smell of seaweed on the culvert, the tide curling in and out, the line of waves breaking along the shore, all that had a disturbing effect on my rural sensibilities and innards before I even knew myself to be Piscean.

Little grains of sand dislodged themselves from the slope of the bank and slid into the stream; I felt the suck and drag under my feet separating my toes and pulling me in. Distant figures were crossing the metal footbridge at Greystone station, where Dado (true to form) was pally with the stationmaster. He seemed to cultivate stationmasters, for he was very pally with Mr Dooley at Hazelhatch.

Then, out of a clear sky, the bolt fell.

The gulls continued to squawk over the culvert, the waves

43

were calmly curling in, the Dote was up to his waist in a
hole he had dug in the soft sand; and coming towards us
was the very last person in the world that I ever wanted to
see anywhere, lunging in our direction with a broken stride.
That morning I had been bold and Mumu had told me that
she wouldn't smack me but I was a disobedient little brat all
the same and she had a good mind to set the Bogey Man
on me, to teach me manners. And now he was coming to
get me, Mumu had had a quiet word with him; from afar
he had me spotted and now I was for it.

The fresh breeze blew from behind him, whipped the
tails of his greatcoat, the sort that coach-drivers wore in
the olden days, and incoming waves curled over the culvert.
He wore big brown boots and a wide-brim brown felt hat
which he clutched to his head with one hand, the other
reaching out towards me, summoning. I watched this holy
terror come plunging towards me like a meteor; unable to
cry out or run away, I awaited my fate.

The Dote was preoccupied in his hole, now submerged
up to his shoulders, still patiently digging. A single figure
on the metal footbridge seemed to be looking in my direction but the quarter of a mile that separated us might have
been the width of the Atlantic Ocean and all the pebbly
foreshore of shingle the terrain of the Bogey Man and those
whom he wold punish for their misdeeds were corralled
into it. His method of punishing would be uniquely his own,
uniquely horrible. I imagined that he would run upon his
victim, fix his lips to my lips and blow all his foulness into
me, his badness, as you would blow up a frog by sticking a
sharp thrawneen through its skin. The victim would be filled
up with that foulness and expire on the spot.

I sank down into the bank as it approached and tried to
make myself invisible. But what a hope!

Arriving by the stream and not even bothering to break
his stride the Bogey Man leaped across to my side, the tails
of his greatcoat spread out behind him; confronted with the
spectacle of me cowering there, abject, he halted in his

tracks. Bending down as if to verify the truth of this emaciated creature who abjectly cowered before him, he brought his twitchy face close to mine and the smell that came reeking from his stomach was hot and savage, a compound of stale porter, shag tobacco, hyena cage, burning slack, an open cesspool wriggling with fat white worms, rotting fungicide in a winter wood, as if he was decayed or had beshat himself.

He asked in a breathless panting voice if I had ever been to London? Or seen the King?? Did I know Gamage's of Holborn??? I shook my head, pinned to the sandbank by his brown anxious eyes, his panting breath, his shadow, his vileness. For I had never been to London, never seen the King riding out of Buckingham Palace in his coach with the Queen by his side. All I knew or feared was that it was foggy there and Soho lay underground and race-gangs knocked the points of railings and filed them down to dagger sharpness and gangsters from the Gorbals – the very worst, the hardest criminals – concealed razor blades in the peaks of their caps, for slashing the faces of opponents. And they fought in gangs in the underground city always obscured in thick fog. These undersized taciturn dangerous men were under-nourished and would think nothing of slitting your gizzard if you as much as looked sideways at them. They were very touchy.

'Then you know nothing,' spat the Bogey Man with a gush of fetid hyena breath right into my face, dismissing me.

With upraised hand he seemed about to swipe me across the face but glancing furtively around he quickly touched my knee with a claw scratchy as a badger, brought himself upright, preparing to move away.

'You could do with some fattening up,' he called back in a hoarse broken voice.

I watched him pass out of sight, plunging through the wet sand of the foreshore as if in a quagmire, pounding along until he had rounded the blocks of cement and disap-

peared off in the direction of Kilcool. Little grains of sand
escaped with the sound of a sigh and running together
collapsed into the fast-flowing stream and my heart (that
had stopped beating ever since the Bogey Man had first
addressed me) could begin to beat again.

The Dote called to me from his hole in the sand (where
he was now up to his neck) and held up a crab. Gina
Greene had tucked up her skirt and was slowly wading in
our direction along the edge of the sea.

Dado said that Greystones was a place where Protestants
came to die, like old horses put out to grass when their
useful days are over. Mumu said he shouldn't say such things,
but Dado only sniggered, a silk cravat knotted about his
neck like Freddy Brown, and rustled the *Irish Times* at her.

In a silken kimono of vivid Japanese lozenges inset with
dragons and wearing plimsolls on her bare feet Mumu left
the Grand Hotel each morning when the sun shone, going
by the esplanade to the south beach for her morning dip.
Her woollen bathing costume of horizontal blue and white
stripes with midnight blue trunks that reached to near the
knees but left most of the back bare could be seen crossing
the shingle below the icecream hut and the turnabout
where the trains reversed for the journey back to Dublin.
Flinching she cautiously entered the sea to perform a stately
breast-stroke. After breakfast Dado drove to the golf club
for a morning round.

The distinctly posh aromas of the Grand Hotel overwhelmed me, always overly sensitive to smells and their sig-
nificance: the intractable odours of fine furs, tobacco and
violets, velvet brocade and polished woodwork, the whole-
some smell of furniture wax mixed with the coarser aroma
of roast mutton; carpets and drapes, perfumes trapped in
an airless vacuum where uniformed hotel servants bore trays
of afternoon tea, drinks. A plush and satin parlour, cloth of
pearl and coral, a musky chamber. The effluvium of plenty
was strong here; an aura of privilege and opulence.

5

The Bowsy Murray

Grogan (breezily): 'The hard Bowsy! How's the form?'
The Bowsy Murray (gravely): 'Hardy aul day.'

T he Bowsy was crippled with the arthritis. Yet he had a
positively Homeric way of mounting and dismounting
from his trusty butcher's bike, lowslung and very
prone to punctures with a black-painted hand-tinted sign
slung between his legs, from the crossbar on which was
inscribed in white lettering:

J. J. Young, Victualler
Celbridge 4.

The act of throwing a stumpy-booted and gaitered leg
athwart the low saddle was a grave gesture both ceremonial
and heraldic, man and machine (wrapped in symbolic
flame, suggesting Mercury) emblazoned on some obscure
escutcheon invoking Subordinacy, Humility, Obeisance,
Homage, Destiny, *Victualler*! He threw or rather cast his
weary leg across the accursed saddle (he was afflicted with
piles) with all the easy grace of long custom. He stank like
an ancient Irish battle long lost. The triumphant victors
having given three rousing cheers and stumped off, brandishing their bloody weapons, to dine in high style that very
evening off the finest plate, served by henchmen and lit by
ranks of wax candles dripping from Georgian silverware; the

defeated left dead on the cold field as wolf-fodder, crow-bait and spoils for pillagers.

The Bowsy was a strong stumpy little man who got about, when not awheel, with a pronounced limp (on which more anon); about his middle a broad leather belt with studs to augment coarse country braces or what he called galluses and, tucked into the long-johns (combs), a labouring man's collarless cotton shirt known as Grandfather, never washed but worn until it could walk off him. On his broad cranium the same cap worn in all weathers all its long natural life, a greasy sweatsoaked affair crushed in his hands and wrung out when confronted with the Gentry, who were always out and about.

He habitually wore a bloodstained blue and white striped butcher's apron tied behind, dirtied with gristle and mince-meat and snot (for he contrived manual emissions of snot while in motion and some of it came back on him, in high winds) adhering to it, a seal of his worth. A sack was thrown over the shoulders in foul weather or snow, more token than actual cover; and when it was teeming with rain, and don't forget we're in the Midlands, he arrived agleam in black oilskins with tam o'shanter like Skipper, the herring fleet captain, as if he were a fish (a flounder) or had come by water, so drenched was he. But always cheerful, always cheerful, leaving his puddles behind, and not a word of complaint, never a word.

He cycled miles in all weathers on his stiff delivery bike, stubby *pipa* clenched between stumps of broken brown teeth; soaked in sweat, running with rainwater, to deliver the meat and sausages and silverside and black and white puddings that were the staples for the not-so-well-off so addicted to rashers delivered safe and sound into the hands of the poor recipients.

Neither he nor his trusty machine was 'able' (as he put it) for the slight gradient on the front avenue, so he was obliged to dismount and push it the rest of the way. Every Saturday afternoon regular as clockwork he arrived with the sirloin of beef wrapped up bloodily in yesterday's *Evening Mail* and, like Olympic athletes passing on the flame, conveyed this safely into the hands of old Mrs Henry, for her to tell him that it was 'a nice piece of meat', and carry it off to the larder; hardly in the larder door before she came hurrying back to do the honours, offer him a bottle of Guinness to slake his thirst and beg him to be seated and take the weight off his feet, with which he gratefully complied and always with the same formality, washing his hands in coarse soap at the scullery tap while Lizzy set to work with a corkscrew, so that the hero full of village gossip, saddlesore and battlesore, could blow his nose into the sink and sit on a kitchen chair, to stink up the kitchen as he indeed made himself 'at home'. Mumu confessed that she thought the world of the Bowsy Murray, and Dado said the Bowsy was no fool.

With a dextrous turn of the wrist old Mrs Henry took the poker to one of the covers on the range and had it open to feed in more coal from a tilted scuttle, stoked up the fire and made it go roaring up the flue, before setting the big sooty kettle on the hob. Lizzy told the Bowsy that he was being treated like a prince and the Bowsy, pleased, looked down complacently at his stumpy little legs outstretched to the blaze. He wore leather gaiters winter and summer, liked to pour his own pint, keeping his little finger crooked as if he were taking tea with a grand lady, not porter with the cook. He drank tea and Guinness *together*, taking a mouthful of bread thick with butter, then a swig of tea, munching away at the sops like a cow chewing the cud. He put his thumb through the handle of the cup and swallowed as if from a goblet.

Now he took a good long swallow, drew his fingers through his walrus moustache and brought up a low rumbling belch from the interior of his stomach.

'Nutten lika gude suppa tay.'

'The Bowsy just let out a rift,' I informed Lizzy Bolger.

Mumu called a belch a rift; rifting was rude, but it was all

right if you covered your mouth with one hand and said
Excuse me or Oh-I-do-beg-your-pardon in a genteel voice.

Old Mrs Henry sliced off generous cuts of bread and I
put the poker through the bars of the range and when it
was red hot laid it across the bread spread with brown sugar
and made a game of noughts and crosses that in the mouth
tasted of treacle; for I ate only dry bread, was allergic to
butter, put sugar on all my food.

'That stomach of yours must be wan mass of worms,' old
Mrs Henry said, sniffing. I saw loose yellow hair about her
crumpled ear.

Screwing up her eyes and tilting the big empty teacup
this way and that in her hand she prepared to read the tay-
leaves, the backs of her old working hands speckled like a
bird's egg, flecks of amber in her tired old duck-egg blue
eyes, strands of white in her grey hair. She wore brown
worsted stockings that went halfway up the calf, held in
place with black garters that were always slipping down. She
had a comforting homely smell off her like an open tin of
biscuits.

I smoked on the sly with shag tobacco that the Bowsy had
pared carefully into his calloused palm with a claspknife,
giving it to me mixed with a Wild Woodbine ground in the
heel of his fists that he swore would give me a grand mild
smoke.

Meanwhile old Mrs Henry saw dark strangers, journeys
across black water, good or bad fortune on the way.

As she read the headlines of the *Evening Herald* she moved
one finger below the line of print; her lips saying the word
before she pronounced Aby-ssinnia! She used a hairpin to
underline more difficult words. The Italian soldiers were
slaughtering Fuzziwuzzies in the desert, the naked tribesmen
armed with spears and Mussolini's son machine-gunning
them from an aeroplane.

'An dey oney poor bloody savages,' the Bowsy said.

Lizzy lowered the clothesline. It was a long bar held in
place against the ceiling by a rope looped about a stanchion

near the famous mangle; the nursery was above this and in
bed at night I heard it squeaking and gibbering down like
the damned screaming in distant Hell.

I walk on uneven paving-stones that sweat, down the corridor below a line of dusty bells, past a whitewashed wall
covered in drawings of Spitfires and Lysanders and Stukas
and Dorniers drawn in pencil by myself and my three
brothers. In the kitchen old Mrs Henry and Lizzy Bolger
are cleaning and plucking beheaded pullets killed that day.
With their feet in feathers and their hands bloodied they
pull out entrails, winking and laughing like a pair of witches,
their reddened hands methodically plucking feathers. I
smell cold guts.

'Where's Ma?'

'Yewer Mammy's run off with a sailor,' Lizzy says, leaving
a smear of blood on her forehead.

'No.'

'Yewe'll see soon enuff, Mister Smarty!'

I run from the cackling witches.

A barrelchested sailorman with red hair pulls steadily at
the oars, smiling at my mother who sits facing him in the
thwarts. She is dressed for a long journey. The sailor has
gingery hair and bottle-green eyes; behind them a ship rides
at anchor. My mother is leaving without a by-your-leave,
without a goodbye kiss, without a backward glance. Up
anchor at full tide and away! A rowing-boat approaches a
wooden jetty by moonlight, in silence but for the soft whirr
of Ger Coyle's projector and I imagine that I can hear oars.
A mysterious passenger shrouded in an overcoat, with face
shadowed under the brim of a hat, bends forward, gazing
steadfastly at the rower. The prow touches the jetty, the
passenger rises, begins to turn, but before I can see the face
the film ends. The film has no beginning and no end. A
hunter enters a cave after a bear, savages run down a jungle
path. Who is this traveller?

Mumu is leaving us. Choking with misery I lie in the long
smothering grass.

I sat on the Bowsy's leathery lap and asked him to tell me again about his time at war.

It was like this (said he): 'Dim Jairmans made mate a-dim.'

One Sunday following a bombardment lasting a week he advanced with his platoon with bayonets fixed across a hill covered in corpses that had bloated up and gone black in the sun.

'Did you ever,' he asked old Mrs Henry, 'hear tell of the Vimy Ridge?' She never had, had never set foot out of Ireland, as her mother before her.

The men killed in the shelling had lain there and the stretcher-bearers couldn't reach them, swelling up and slowly turning black.

'Lost in action,' said the Bowsy, looking at me with his blue bemused eyes, 'so dey do till the next-a-kin. But glory be to God summa dim lads wint out over dim failds in bits an' paces.'

He told it to us all again (it was like Dado and the time when *he* escaped from hospital, letting himself out the window on knotted sheets; the to-be-continued tale of his mistrust of surgeons. The Higginses were all like that, Mumu said, afraid of the knife.): The explosions that would pull your bowels out, the scream of pain, someone had bought it. He took a terrible blow on the chest over the heart (here the Bowsy struck his heart) and the air over Vimy Ridge began to turn grey with little grainy black spots falling everywhere. He lay stretched out amid the corpses. 'Our lads an' their lads, God help us'.

Presently his officer was staring down at him asking, 'Anything wrong, Gunner Murray, are you hit?'

No, Sor, nothing exactly wrong, Sor, only the air of Vimy Ridge was turning mauve and his boots began to fill with blood.

He was carried behind the lines on a stretcher; from field hospital by troop-train across Belgium to a ship preparing to leave; the wounded Irish were returning home. After a slow voyage (dodging U-boats in the Irish Sea?) they reached an unknown port at night. The Orderly who had sat with the wounded stood up and said: 'Okay, Paddies, home. All you lucky blightahs for Blighty! Any of you perishing Paddies got relatives 'ere?'

'Where are we?'

'Dublin.'

Dublin! Glory be to God, he was back home.

He was put into an ambulance, carried in a stretcher into Mercer's Hospital. In the field hospital the surgeons couldn't find the shrapnel inside the Bowsy but in Dublin he would be examined by specialists. Sir James Ware walked through the wards followed by a retinue of internees making copious notes. There was a hole in the Bowsy's chest, covered in a sort of cobweb of filmy skin that blew in and out as he breathed; dark blood from near the heart had pumped out.

Sir James Ware examined him and made a mark with an indelible pencil near his heart (the Bowsy indicated where and Lizzy and old Mrs Henry stared) and told the Bowsy not to go and rub it out. They should X-ray at a certain angle, Sir James said; the X-ray showed the piece of shrapnel lodged near the heart. Sir James Ware removed it.

The Bowsy left hospital for home. He became a game-keeper on Lord Portarlington's estate at Emo Park, where he was a gun-bearer to King George V, a guest at shooting parties, who always asked for the Bowsy.

'Did you know the King, Bowsy?' I asked him, inhaling his smells, tea, Guinness and shag tobacco, his long-sweated-into working clothes. 'Did you spake to dey King?'

'Shure I knew him as well as I know your own Doddy,' said the Bowsy, shifting my hot bottom on his lap.

I looked at the mottled hands of the soldier and slaughterer who had walked with his platoon one Sunday across Vimy Ridge; had stood and received orders from Lord Portarlington; had handed a gun to the King of England in the hide.

Here the Bowsy took out a stubby pipe from his overall pocket, struck a safety match, touched it to the bowl, sucking his hollowed cheeks, going Mmmm, mm, mmm, holding up the match for me to blow out.

One unlucky day in summer he was walking alongside a hay-bogey and didn't the load shift and the lot came down on the road, but a pitch-fork went through his right knee. Nothing would persuade him to go into hospital to have it seen to; he had enough of hospitals and surgeons. For nine years he suffered on and off; at the end of that time a Dublin surgeon had crippled him for life.

('Don't go *near* those buckoos!' cried Dado.)

But the pain had come back too often, he couldn't sleep, putting his foot on the ground was like putting it into a furze bush, he decided to have it seen to. The choice was between two surgeons, Dr Chance or Dr Cherry. 'I took a chance on Dr Chance,' the Bowsy said with a heavy sigh. ''Twas the wrong choice.'

'How long have you had these?' the surgeon asked, tapping his varicose veins with the stethoscope. 'We'll whip those lads out too.'

The Bowsy drew at his pipe and stared into the fire. 'He was whippen everting outa me.'

He was given sedatives and a hundred injections, put to sleep and operated upon; to wake up a cripple. He wasn't to know this until later. Convalescence was endless; after five weeks he demanded his clothes back, he was signing himself out, returning home, he had work to do, his Lordship would expect to see him. Dr Chance told him: 'You go out that door at your peril, Murray.'

He dressed, walked out, took a bus, took a train, walked three miles to Emo Park, where all was in disorder. A thick country buck had replaced him, doing the rough work, feeding the pigs. The Bowsy's temper had become short, the pain hadn't gone away, he was limping about. One evening while sitting there at supper the sucks began screeching.

'What ails the sucks?' he asked the country buck. 'Didn't yew fade dim?'

The country buck looked shifty, brazening it out. 'Yarra why should I fade dim, isn't wanst or twiste a wake enuff for dim sucks?'

That did it: the Bowsy rose up, he was as strong as a gate, his rage when it came was terrible, he was livid. The country buck spat on the floor and scraped it with the toe of his boot. 'Why should I din?'

The Bowsy broke past him in one lunge ('Iffa he hadda touched me he was a dead man'), the claspknife already open in his right hand, and went for the screeching sucks, intending to slit every throat in the stye. The blade entered the side of a suck's neck; but didn't the Bowsy slip and the knife jumped out of his hand. The suck was bleeding and screeching in terror but the Bowsy had come to his senses; he let the country buck help him to his feet.

A silence fell on the kitchen but for the sound of the fire. I slipped from Bowsy's grasp and stood up.

'The sucks is skraatchen! The sucks is skraatchen!!' I screamed at the top of my voice and seizing the long deal table by its middle part with superhuman strength toppled it over with the Boland's loaf, crockery, a two-pint jug of milk, butter and jam, the Bowsy's cup and saucer (he had risen in alarm, was holding fast to his half-swallowed glass of porter); all crashed in a loud satisfactory manner on the flagstones of the kitchen floor, a noise greatly augmented by a high keen from cook and Lizzy's unhinged screeching, all of which was so much music to my ears as I fled from the scene of the crime.

'Ah cummere to me now me old shegoshia,' Grogan coaxed me in the yard, and his cruel cat-stretching hands reached out.

'Don't be at him, Grogan,' Lizzy said. 'Yewer always at him. Lave him be – he's in disgrace.'

She was on her way to the bleach-green with a tub piled

high with washing; had set it down to catch her breath. But
the cruel torturer's hands held me in a vice. 'Now we'll see
who's strong,' Grogan hissed into my ear, doubling me up
in a fierce wrestler's grip, with my head upside down
between his knees. 'Ever hear tell of the Irish Whip? Or of
Dan O'Mahoney of Ballydehob?'

The blood has gone to my head, I feel faint.

'Let him go, Grogan. Let him be.'

In bits and pieces I fall onto the gravel from Grogan's
smothering grip and run after Lizzy into the bleach-green
where she has begun to hang up big sheets on the line.
Rita Phelan came singing onto the bleach-green with more
washing.

> Kiss me wanst and kiss me twisst
> An kiss me wance agin,
> It's been a long, long time,

sang Rita, holding up washing.

'Daffala does have me heartscalded,' Lizzy told Rita.

'Now yewell catch it hot on the BTM, young fellah-me-
lad, so you will,' Rita said spitefully.

'Don't care.'

'You will when your Doddy comes home.'

'Won't.'

'Will, cry-babby!'

'He's a caution,' Lizzy said.

Ah, Dado!

I had not seen them set the table on its legs again and clean
up the mess on the floor or Bowsy clap his sweaty cap
back onto his matted hair and hoist the empty bloodstained
basket on his right arm, bid old Mrs Henry and Lizzy the
time of day and stump from the kitchen, but from Mumu's
window in the window embrasure behind the drapes I
watched him cycle off down the front avenue, cranking
down on the stiff pedals, one shoulder crooked, the skirts

of his coat fluttering, going easy on the gradient. J. J. Young
(Victualler) was a mile away in the village. Cattle and sheep
were driven towards J. J. Young from all quarters of Kildare,
sheep and pigs and lambs, lowing and bleating and baaing
and grunting, their fate already sealed when paper money
had changed hands in some dim and dirty pub. And then
they had only to wait for the Bowsy to arrive, with a grimy
bloodstained sack about his waist, a crowbar in one hand,
the butcher's knife in the other, sharpened to razor keen-
ness on the whetstone.

I tried to see the Bowsy (Gunner Murray of the Irish
Fusiliers) in puttees and wrinkled uniform, a tin hat, carrying a heavy Lee-Enfield rifle out of which a bayonet sprouted
in an alarming way, a heavy pack on his back, gone to
fight for King and country (the wrong King and the wrong
country), the same gamekeeper and beater who had driven
hares and pheasants towards the King, or handed him his
gun, the King whom he knew as well as he knew my own
father, Dado of the Knotted Hospital Bedsheets.

The Bowsy herded them into J. J. Young's yard with its
ominously sloping drains. Soon blood would run down those
slopes. Did he whistle through his teeth as he approached
to stun with crowbar or slit throat with butcher's knife, as he
did habitually while waiting for his tea to cool? Sometimes I
heard what I took to be the sounds of their distress mixed
with the church bells Protestant and Roman Catholic that
came jumbled together on the wind, the irate highpitched
screeching of stuck pigs in the village a mile off.

Wisdom of the Bowsy Murray:
> You can't bate a good strong potta tay.
> You can't bate a good supp tay.
> Nutten like a good potta tay.
> Tay does be a rale drug.

Wisdom of J. J. Young, Victualler:
> Of course when you're dead the kidneys are no
> damn use to you.

> Turkeys are down on last year.
> They do say the bowels of Strongbow are buried
> above in Dublin City.

The upended carcase of a buff-skinned pig was slit up the middle to expose its rosy entrails and red innards, suspended from a hook so that its trotters hung down and its snout bled into the sawdust alongside the decapitated body of a speckled cow. Rows of dead poultry and bloodied game hung from smaller hooks; a sad array of fur and feather amid the chill stench of entrails.

A great stag's head protruded from the wall above the chopping-block, its glazed eyeballs sad and weary. The office was a cabin under the roof, reached by spiral steps; Mrs Young ran the business from there and kept an eye on all movements below, handing down change to J. J. Young.

J. J. Young was a tall taciturn man with a beaked nose. He wore the blue and white striped butcher's apron tied about his waist and a set of carvers in a leather pouch like sixshooters in their holsters; for had he not once saved me from the rough lads of Tay Lane who went off to steal kindling from Killadoon and had menaced me, or pretended to, on the brow of the hill, on their way home?

I had always considered J. J. Young's to belong to a peculiar and even fabulous end of town, quite unlike the grandeur of Castletown gates at the other end. Little donkeys that brought the turf carts from as far away as Birr were hitched to the disused mill windows with sacks of fodder hung from the bars. The fire from Darlington's forge lit up the houses opposite (like a stage-set when the electricity failed) where gossipy women stood about with folded arms. The forge furnace lit up the betting office where Nurse O'Reilly put down cautious bets of tanners and bobs and half-crowns from the tips she received from Grogan and Burke, who were in the know, or said they were.

A penny-farthing bicycle, peculiar and out-of-place as a giraffe, was suspended outside Flynn's bicycle shop as a sign, and around the corner of Oakley Park demesne wall was the thoroughly peculiar Death House near St Mochua's from where the rough lads set out on their marauding expeditions.

The kindhearted J. J. Young had laid his hand on my shoulder and enquired had I got the collywobbles. His wife was nodding down from her eyrie, smiling and nodding (I used to think that she had no legs or body, just a nodding head) and J. J. Young snapped the twine on the parcel with one jerk, as he might wring the neck of a pullet, and handed it over to the customer who stood at the open door, gaping back at the red single-deck bus that had come off the bridge and was stopping before Breen's Hotel.

'Dus dat buss gwantah burr?' he asked.

J. J. Young said that as far as he knew it did and (to me) not to mind those fellows, referring to the Tay Lane toughs who had come back laden down with kindling. I should not worry too much about them, J. J. Young said, giving me the benefit of one of his rare sad kind afflicted smiles.

6

The Great Wall of China

B ut 'in the heel of the hunt,' Mumu would say, meaning
when all was said and done, they didn't go and sneak
on me; they said nothing. Grogan told me that it took
Lizzy, the Bowsy and young Henry (who had come in from
the fields) to get the table on its legs again, and that I must
have the strength of ten men when my dander was up. I
told him I was strong as an ox.

When I strolled into the kitchen there was a silence.

'Up Dev,' I said.

'Yule cotch it hot when yure Doddy hurs of duss.'

Who sailed in but Mumu, who had been alerted by the
commotion belowstairs.

'One fine day that rotten temper of yours is going to get
you into trouble, Sunny Jim,' said Mumu frostily.

I retired behind the mangle where the cats made their
stinks. It was my glory-hole, Mumu said. I smell the dirty
mangle water in the bucket squeezed and wrung out of
sheets; the rollers exude black grease that comes out in
thick globs. Lizzy gets all flushed at the mangle, her stockings coming down, her hair in disarray, groaning and sighing at the hard chore, slowly at first and then in a rush at
the end, dragging the handle, manhandling it, sweating.

'Let him stay there and cool off, Mrs Henry,' Mumu said.

'Oh but hasn't he been bold, Mrs H.!'

Ba, ba, ba, I thought to myself; womanly loyalty! Sour milk!

'No supper for yew,' said Lizzy, putting her oar in.

'O'Duffy's your man,' I said.

'Cheeky.'

I wanted to run away from home, to China. I would prefer to be walking along the Great Wall of China, looking about me with slitty eyes, flouncing my pigtail. I did not love Mumu any more because she was Dado's sneak, nor old Mother Henry who was a lickspittle, nor Lizzy Bolger who was deceitful when it suited her, I did not love any of them any more.

Then I heard the klaxon blare at the gate and presently the sound of wheels crunching over gravel and slowly entering the yard and even more slowly backing into the garage and the sound of the garage doors being banged shut and then my father was wiping his feet on the back door mat and walking away from us towards the study, calling out, 'Anyone at home!'

'Here,' I whispered.

They were silent before him and I was not punished. After supper I escaped into the shrubbery, riding at full tilt on a little wild thing, a pinto, myself a Pawnee brave on the warpath.

Rogation Days meant heat and offerings. The warmth of the sun and the closeness of the cloudy days sickened me. I walked slowly through the Crooked Meadow and saw a cock and hen pheasant on the bank; my sandals were covered in yellow pollen.

7

The Bareback Rider

Mulligan's Field, where film shows were given periodically in a marquee, was out on the Dublin Road before you come to Sir Ivone Kilpatrick's gate. Faded old four-reelers made even more indistinct by the daylight filtering through canvas, showing jumpy episodic sequences of cowboy films, a ghostly Joe E. Brown reduced to a grin in *The Six Day Bicycle Race* and even ghostlier Charlie reduced to bowler hat and black moustache in *The Rink*. Fossett's brought their circus there.

Lizzy Bolger took my young brother and I with her pal Rita Phelan; the two girls powerfully scented wore alarming scarlet lipstick for the big occasion.

The stained canvas of the marquee smacked against its braced supports, sinking and rising as if taking great breaths as the wind dragged at it. The band, up on a makeshift platform of planks, played old circus tunes. The trampled grass gave off smells of the damp earth. We sucked boiled sweets from paper bags handed around by Rita Phelan. A white-faced clown with a bulbous red nose and orange hair stumbled across the ring in outsize boots and baggy pants to trip over the low barrier and fall into the lap of an embarrassed countrywoman sitting in the first tier of

wooden seats. He began to bawl, rubbing his eyes and pointing, calling her his Ma. The crowd roared laughing.

Obscene was the stare of this clown now joking with the
audience, codding and raising his painted eyebrows, as he
cocks one leg. Obscene the angle and position of the flower
he carried. He walked with a slowness amounting to criminal
intent, his gestures licentious and provocative in the
extreme.

He lifted one foot, then the other, to examine the soles
of his big boots for dog turds; he had wet himself or done
it in his pants, drawing out his striped clown's trousers,
opening his mouth wide to stick out an astonishing tongue.
He shouted at the band, who brightened up to call back at
him. He was everywhere, held it all together with his coarse
innuendos.

A circus man in a blue boiler suit held a zinc bucket near
where the animals made their entrances and exits; the Lion
Tamer doubled as Strong Man, bare to the waist he cracked
his whip to make the jungle killers lay back their ears, and
Rita Phelan sucked in her breath. The great lioness emitted
a bloodcurdling growl and slunk along the bars while the
lions sat up on tall tubs and yawned at the audience. The
Lion Tamer lay down on the lioness and feigned sleep; then
he kissed the lioness. More fellows in blue boiler suits ran
in and dragged the cage out and in came the performing
dogs, pissing with excitement, followed by a lady dog-trainer
in riding britches fairly bursting at the hips. The dogs were
all over the place.

I followed the jauntily swaggering hips of the trainer; but
it was the bareback rider coming next who was to sweep all
before her. The band, brightening up again, played her
signature tune, and in she came. First she circled the ring
astraddle two trotting white ponies, her actressy eyes catching the light, she held her bare arms out for applause, I
watched her spine and rounded knees as she jumped
through a blazing hoop.

She was all movement, all mystery, struck no poses but

those of her craft, beautiful beyond compare. Now two quick-stepping white ponies with dusty pelts and red plumes circled the ring; she left one dusty back for the barrier and left it for the other broad back, facing forward, then backwards. Following her progress in a smaller circle the Ringmaster was speechless, strode in a tight circle with his long whip folded, as if witnessing perfection itself, never taking his eyes off her as she leaped through a whole series of hoops.

Under the swinging electric bulbs the marquee looked less shabby, the ponies whiter, brisker in their trotting as a heavy shower of rain pelted at the canvas and an ostler stood with his mouth open, holding under one arm a bucket of sawdust and lion dung and finished a long yawn.

And now she jumped from the dusty back of the pony for the last turn and the Ringmaster had his arm about her waist and his whip upraised for applause, and then he swept his hat off and ran after the ponies who were galloping out by themselves. From their short jogging legs to their nod-ding plumes they were all joggy movement, advancing in time to a music out of Time (the excited trumpeter was on his feet, holding what appeared to be a red chamber-pot before the mouth of his instrument, blowing like Tommy Dorsey) and the top of the marquee slapped against the high poles, and the lights fixed around the ring were shining on the top hat of the Ringmaster and the eyes and teeth of the bareback rider. The young equestrienne seemed to drift; she walked out to the centre of the ring, bowed, ran off.

Wild horses came in at full gallop with a handler being dragged off his feet, pulling at the traces for dear life. The handler went 'hup-hup-hup!' and the big speckled horses tore around to the music, the band could not keep up with them. 'Hubbledebay!' The lions, pulled in again, dragged their fur against the bars of their cage and pissed violently, and Rita Phelan again hissed between her teeth, hot as a furnace on the high wooden plank. All passed, the animal too. 'Allyoop!'

Disguised now as the Strong Man in leopard skin which left half his chest bare and exposed a hairy male nipple, the Lion Tamer came back, on his feet Roman sandals, on his powerful wrists leather thongs with buckles. Arching his back and puffing out his cheeks he lifted an impossible weight previously carried in by four men, two of them ostentatiously staggering; raised one arm with ponderous slowness to display an awesome underarm forest.

The bareback rider now dressed all demurely in a shabby raincoat sold raffle tickets between the rows of seats. During the intermission, when Lizzy and Rita puffed their fags outside, the Strong Man had changed into a dark blue suit with thin white stripes, ox-blood shoes and an open-neck white shirt, and talked to the bareback rider by the entrance, flashing his white teeth, resting one hand on the small of her back and killing himself laughing. Under the shabby brown raincoat she wore a tulle skirt and wellington boots. I saw again the pleated underskirt pressed to her thighs, rising and falling as she stood facing the wrong way on the pony's back, turning up her wrists and looking about with bright eyes, deep into her act, untouchable, pulled hither and thither by the music, by the ponies, by the Ringmaster's languidly twirling whip, by the turning Earth itself.

Then the band stood and played the 'Soldier's Song' and the lights were being taken down and we went out and I heard a tractor belt humming and there was the Strong Man on the steps of his caravan, talking to the bareback rider, now in headscarf and fur-lined bootees. They would travel all over Ireland together with Fossett's Circus. Rita Phelan asked me had I liked it. Had I Hell! The bareback rider! The bareback rider! Where would you find her equal in tights today?

8

The Protestant Gate

'Would you two lads like a spin?'

The Overland had a richly purposeful odour of leather and mahogany and Dado, a very indifferent driver, in wide-brim tweed cap and pigskin gloves with the tops rolled back, now with a casual touch of his fingertips on the rubber klaxon had summoned the Keegans (as genii out of a bottle) to throw wide open the heavy front gates, with a resolute blare of the horn.

He drove it in a highbacked lofty manner as if controlling a dromedary with a touch of a bamboo cane; the yellowing side-windows (not glass but some material before perspex) sagged and flapped in the breeze of our passage as Dado let her out, the speedometer wobbling at fifty and the floorboards heating up. It was grand airy motoring in high style and the Dote and I rode on a howdah, looking down benignly at our native bearers.

Dado drove us to a sweet shop on the road to Clane, where in the early winter dusk we saw the lights of CWC shining like an ocean liner out at sea, the castle of the Wogan-Browns by the Gollimockey stream, visible over the low hedges.

A black dip-stick with white calibrations down the sides was wiped in an oil rag, one of Dado's discarded shirts, and thrust firmly into the petrol tank, Dado having unscrewed the cap with its silvery winged Mercury, for he never knew how much petrol was in the tank, or whether she was dry, ordering sixteen or more cans from the village pump. A spare can was strapped to the running-board.

And so we would set out grandly. There were few cars on the roads. Dado drove the sky-blue Overland at a stately pace through Clane and Sallins, like Baroness Blixen driving to the Muthaiga Club in Nairobi, the guest in highest places, friend of big game hunters and titled people, Sir Northrup McMillan, Eric von Otter and the Prince of Wales.

But it is not of the Overland's travels around Kildare, now speeding, now crawling, for Dado refused to buy a driving licence, preferring to bribe the Guards with parts of trees chopped into logs, that I would speak; but of the enigmatic posture of Protestant gates. Postern gates.

I am thinking now of a certain gate in the townland of Donycomper opposite the Catholic cemetery. An imposing front entrance leads into some hidden Protestant estate. A wide gateway – more doorway than gateway – of some smooth hard expensive pale wood, birch or beech finished with layers of tongue oil, meshed with cast-iron cross-pieces and wrought metal scrollwork fastened with many nuts and bolts and latches and padlocks and rivets and deadlocks, faced the road with an inflexible Protestant gravity. This formidably wide gate was permanently closed, like an Anglican church, leading no doubt to tonsured lawns well and truly mowed by greyfaced Protestant gardeners, by scuffled driveway where a severe lady walked absently under a wide-brim sunhat, carrying a trug, followed as absently by the half-closed eyes of large somnolent comatose pedigree hounds; all would be protected by inherited wealth in that hidden demesne where I had no right to be.

It was – to borrow one of Mumu's formulations – the 'very epitome' of Ascendancy stuckupness, a very Protestant entrance which refused entry, but gritted between clenched teeth: KEEP OUT!

It was formidable as the striding giants of yore in their
seven-league boots, to a nipper in shorts and openwork
sandals soiled by cowshit that I had trodden in, yellowed by
field pollen and dandelions and buttercups, who liked to
consort with the snotty-nosed brats of lodge-gate tenants
very lax at paying their rent; impassable as the 'grim eight-
foot high iron-bound serving man' mentioned by John Donne.
The gate was shouting out in imperial fashion, 'Clear off
you bally Catholics – these are *Protestant* grounds! Take care!
Off with you now or by Christ we'll set the dogs on ye!'

And already we hear the deep baying of the killer pack.
Oh dear God didn't we take to our heels and off with us
down the slope; before us the shell of the mill, then the
humpbacked bridge; the Liffey pouring out through its five
arches and old Granny Greene herself sitting outside her
doorway, smoking a clay pipe, driven out by the turf smoke,
getting a breath of fresh air before venturing back into the
dark warren where all the Greenes lived in the dark.

'Lowry Maher floggin' de bar!'

'Burst the goalie!'

'Frig the fecker!'

Mumu referred disparagingly to those beyond the Pale as
'fishwives' and 'guttersnipes', hooligans and Yahoos. She
never joined us on those carefree Safaris for boiled sweets
and Liquorice Allsorts. The Dote and I, sons of bigots – as
befits those lucky ones born into privilege under the right
auspices – read P. C. Wren's *Beau Geste*. Our proud parents
would tell us how a fortune had been taken from the ground
by a resolute Higgins.

Bisbee and the vanished copper-mine towns (haunt of
ghost-town buffs) adjacent to doomed Tombstone near the
Mexican border of old Sonora was where my grand-uncle
Tom Higgins had made his pile in the 1860s. Now all had
gone back again into the ground. Waste dumps, headframes,
test holes, open pits, abandoned copper camps and railway
stops dot the region; a timely reminder of mining's fickle
nature, there under Mule Mountain.

9

Zeno's Café

Two European gentlemen sit facing each other diagonally across the carpet in deep leatherbound armchairs that smell of hot hide, their legs stretched out luxuriously to a heaped coalfire roaring up the chimney.

One is grossly corpulent with protruding boiled eyes who wheezes like a Pekinese while puffing away at a thick cigar. This is Fatty Warnants, the Belgian envoy to Ireland. Pale and bloated as a toad and sweating profusely, one chubby hand folded across its fellow and both resting on the immense tweedclad belly that rises and falls with each stertorous breath, whilst wallowing in the depths of the armchair like Mr Verloc, sate Fatty Warnants who ran the armaments business *Fabrique National,* supplying armoured carriers and FN rifles and ammunition to the Irish Army.

Fatty is a friend of Zeno Geldof, another Belgian, who owned The Broadway Café in O'Connell Street, known to Mumu as Under the Ocean because it was below the Ocean & Accident Assurance Co. Warnants is a friend of Joss's and Zeno Geldof, the Moorkens' fishing tackle and firearms shop in Upper Abbey Street not being far from Zeno's Café.

The three friends met in July each year at the Belgian Embassy in Ailesbury Road to celebrate the National Day for the King of the Belgians. A formal invitation was sent

out: *L'Ambassadeur de Belgique a l'honneur de vous faire savoir
qu'une Sainte Messe* . . .

Fumes of black tobacco drifted over their heads to collect
near the ceiling and through this acrid smokescreen they
boomed away at each other, above our heads, eavesdropping
behind the sofa. They seemed to be clearing phlegm from
their windpipes or gargling (in fact they were talking to
each other in Flemish).

The Flemish larynx was a darkly constraining sound-box
that emitted unheard-of gargles and groans, signifying God-
knows-what; the gorilla-speech of grunting Calibans. They
spoke as the Bogey Man spoke, in intense and compromising
vagaries, that or muttering incomprehensible gibberish; for
this was how men communicated on the Continent – this
dark talk would give you the shivers. And the women of
Belgium, how did they talk? Quacking like geese? Oh horrors! *Bedlam!*

The drawingroom seemed to have shrunk, congested by
the dense fumes from Fatty's thick cigar and Joss's bulldog
pipe. The Dote and I hid behind the sofa until driven from
the room by fits of the giggles; we were obliged to crawl
hurriedly away, in stitches.

The two gentlemen were silent for a moment, but halfway
up the stairs we heard them resume their dark Calibanish
grunting. Flemish swirled around the room, mixed with
tobacco fumes, suggesting distant places and savages, as
Lizzy Bolger came with eyes out on stalks starting from her
head, white as a sheet, summoned with the drinks tray by a
strong yank at the bell-pull.

One of the Moorken girls of Herentals and Antwerp had
married a Lieutenant-Colonel Edward Ghys who had served
in both wars. Another sister – Emilienne who was called
Tante Mil – had married Albert Buyle, the director of a
radium factory at Herentals. The Schelde at Antwerp, where
Joss's family were born, is wide and pushes a great tide
onwards.

Fatty had a French wife called Cleo; his real name was Gustave. Yet another Gustave.

When you stood at the urinal of the Grafton Picture House in the steamy atmosphere of gurgling pipes and the antiseptic tang of air-sweetening cubes dissolving at your feet in the piss and looking up at the shadowy forms of male and female pedestrians passing overhead, distorted in the rhomboids of thick glass, you would suppose yourself to be in a submarine.

When we walked up the white marble staircase of the Capital Cinema under the pictures of the stars, Robert Taylor and Spencer Tracy, Lana Turner and Merle Oberon, to the ticket office where complimentary passes were handed over by a female attendant in a purple uniform and pillbox hat with strap under the chin, her face made up like a mask, it was like being in a palace.

Sometimes on a winter's night we heard the sinister drone of Dorniers and Heinkels passing high overhead. Ours were no match for these. Lysanders and Avro Ansons (motto: 'Small But Fierce') took off from Baldonnel, flew out over Celbridge, over Killadoon wood, hid in the clouds until the danger had passed.

10

Wurung

Looking longingly once more through *Paris Salons* etc., and feasting my ravening eyes again on the shadowy nude ever stationary who never turned to face me under the studio skylight, I chanced upon some elongated Art volumes devoted to the Pre-Raphaelites and opening one at random was shocked to encounter the par-boiled eyes of the Bogey Man fixed steadfastly upon me.

He was sitting with a moony-faced woman with goggly gooseberry eyes who might have been his wife or sister, dressed in a windswept cape and bonnet. They were seated close together for reassurance and warmth in the stern of a ship just leaving for foreign parts, perhaps Australia. Wrapped in travel rugs about their knees both were staring as if mesmerised back at the receding quayside and the land they were leaving, staring straight at *me*, as if accusingly.

The unsettling windy daylight that suffused the painting suggested a port of departure where floods of tears might be in order and not far off; redolent too of a hospital forecourt where patients assembled, still weak in the legs, resistance still low, bidding adieu to doctors and nurses who had looked after them. The picture reeked of convalescence, as if tilted by sickness (no one there looked well); it was called *The Last of England*.

I asked Gina Greene to go with me into the cellar and

hand in hand with candles lit and wavering in the fetid updraught we descended sixteen steps by mildew and cobwebs into the stink and darkness below. To the arrowheads and mouldy masks of dragons and racks of empty wine bottles discoloured and hazed up, and there around the corner in the furthest recess was a damp sack by the wall, where he must have slept curled up like a dog. But of the Bogey himself there was no sign. The cellar was empty.

He had sailed away with his sick wife or the mad sister to the Antipodes, the hot continent of extraordinary creatures, buck-jumping kangaroos and sandblind upupas and leaping wombats that would come as no surprise to a pair as strange as they, perhaps already living in a shack in the Outback, in some remote place like Dajara or Wurung on the Flinders River near the Gulf of Carpentaria, far away, far away. Perhaps they had started a tannery there?

11

The Hand & Flower Press

Mumu, herself a voracious reader, had turned the Dote and myself into bookworms. The initiation came when we were six weeks in bed with measles in a darkened bedroom (we were moved to the Dodo's for a view of the Dublin hills) and not allowed to read. She read Hans Andersen to us; it was a revelation. Mrs Warren's library was there to be read; all Dickens with Boz and Cruikshank illustrations in a matched set, Scott's *Waverley* novels, which I found dull. P. C. Wren, Baroness Orczy and the rest in shelves that reached from floor to ceiling in the study. The first discovery of our own was Clarence E. Mulford. For some years a 'present from town' was invariably another two Hopalong Cassidy novels at two shillings each from Eason's in O'Connell Street, which Dado would bring back home in the bus, to find us waiting at the gate.

The packages were not to be unwrapped until we reached the house; I imagine so that Mumu could witness our delight. Hopalong and Mesquite Jenkins and Red Connors were our Wild West pals. Our next discovery was Sapper, all the Bulldog Drummond stories. We too became voracious readers. Dado did not read books but had on order a quantity of Irish and English newspapers in addition to the huge American newspapers that came from Los Angeles with his dividends.

The Dote and I were addicted to 'Mutt and Jeff' in the *Evening Herald* and 'Mandrake the Magician' in the *Evening Mail.* We had no dictionary in the house but Mumu could explain the hard words until she pretended to be stumped by '*Crime passionel*', by which time I had begun to put aside childish things. I was in the pram until no longer able to fit in it; would always be two years behind in my schooling, because the Dote had to begin with me and I was 'held back'. When already into puberty I beshat myself with excitement and Mumu ran a shallow bath and cleaned me as if I was an innocent again, handing me a large sponge when she perceived my embarrassment, to cover my shame.

Lizzy asked the Dote what he wanted to be when he grew up. The Dote answered stoutly: a crow. Mumu said he was stubborn as a mule, he dug his heels in and would 'go far'.

She said; 'Wanted: a detective, to arrest the course of time.'

'Steady the Buffs and let the Rangers pass,' said brother Bun, just arriving.

As a lad I was much given to melancholy brooding and bucolic reverie, oft sunken in apathy and sloth, addicted to daydreaming on or around lewd subjects, never in the best of health, wandering about in a dream, chronically anxious, chronically constipated, spending hours in the lavatory. It was my long puberty. Ah, puberty!

Mumu said that some girls were 'low', without going into too much detail. The big hot girls on the back road smelt of tea and jam; mouths daubed with lipstick seemed to bleed.

They coaxed: 'Ah, gizzakiss! Ah do! Ah g'wan!'

They threatened: 'I'm gona tell on yew so I will!'

They kicked football with us in Killadoon, screeching in the tackles or squatting on the embankment to watch us play, Patsy Keegan urging the kicker to 'burst the goalie'.

'I'm black out wiff yew!' Rita Phelan screeched naggishly at Grogan.

Even before I was assailed by dirty thoughts or unchaste desires, I felt a blush coming like a wave that must bear me along with it; the Cattle Trough Guilt had me blushing to the roots of my hair as fleshly temptation strode into view in the shape of two dozen hefty Protestant girls with fresh complexions out from the Charter School. Rounding Brady's Corner, chattering like starlings, with a few teachers pacing behind, out for an airing to Odlum's crossroads and the Hill of Ardrass; and all their Protestant shadows flitting by along the wall and the chattering and giggling risen to a crescendo as I appeared on my Raleigh, mortified as sin and already blushing. Sometimes I would turn about and pedal back up Springfield front avenue as though I had forgotten something, and cycle down the back avenue to see the tail-end of the crocodile passing by Miss Coyle's cottage. Tail-ends were *Verboten*. My confessor urged me to pray for the grace of holy purity.

Dado warned us that we would 'ruin' our eyes by too much reading. We were blinding ourselves. He himself had no interest in books but did much browsing in newspapers. His heroes all tended to be stereotypes of himself – Gordon Richards who had ridden more winners than any jockey alive; the diminutive brave Irish fullback Con Murphy; the skinny runner Tommy Coneff of Kildare; and the even skinnier boxer Jimmy Wilde, the ghost with a hammer in each hand.

He spent much time gaping vacantly out of windows, revolving a spent match in one ear, then the other. In those rapt vacant times perchance he was invoking and evolving the fabulous creatures so colourfully involved amid the flora and fauna of his stories of Finn MacCool and Jack Doyle and Dan O'Mahony, famed for his Irish Whip. He had a repertoire of yarns that involved giants, ogres, hobgoblins, monsters, not forgetting the resident fairy that was to be seen – if you were quick enough – in the rose bushes by the summerhouse.

He spoke often of the olden days and of 'Aten Matches' or eating contests between a couple of legendary trenchermen pitted against each other, in consuming legs and (if up to it) thighs of 'dunkeys' roasted over a spit for the occasion. When one contestant could eat no more he gave his opponent best. The champion said to fetch in the mother (mudderdunkey said Grogan in the re-telling) donkey and he would eat some of her too.

I know that in our heroic ages, the apocryphal time that may never have existed and certainly not as we imagined it, in those lost and forgotten times, when the hindquarters of a Wicklow deer or Irish elk were served up, the bravest warrior present had the right to the thigh, it was the champion's portion and woe betide any man present who laid claim to it or gainsaid him; for then both would seize their swords and go at it hammer and tongs in a 'fight to the death', Dado repeated with relish.

These were not Grimm-like tall tales and folk yarns about greedy German giants, I see now, but rather folk-tales reflecting fears or tremors boding ill, passed on from father to son, my father having heard it from his father as he from his, so that those terrible times of famine would not be forgotten.

When Mumu asked me to pass her the big scissors I carelessly tossed it to her as she lay propped up on pillows on her bed covered with newspapers, their sheets buckled and scattered amid *Good Housekeeping* and *Woman's Own*, and her boobies loose in a thin-strap nightdress. She threw me a quick censorious look.

'That's very rude. You mustn't throw things at ladies; you could rupture my breast.'

I heard 'rapture' and 'my breasts' and had a sudden twinge of Old Adam and instantly assumed The Guilty Look. For in our family I had two faces: The Guilty Look and The Bear's Face, one developing from the other, compounding chagrin and intense embarrassment at being found out.

Eau: Faiblesse devant les tentations.

One Sunday after Mass in Straffan I took a bundle of
London newspapers into the rockery for peace and quiet,
in order to study the long sinful legs (ungirt was unchaste)
of the variety girls without any inhibitory checks in the
Sunday Dispatch.

Among the books in the study I had come upon *Paris
Salons, Cafés and Cabarets* by Sisley Huddleston and spent
much time poring over a monochrome nude posing in a
shadowy studio. On the orderly shelves of the Dodo's reference library I found neat piles of *Lilliput* and in them stark
naked English ingénues photographed by Douglas Glass in
a field of English wheat.

'With yourself or with others?' questions the priest from
behind the wire grille partition that separates us. I see his
tilted profile, hand to brow. He does not look at me. The
nuns told us that the secrets of the confessional are 'sacred',
and in any case always forgotten by the priest the moment
he steps out of the confessional. I smell the sacred wood
and the priest's hair-oil. I have been pulling my wire again,
while 'entertaining immodest thoughts'.

I take a breath; falling back into deep abasement. 'Wiffme-
self Fawdur.'

The priest shifts in his seat, the face comes closer, the
whispery voice asks, 'How many times?'

I must not let this sin catch hold of me. For my penance
would I say three Our Fathers and a Credo. Did I know the
Credo?

'Yis Fawdur,' I whisper.

'Go in peace then, my child,' the priest murmurs. 'Say a
prayer for me.'

The little Judas slides shut.

And now, trembling as if in the presence of something
sacred, summoned by a surreptitious joy, I quickly undress

and already stiff slide feet first into the tepid brown water in the ditch that embraces me. Eel-like I push it into the yielding mud, fornicating with the bank that bulges up at me in an obliging feminine way. The muddy water of the stream shat into by cattle holds me fast; the roaring in my ears is the circulation of the earth's blood, I smell the fresh trampled grass where the beasts have come down to drink and I am one with them and all creation shitting and shameless. Fibrous white stuff floats out of me and I see my rapt face reflected in water like the moon in clouds.

Drained by self-abuse I crawl from the ditch like Crusoe from the wreck, to dry myself with a linen pocket handkerchief and dress by a bed of nettles.

The Hand & Flower Press! The Hand & Flower Press! A fig to the fiction of holiness, to all lay priests!

I began to cultivate a taste for meditation and vague daydreaming.

A definitely risky word was 'suspenders' (suss-spend-ers) that hissed like a snake, even if Dado wore men's suspenders to hold up his socks with little clasps that clipped on like ferret's teeth. Whereas Mumu, ever coy, wore a lady's suspenders fixed onto a hidden corset that required much artful wriggling and bodily contortions with a quick catching of the breath in order to bring stockings and garters of crushed strawberry into alignment, that brought a gratified flush to her powdered cheeks.

As with halitosis or the toadstool reputed to be poisonous (emitting a sudden puff of decay when trodden on unawares), another unsettling word that sometimes cropped up in my reading was 'chastity' (chas-titty), ogling me, invoking the somewhat shameful spectacle of shy Mumu nipping up her tweed skirt to adjust the slipping garter, revealing a guilty border of corset with fancy stitching and lubricious lace-bordered trim of fine crochet-work in off-white already suspiciously stained; the buff and subtle dove-grey overlaid by some heavy usage, depicting the god Pan and a primordial scene in full rut in broad daylight, shamelessly copulating.

The bedroom was far away, the chamber-pot always in use. When Mumu got out of bed for her ablutions (and she was to spend years in bed when her nerves went against her) and went off in her Japanese kimono of writhing dragons and sluttish slippers to the bathroom to cut her corns, I saw the soiled and discarded corset thrown down on the bed and felt uneasy in its presence. It had a strong purposeful female presence all its own; a clinging gluey smell, sweetish – the disturbing spent whiff of warm plasticine.

Kitted Out for Killashee

The Dote and I were fitted out with:

2 Dark Grey Suits, 1 extra pants,
4 Shirts – 2 grey and 2 white,
2 Grey Pullovers – V neck (long sleeves),
3 pairs Pyjamas,
3 pairs White Socks,
3 Pairs Grey Stockings,
12 Handkerchiefs,
3 Hand Towels,
1 Bath Towel,
1 Laundry Bag,
Dressing Gown, Slippers, Toilet Requisites,
Clothes Brush, Shoe Cleaning Materials,
1 pair Walking Shoes,
1 pair Light Indoor Shoes (black, laced),
1 pair Brown Sandals,
1 pair Wellingtons,
1 pair Blankets,
3 pairs Sheets,
3 Pillow Cases,
Rug or Eiderdown,
3 Table Napkins,
Breakfast Knife and Silver Fork,
Silver Dessert & Tea Spoons (All engraved
with pupil's initials), All articles of clothing
to be marked with pupil's name and, in addition,
the number '26' on articles for the laundry.

FOOTBALL: Green Jersey,
White Togs,
Green and White Socks,
DRILL: All White – Woollen Jersey,
Twill Pants (short),
Drill Shoes,
all procurable at
'Our Boys', 24 Wicklow Street, Dublin.

I write 'A.M.D.G.' on each page top of my lined theme book, meaning For the greater glory of God. When the page is full I write 'L.D.S.' at the foot, meaning *Laus Deo Semper*, Praise God always. So that all my work, full of errors, is always in His honour. I miss Springfield: the Place That Never Changes. Our serious Catholic education begins.

Sunday was visiting day but Mother Mulcahy advised Mumu not to call for a fortnight, to 'allow the two boys to settle in'. Dermot Doorley from Longford would show us the ropes. The Christmas vacation seemed far away. Our Lady's Bower felt cold and austere. I thought of Haffner's peppery sausages bursting open in the pan, Dado crossing his legs (in plus-fours) and shaking out his napkin at supper. We marched through Killadoon wood with the Keegan boys, all Republican Irregulars, chanting:

> I stuck my nose up a nanny goat's hole,
> And the smell, it nearly blinded me!

Walking backwards in a dream, staring up at the sea-green dome, the daydreamer Glynn fell with a weak little cry into the goldfish pond. He wears teeth-braces and is very vague. Madame Loyola gave him a special exercise book for him to compose his stories. He wrote ('I had been forestalled . . .') of Knights at the Crusades, ancient times. I saw only a jackass looking over a gate as it begins its atrocious bray.

We wear coarse jerseys of sackcloth on play-up days and our faces turn strange colours as we struggle in the thick grass. The Dote wears a loose cardigan of greengage and candy; he unknots his school tie, laces up his football boots, totters out into the playing-field.

At Christmas Springfield appears to have shrunk. We put on grand airs before the rustics; wear ties, become proper little gents, snobs. Prigs.

A fire was lit in the nursery and as a treat (for it was the last day of the holidays) we were served tea and scones with Mumu hovering around, all solicitude, our trunks packed and Dado already backing the Overland out of the garage. We prayed that the Guards would be out cycling on their big black bikes, so that the unlicensed Overland could not pass through Sallins, Clane or Naas, and we would miss the sad churchbells of Clane, the fancied temptations of Manzer's. I had discovered Sir Arthur Conan Doyle and was immersed in *A Scandal in Bohemia*.

Finicky about food and who served it to me, I would starve in Killashee, for I would not eat buttered bread and was reduced to licking toothpaste to kill the pangs of hunger. Coldsores on my lower lip went septic and I was picking at this in class where Madame Ita Magdalen was raging, had instituted a reign of terror. She made Hugo Merrin and myself wear leather gloves in class, a stigmata like dunces' caps. Madame Ita Magdalen had russet coloured cheeks like Bramley Seedlings with the hoary aura of apples about them, a down of fine white hair visible in slanting sunlight. For evening devotions she wore a veil over her wimple.

Madame Patrick Clare took us for walks through the sunken Pleasure Grounds, down hundreds of steps to the swimming pool long out of use, emptied of water, with clumps of dead leaves and crow droppings. We walked along the path covered in moss and overhung by rhododendrons. Madame 'Paddy' Clare was a stout calm nun, but the tall and angular (and often angry) Madame Ita Magdalen was a storm. Culprits were told to stand in corners, then outside the classroom, then put in solitary confinement in the dark store cupboard opposite. Jolly visiting priests called for half days, asked that some of the boys put on the gloves and box for them, at which Madame Ita Magdalen flushed and showed her great horse teeth, taken by the spectacle of footwork and feint as blows rained down on bare boy-flesh and the stoutly perspiring visitor looked as if he might put on the gloves himself and try a few rounds with Madame Ita Magdalen, who had put a coy hand up to her face, discovered blushing like a bride. The boxers fought in a hypothetical sort of ring formed by the desks pulled back in the classroom where Madame Loyola (who 'took' French) had written on the blackboard:

> un petit ruisseau comme un ver, la forêt
> en automne, la mer iodée et tumultueuse,
> les ports.

Madame Ita Magdalen's face had a saltpetred fuzz of fair hair over a maroon complexion that flooded with dark blood like the wattles of a turkey-cock when her dander was up. At the head of the table in the refectory she sat between her pets, lashing into her lunch; a great engine of resentment was being stoked up as she cleared her plate of gristly meat and turnips and spuds, taking great draughts of water from the jug, and then putting away a sago pudding with prunes; a repast that might have ended not with a prayer but with a resounding belch.

But no, for she was sucking in her great herbivorous buckteeth and rolling up her napkin to fit it into its plastic ring and rising to say grace, indicating that the meal was over.

'All in!'
'All out!!' went the bells and whistles.
Walks were 'off', Scarisbrook was ordered into the mop cupboard. There was a distinct impression that boys if left

to their own devices could only get into trouble, would get out of control. Mr O'Neill the Games Master ran up and down blowing a whistle. Domination was a kind of sexual play. The huge fat priest heard confessions sitting on a chair at a prie-dieu, the sinner perfectly visible, kneeling with bowed head, murmuring his sins. The whole school walked in silence up and down the corridor, as punishment. I thought, these thwarted nuns might have found their true vocation in a field hospital or leper colony.

I wouldn't eat butter, which I associated with cows and lactation, the softness and sickness of womankind. Meat had to be cooked to a cinder or I wouldn't touch it. ('Don't play with your food!') I blushed to the roots of my hair when I felt the Cattle Trough Guilt swooping down over me again. 'Immodest thoughts' tended to involve the darkly attractive Molly Cushen with the deep silky voice who lived up Temple-mills way near the weir.

Running water was an aphrodisiac before I knew the meaning of the word: the flushing of the nuns told me something before I could put two and two together.

I pronounced Thames as 'de Tams', and the class tittered.

Madame Ita Magdalen said we were no better than savages and the whole class was put in detention. Imperator Basil Fogarty had read aloud an account of ancient Rome for the whole school at lunch and our class had been caught up in a game of make-believe in the long grass of the playing field, where slave struggled with slave, caught in nets, and cruel Caesar gave the thumbs-down sign for the victim to be dispatched, whereupon Madame came out (gone the colour of a turkey-cock) and blew her whistle for the entire school to go indoors. She said she would not have us behaving like savages. Anthony Scarisbrook showed us the discoloured and enlarged veins of his wrists where Madame had punished him with the stick. 'It's not right,' he said. He would write home and tell his parents, so he would. But all our outgoing mail was read and censored; we were held in trust never to say or write anything derogatory about Our Lady's Bower, ever. We were honour bound.

We hear of Eck, Hus, Zwingli, Euclid, the Diet of Worms. We walk the corridors in silence, it's punishment for the whole school, Madame's pets are encouraged to sneak on us. Madame takes out the stick, sucks in her buck-teeth, goes white in the face. Speaking is forbidden at lunch and supper; we retire to bed in daylight, where speaking is also forbidden. In Madame's classroom a reign of terror begins. I am sent into the dark cubbyhole where the mops and brooms are kept. Madame says I have a bull neck. 'If I have to spend all day,' Madame says up on her rostrum, drawing in her breath, 'if I have to spend all week, you'll get this right.'

I am struck on the back of the head with the tin edge of the ruler, which does nothing to help me remember French irregular verbs.

'No surrender!' cries Louis Noonan.

Wednesday night is bath-night. We wear full-length bathing drawers in the bath and are forbidden to lock the door, it must be left wide open. Madame shows us how to soap ourselves and cover up again. Sometimes oh God in she rushes to empty a bucket of cold water over the bather. Madame comes from Kerry and could kill you if you did not know your French verbs. Louis Noonan says we should all march out down the front avenue, with drums playing; a revolution!

Madame storms in, mounts the rostrum, takes a handkerchief from her habit and with both forefingers together delicately blows her nose.

Platters of thickly buttered bread are set out on the refectory tables; the light shines on the glasses and silver, all engraved with pupil's initials. I can see the trees in the Pleasure Grounds, silently I beg permission to rise, walk to the kitchen entrance where an old nun hands me a plate of dry bread and a small portion of jam to spread on it. If she forgets to come, I am too timid to complain, and go hungry to bed. I drink cups of water in the dormitory, it is still daylight outside, I hear the birds, lick paint off lead soldiers and hope to die.

Basil Fogarty reads *Hiawatha* for both classes; Hal Hosty sings 'South of the Border' and Madame goes red with embarrassment again; bending low before the altar, the stout wheezing priest (who hears our confessions and the nun's confessions) strikes his breast and intones, *In principio erat verbum, et verbum erat apud Deum,* and Eric Sanderson rings the little bell. The whole school sings the *Veni Creator.* Madame wears a veil over the shell of her coif, which she raises to receive Holy Communion on her tongue. Mother Superior (Mother Mulcahy) looks just like Eugene Pacelli; she comes every Friday to read reports and give out class cards. She gives us a spiff. Madame Loyola beats us; we are hidden away in Our Lady's Bower, Killashee, Naas, County Kildare. It has no end; the long term engulfs us. We sing:

> This time ten weeks where shall we beee?
> Outside the gates of misereee!

Ten weeks: an eternity.

My young brother and I are in a class together under Madame Loyola. When we go up a class we will be under Madame Ita Magdalen. And then God helps us. Our class

Pat Rogers,	John Quirke,
Jim Morris,	Cormac Brady,
Liam Lynch,	Hugo Merrins,
Eugene McCabe,	John Glynn,
Eric Sanderson,	Tony Sweeney,
David Hogan,	Peter and Aiken Austin,
Ted Little,	Jimmy Donnelly,
Michael Cuddy,	Pat Pullen,
Frank and Joe O'Reilly,	Pat and John Markey,
Aidan and Colman Higgins.	

Subjects taught as prescribed by the revised Primary

School Syllabus. Optional subjects: Piano, Riding. Fees
to be paid in advance.

In the melancholy matter of so-called self-abuse the Piscean
preference has always been to do it in water, take the *soi-
disant* wriggling beast Thingamajig in a cattle-trough in
August and September heat. Above me the vaulted sky of
Clare's madness.

Alongside the cattle-trough stood the ring-pump which
brought ice-cold water up out of the ground. A galvanised
wrought-iron chute was bent and attached by wire to the
mouth and water pumped into the trough. Heifers and polly
bulls with dusty polls stood in liquid dung and laid their
heads across each other's shoulders, rolled their oily eyes
and beshat themselves and then dipped hairy chins into the
icy water that held my member as in a vice. They slurped it
up, making a noise like suction pumps, ignoring the desperate exertions of the pale nudist (Crusoe hauling booty from
the wreck) with his tool stuck into the mossy side as if into
female pubic hair. And meanwhile what was the Dote up to?

Why, adding to his stamp collection, fiddling with tweez-
ers. Having saved up sufficient pennies and tanners he had
taken out a subscription for *Wide World* and began an intense
study of its contents. He had progressed in one hop from
Wizard to *Wide World*, from Clarence E. Mulford to Charles
Dickens. He was reading *Martin Chuzzlewit*, then it was Henry
Williamson's *Chronicle of Ancient Sunlight*, then Tolstoy's *War
and Peace*. There was no stopping him.

13

A Day at the National School

Out on the Templemills Road opposite The Grove and the squat Methodist Church stood the National School, a much-dreaded institute long renowned for the punishments meted out there by the Brothers. The lads of the Convent trembled at the notion of ever attending; for if the nuns were severe enough with the strap, the Brothers were savages altogether with the stick. The Dote and I, all atremble, were dispatched there. For one trying day we suffered under the thumbs of iron disciplinarians and begged that we never be sent back.

The windows were high in the long classroom and the supply of daylight and fresh air limited because of the tall demesne walls opposite and the stand of trees beyond and, a-din the place of torture, the huffing and snuffing of a score or more of uneasy hobbledehoys who stood with hands behind their backs and shoulders against the wall, for a spelling test. Some of the lads we had known in Convent days were now big strapping youths.

We, with Killashee behind us, kept out of the playground at first break, sat on the river-wall and threw heels of our sandwiches down for the fish. Our new schoolmates cat-called and mocked our high and mighty accents until a hand-bell was rung and we were told to close our books and stand along the wall for a spelling test.

'Stand out there, Ned Colfer,' the teacher called, 'and let's hear you spell "patriotism" for us. Pay-tree-ah-tissm.' Pulling a woeful face (for didn't he have a woeful stutter?) and swallowing a frog, Colfer prepared for humiliation.

He had shut his eyes the better to concentrate, to show he was trying.

'Now Ned, take your time. Don't rush it. We have all the time in the world. Pay-tree-ah-tisssm.'

'Pat-pat-pat . . .' stuttered Colfer, gone red as a turkey.

'Take your time, Ned,' purred the teacher, smooth as silk, reaching for the stick.

'Put-put-put . . .'

'Pit-pit-pit . . .' stuttered Colfer, sweating.

The teacher stood up, stick in hand, looking grimly determined now.

'Pot-pot-pot, ppptk!' Colfer swallowed and stopped, his eyes still closed.

'Very well then. Now Colfer, you can surely spell "stupidity"?'

'Stew-stew-stew, ssppsssppppk!'

The cane crashed down on Colfer's inky desk, scored with penknife cuts and abrasions, causing him to jump and his eyes to fly open. Now he was for it.

'Stand out there until I stew-stew you, numbskull. You're the straw that broke the camel's back. Stand out there!' Ned Colfer awkwardly held out a trembling hand at face-level. The teacher brought it down and steadied it, measured his stroke, lifted the cane high. Colfer chewed his scummy lips and got all tightened up, with eyes closed again prepared for punishment.

I heard the crows squabbling in the trees and the murmur of the river running out under the knots in the floorboards and wished myself far away. Colfer had curled up his fingers to take the blows and now both hands were under his oxters and he had his head down as the teacher unrolled an old worn well-used map of Ireland all wrinkled and torn to point out County Kildare with the stick which I expected to see spotted with Colfer's blood.

'Can anyone tell me how many counties there were in the Pale?' Clever brother the Dote, looking around at the numbskulls who had not raised a hand, cautiously raised one of his.

After a serious consultation that evening our kind parents, easily persuaded by our begging ('We don't ever want to go back to *that* place!'), had agreed to send us to Clongowes Wood College, where our two elder brothers had gone, and Cousins Syl and Pompey. Mumu came to tuck us in and convey the good news; that very night she would write to the Rector, Father Fergal McGrath. The fees were stiff, so we would have to work hard. We said, 'Yippee!' and did handstands on our beds. Smiling Mumu tucked us in and told us to say our prayers and be good boys.

We would miss a term. But a tutor would be found in the village to prepare us for the Jesuits. Presently the prospectus arrived. We would be kitted out at Our Boys in Dublin, in hardwearing mustard-brown matching herringbone tweed two-piece suits, feeling very grand indeed after two fittings, standing grave as statues before a long mirror.

14

The Temptress, the Eely River

I had thought always of her as The One. She travelled to and from Dublin by bus. I didn't know her name. Perhaps she was a trainee nurse doing her intern? On one memorable occasion she had sat beside me and I breathed in a ferny scent of hair and flesh that was stronger than cosmetics. When she moved the scent became stronger. She spoke to a friend, craning back, telling of stockings she had purchased at Garnett's in Dublin, and I listened.

I had seen Mumu lift her skirt and seen the mark of garters where they gripped the thighs but never had I seen a young one lift her skirt, and never kissed a pretty Prod, and this one was so pretty, and I wondered what it would be like, to kiss her. I saw her skirt raised above her knees as she showed me the Garnett's stockings and spoke of mesh and size (so difficult to get during the Emergency when everything was rationed) and kneeling down in adoration before her I was permitted to kiss those warm odorous thighs so obscurely craved. You may kiss me there, she whispered to me. Just once, just there, no higher. I fancied that something venturesome peeped out at me from half-closed mischievous eyes; and I did. Her calmness unsettled me; I was too shy to look at her, much less speak to her, I who was too young for her.

When she stared out the window I saw her reflection watching me in the glass, where lights shone and people with parcels had gathered to wait for the bus, and I encountered a glance both moist and disturbing, a quick feminine glance that sank into me before I could turn away. I thought of her walking in the wards and speaking softly to sick ones. The texture of her Proddy skin was glazed and clouded as if greyish blue smoke tinged her living flesh, lent it a down of dusk. Then my furtive and craven Catholic eye fell to the bulge of her amply rounded thigh, to the grey-blue tracery of fine veins at her wrist where bare skin showed in the vee of her gloves, and the teasing bulge of her garter. She wore a small lady-model wristwatch which I imagined would show a different sort of Protestant Time; corncoloured hair was cut to the shape of her face, brownskinned, and the same blue veins throbbed at her temples.

'Actually I did,' she told her friend.

Her breath told me what she had had to eat. Actually I didn't, actually I wouldn't... actually I just might. She glanced up at the parcel on the luggage rack where the advertisement said, 'We lead, others may follow'. And a hobbledehoy with flaming ears lifted it down before she could stretch up for it and she thanked him, dipping her eyes. She rose up, preparing to go, and I let her out into the aisle.

I had felt embarrassed when sitting next to her in an untoward intimacy of odours and intake and exhalation of breath, and imagined that a sort of counterfeit intimacy had sprung up between us and been wordlessly shared, even if I could not bring myself to speak to her. She for her part had probably been relieved that I hadn't. I followed her, Dado at the front of the bus making a great show of letting her go out first before him, doing the gallant. Her calves quivered in high heels as she walked away, going to a girl-friend who came with her bicycle, holding it by the handle-bars. She had a neat feminine way of mounting, thrusting herself forward on the pedals and then subsiding onto the saddle. She began to move off, pushed by the friend who walked alongside. As she went a sense of evening accompanied her and the pain which I had hardly felt at first kept on growing. As she went away a part of my unformed life went with her.

Heavy rolls of the evening editions were being hurled from the roof of the bus with the bicycles stacked there lifted down and the driver had stepped into Breen's to slake his thirst. She, sadly departing, waved back. She combined blonde and brunette elements of two film actresses I secretly desired: Priscilla Lane and Evelyn Keys.

Oh but she was evermore The One!

Shriven by the handsome curate whom we call Father Basilica, who was a novice in Rome and cannot forget the Holy City (it features in every sermon and the great basilicas are named), and feeling very pious, I carry a prayer book about with me, the squat size of the *Mickey Mouse Annual*, and take it up the fields in order to pray undisturbed and to commune with nature. It has a white laminated cover of horn or ivory with IHS embossed in silver, shooting out static flames, with a purple book-mark to hold my place.

I kneel rapt in prayer before the frog-infested pond near the fox covert and watch the frogs rise and sink with out-stretched skinny arms, leaving trails of bubbles as they go, kicking up powdery clay from the bed of the pond, or breaking the surface to slowly open the portals of their wise old eyes as though it were the first day of Creation. They are the image of nude old men, bald-headed with their mickies wizened away to nothing, floating through clouds, they sail up and down for air, jerking spasmodically with long obscene hind legs. They burrow into the powdery clay that rises up like smoke, digging themselves in until only their bums stick out.

The tadpoles devour each other indiscriminately, feeling no pain, working up from the tail; two or three of them stuck together, feeding, the middle one half-eaten by the

end one, and only the head of the foremost one remaining.
Rita Phelan calls them pollywoggles.

A labouring man with his coat off in the heat, wearing
what Rita calls 'galluses' (his braces) looks over the hedge
and discovers me kneeling by the pond.

'Grand day out!' he calls.

'Grand!' I simper, feeling very silly, a right eejit.

His red-faced brother discovered me a week later, the
heatwave continuing unabated, kneeling naked and poring
over one of the Dodo's *Lilliput*s with English girls in the
nude up to their bums in an English wheatfield. A coarse
amiable voice called out in derision as I crawled into a bush,
dragging my shirt and shorts in after me. I watched him
cross the field when I was decent and dressed. He wore big
hobnail boots and carried a blackened billy-can; without
breaking his stride he jumped the ditch into the next field,
striding onward, whistling, not a bother on him. I heard a
cuckoo calling in the Crooked Meadow. Where I stood was
the limit of Dado's seventy-two acres; beyond lay Matt
Dempsey's land and Major Brooke's land again, where the
hare-coursing took place, the killing on the slope.

'That Phelan girl is a right h,u,r,e,' Dado said, sucking in a
morsel of gristle in his teeth.

I kept my eyes fixed on my plate.

'May I replenish?' asked brother Bun in a fatuous way,
holding up the carafe of water. 'Do you use Long Melford,
Sir?'

The days press in. In an aimless sort of way I cycle about,
without any design or purpose. A donkey starts to bray,
drawing in terrible lungfuls of agony; a haycock begins
steaming. I feel the bridge wall vibrate. Two hundred yards
away in the shallows two young women of surpassing beauty
wade in their bathing costumes below Straffan bridge. Water
invites, the whole earth breathes; I sink ever deeper into
shame and abasement. Confession is torment. I tell my sins

to Father Basilica. My sins are always the same, dirty thoughts.

I float with the current that drags me down, pulling at myself, swallowing water, half drowning, sinking ever deeper into shame and abasement.

Behind the fretted baize in the wired-up and domed valves of the wet batteries a red light pulsates, electrical discharges begin to squeak and gibber, bubbling away with static, and a throaty seductive female voice calls out voluptuously, 'Hello, hello, we're gonna play rolypoly today!' and is instantly cut off by howling frictional electricity, spluttering and gurgling with the hydrogen gas being emitted from sulphuric acid. The heat is sweltering. The word 'stall' excites me.

The river is full of eels, Josey Darlington tells me. He is working in the forge for his father the blacksmith. Two pretty cyclists pass Sadlier's Harness Parts and ride onto the bridge where a breeze makes their thin skirts fly up. I see their shadows pass on the bridge wall opposite, hear their startled cries.

Dado tells Mumu that Rita Phelan is a brazen hussy.

Stunted Grogan the cruel stretcher of cats has started going steady with Rita Phelan. Rita is his moth; Grogan is no Molly. Mumu says they are well met.

Whistling between his teeth Grogan curry-combs Sally the mare, mounted on a small foot-stool to reach her spine.

I ask whether Sally likes it.

'Begob she loves it,' Grogan says, whistling tunelessly, and feeling hocks and tendons, pushing the bay's flanks.

A huge inquisitive horse-eye regards me.

'Whoa there, me beauty!'

Sally's hooves strike the cement ramp with a ring of steel and sparks fly.

Dado collected two free balcony passes in the booking office halfway up the grand stairs at the Capital and retreated down to the street as we passed in through the purple curtain with our bags of fudge, going by the framed photographs of Hollywood stars, Robert Taylor, Spencer Tracy, Ida Lupino, the usherette going before us with a torch into the dark, leading us to our seats, and into the middle of my most secret and fulfilling dream come true: the secret island under the sea! *Bahama Idyll* starring Madeleine Carroll and Sterling Hayden is in technicolor, both have blonde hair and are very tanned, the sea is absolutely blue. Even the title intoxicates me: *Bahama Idyll*! Idyll means lounging about in the sun, Bahama is an atoll in the Gulf of Mexico. In an office in a skyscraper in the big city (Chicago or New York) Madeleine Carroll removes her stockings behind a screen. With strained anxious faces they approach each other in a cave under the sea. We see it through to the end. It begins again. The curtains part and lights like an Aurora Borealis flood the screen and the film, which we have seen from the middle, begins for us.

Something light as a feather tickled my bare hairless leg in my first pair of longers and instinctively I had one hand to it as it reached my knee and drew out not a woodlouse, spider nor a cockroach but a small house mouse which I dropped over the balcony rail without second thoughts. Not a sound came from below, where some matinée idlers were coughing in the poorer seats, utilising the toilets.

We chew fudge and observe Madeleine Carroll move behind the screen to unzip her garter and begin to remove her stockings again, while Sterling Hayden, for modesty's sake, waits on the other side of the screen, and the Dote is whispering, 'This is where we came in.' Reluctantly I follow him up the dark aisle with the little spotlights under the steps where the usherette points her beam. We pass out by the curtain and Dado is waiting for us. Gallantly he asks whether we have been any trouble to her. 'Oh none at all,' she says. She wears an extraordinary bellhop uniform in purple with a purple pillar-box hat worn at a rakish angle with a strap under her chin. Dado has been across the street in the Gresham Bar where no doubt his cronies, the lounge lizards, congregate.

I think that Dado's cut-down trousers are not as smart as Sterling Hayden's but about Madeleine Carroll's shorts I cannot even begin to think. I get sick in the bus going home in daylight. Mumu asks us what we saw and did we like it. We tell her something about *Bahama Idyll.*

'It wasn't like *Coral Island,*' I said.

Mumu had the cards set out for Pelman Patience.

'I have a crow to pluck with yew, mister!'

Patsy fixed me with an implacable glare and took a step closer, rolling up his shirt sleeves to demonstrate the stringy muscles of a labouring man's son. His face had gone a curious colour, pinched white about the nostrils.

Patsy's face changed colour with his moods.

'Don't I have yew now!'

The sudden blow – when it came – arrived from far away, striking me high up on the chest, knocking all the wind out of me.

'Don't!'

'I have yew now!'

'You haven't, you know.'

Patsy raised his fist as if to repeat the blow, then put his arm about my neck and wrestled me affectionately to the ground.

I strip naked, roll in dry horse-dung, swallow frogspawn, crawl through the wheatfield. The roan stallion prepares to mount the bay mare. Drawing back hairy black lips to expose great horse-teeth in a terrible grin, the stallion mounts from behind. Awash in sweat, the pair of them seem unusually naked, stripped to necessity, stuck together in a field of rolling hillocks. Like angels struggling to fold their heavy wings they go dancing over the hillocky field, kissing and biting through manes of hair, snorting and whinnying.

Brother Bun squirts cold water over me from a garden hose. He is dressed in a black bathing costume that sags and reaches halfway down his freckled legs and I see the limp outline of his little willie outlined in the damp cloth. Silently I chase him out of the garden, over the paling, down the front meadow, over the paling onto the front avenue, across the second paling, into the paddock; he slips through a five-bar gate and runs bleating away. I take a breather at the gate, watch him run away from me, and my great anger subsides, subsides.

The brazen hussy puts a thrawneen into my mouth and dares me to race her to a knot in the centre.

'I dar yew and I double-dar yew,' she challenges me.

Her breath steams in the cold air, her nostrils flare as she clamps her mouth on the thrawneen and begins ravenously eating it. I see her approaching eyes, her working mouth, I bite the thrawneen short and give her best, it hangs from her mouth with my spittle on it. She makes as if to strike me.

'Take a coward's blow!'

We stand face to face. She reaches out and touches me.

'Give us a coort. Ah give us a squeeze!'

She turns on her heel laughing. I smell her cheap perfume and her lipstick. For me she feels nothing but contempt. The frozen pump behind her is trussed up like a madman's trousers.

She and Grogan slip into the hayshed. When they reappear an hour later Grogan looks pale and drained. Is she his moth?

Josey Darlington pulled the eel trapped in his night-lines out of the Liffey. Dragging the hook from its obstinate black jaw he threw it up the bank where it thrashed in sudden convulsions.

'It's desperate hard to kill an auld ale. It's desperate killing

wonna dim lads. De oney way is to spit tobacco juice down
its nick. Be careful. They'd bite the hand offa you.'

The river, gathering speed as it neared the weir, suddenly
dropped from sight. Swallows were dipping for insects. 'By
my sowl . . .'

Neddy Keegan broke the necks of rabbits under the heel
of his boot or with the hard heel of his hand with a karate
chop. Old Mrs Henry sawed the heads off cockerels with
the carving knife and gave the heads to the cats. The fowl
seemed to take the sudden effusion of blood in their stride,
as a fact of life. They went on scratching for food, rooting
about and clucking, making that droning sound in their
throats that my brother and I called Years-Gone-By.

The eel began to slither back towards the river, but Josey
kicked it away, cursing. He took out his knife and snapped
open the blade. The eel coiled itself without a sound about
the claspknife as Josey dug, grunting, at its neck; bones and
tendons were severed and blood splattered on the grass.

15

That Noble Pile

'Measurement began our might' pontificated Yeats, the Protestant tenant extraordinaire and poet-with-tenure at Thoor Ballylee, humming to himself, up his winding stairs.

Home was where? Home was what?

For the inheritors of forfeited estates and lands it was a surrogate home, a place they would have to get used to; for the very poor, the defeated, home had become a torture-chamber. For the adventurous, it was the place to set out from; for the unadventurous, it was the place where personal property was secure, where one sat down and supped in peace.

Cottages, lodges, bathing houses and temples sprang up about the estate.

Four times a week her Ladyship met the poor of the area and gave them free food, i.e., the kitchen waste with scraps from the diningroom table. To eat well gave a sense of power. Indoors and out her forbidding manner and com-manding presence induced awe in those undernourished and weak with hunger. The childless chatelaine had her own ways; one did not presume to take liberties.

She was said to be 'kind and generous' to the poor; but what does that mean, if she did not offer to abate her high lifestyle by one jot or tittle to help lessen that poverty?

Fraternity cannot be when it is but a disguise to salve conscience; it becomes a condescending philanthropy, a fake charity dispensed with the left hand.

In any case Anglican high charity for the lowly Catholic oppressed would always be suspect, a dubious altruism tinged with self-interest, left-handed charity, dexter charity. 'Charity,' as my dear mother was never tired of repeating, 'begins at home.' The first unwritten rule of the law of survival is immutable: 'Look to your own.'

Lady Katherine and Lady Louisa after her no doubt accepted the poor Catholic villagers as they were: namely, unwashed, evasive, shiftless, fractious (when it suited them), quarrelsome, superstitious, light-fingered, polyprogenitive, impertinent, pushy, deferential, scatter-brained, abject and dumb with embarrassment in her presence. She was a practical woman and saw things clearly, would not tolerate cheek from employees or wastefulness in the execution of their duties; she liked to have her own way, and thought to save the poor by good example, cleanliness, order, punctuality, cheerfulness, good manners, good sense. She wrote: 'They went through quietly... The poor people will find that we are their best friends at last.'

She begged them to put away the pikes, to listen to reason.

Absurd monumental groupings or emblematic fancies wrought in bronze, marble or granite, such as the enmarbled callisthenics of the Laocoon, Cleopatra's Needle on the Thames Embankment or the Albert Memorial in Kensington Gardens are silently intimating something or other like a person pulling a face or a face partly averted while shoulders are being shrugged.

If the Wonderful Barn at Leixlip was built as a repository for grain it was also put up as a threat, the winding stairs and narrow windows part of its defensive system. The preposterous Obelisk was commissioned by the widow of the Speaker Conolly to 'adorn her estate and to honour her husband', after a winter of famine and frost. It cost her £400, with labour at a halfpenny per day. There was something freakish and even threatening in these oddly conceived monuments and follies, with enigmatic elements in their convoluted structures; in some obscure way all were casting long threatening shadows, shadows cast by good King Billy, the victor at the Boyne, signifying 'The Spoils of War'.

Even the sphinxes over the front gate were odd, as if the head and upper torso were modelled on a human model, even if her Ladyship (Louisa) had wanted to put up two couchant stone lionesses (the ones who do the kill while the lions sleep) facing each other; or perhaps she wanted to go the whole hog and have dragons. They were half-human half-beast and halfway to being gargoyles, grim or grinning, hunched up, sticking out their tongues.

Below them Tom Conolly had kennelled his hunting pack and somewhere in the stableyard the bear was chained, ready for the bear-baiting days when the dogs were pitted against him, rearing up and growling, cheered on by the gentry.

The Death House near St Mochua's in particular was freakish, the sort of monument that might have been erected over a battlefield; but the victory at the Boyne refuted, turned aside and 'On Yonder Rock Reclining' sublimated into 'High Anglicanism Enchained'. The Great Lord and the Great Lady, held in a chill classical pose for all eternity in the Death House, threw an even greater shadow: 'The Malign Presence', all dragon lines and killing points.

In her heart of hearts, in her Protestant bones and coursing through her central nervous system was the deep-seated conviction stronger than any prejudice, that the Celbridge Catholic poor were beyond saving, as a hayfield so long subjected to torrential downpours that it had gone rotten, reverted to humus (regard the sorry chapters of their unfortunate history).

On May 21st, 1798 Lady Louisa wrote:

> This last week has been a most painful one
> to us. Maynooth, Kilcock, Leixlip and Celbridge

have had part of a Scotch Regiment
quartered at each place and every day
threatening to burn the towns. I have spent days
in entreaties and threats, to give up the
horrid pikes. Some houses burnt at Kilcock
yesterday produced the effect.

Celbridge was always in danger of being attacked by rebels
coming from their camps at Timahoe and Donadea. A company of the Derry Militia arrived to protect Castletown
House and eighteen of them snored on the floor of the
Long Gallery. Colonel Napier of Oakley Park moved his
family in with the Conollys.

With a firm hand she wrote:

June 1, 1798. There have been skirmishes in this neighbour-
hood; two hundred of
them forced through our gates and passed across
our front lawn at three o'clock on Saturday morning
last but they went through quietly. We are happy
in being able to preserve Celbridge.

Tom was on the side of the property-owners. He and other
prominent landlords formed the Yeomanry Corps to act as
a home guard to help maintain law and order. The regular
troops were posted along the coast to prevent any attempt
at invasion by the French. The rebellion, even if averted in
Celbridge, cast a gloom over Castletown as the Conollys had
relatives on both sides. If Tom Conolly opposed rebellion,
Lady Sarah Napier of Oakley Park, sister of Lady Louisa,
was a committed rebel, and Lord Edward Fitzgerald, nephew
of Lady Louisa, was a leader of the United Irishmen in
Leinster; twice informed against, he would come a cropper:
the twice betrayed one became the noble corpse.

The big houses of Kildare had begun to burn. Lady Louisa
took to walking through the fortress at night, for she slept
lightly, walked silently about, checked the doors, heard the
eighteen Militiamen snoring and farting in their sleep,

hardly a reassuring sound. The flushed face of her hunts-man husband at the far end of the long table was no more reassuring.

She thought to herself: 'May the giving hand never waver. If I sit down again to such sumptuous fare and remove the lid from one more brimming soup tureen, the first guest I pass a plate to will be the Devil. One of these evenings we'll sup with the Devil.'

Some such notion may have passed through her Lady-ship's practical head. For the Williamite victors the consum-ing of grand dinners had a symbolic force; for was it not a further confirmation of a conquest already complete? the ritual aftermath that involved the handing out of medals? While the people of the countryside starved in their mud hovels the rich ate their fill. (Captain Ernst Junger of the Wehrmacht dined one night in 1942 at the Tour d'Argent, and noted in his diary: 'One had the impression that the people sitting up there on high, consuming their soles and the famous duck, were looking with diabolical satisfaction, like gargoyles, over the sea of grey roofs which sheltered the hungry. In such times, to eat, and to eat well, gives one a sensation of power.' It was into the third year of the Nazi Occupation and Paris had begun to feel that they would never go. Paris was no longer Paris but stunned, atrophied; the average citizen lived on very thin rations and was half-starving).

In Madrid Generalissimo Franco, Spain's Caudillo for forty years, had signed death-warrants over his after-dinner coffee, before strolling to the long windows of the Palacio, to admire the gushing fountains before him.

Ruling and holding were done with a heavy hand (for property-ownership is akin to murder) and rulers must be ruthless if they wish to stay in office; others' (prostrate Spain) deprivation whets the appetite with all the purposeful lust of profiteering.

Lady Louisa stirred the brimming soup tureen and thought that others' hunger added a subtle bitter flavour to their own rich repast. *L'art de la civilisation consiste, à allier les plaisirs les plus délicate à la presence récurrent du danger.*

When Tom Conolly returned from hunting in the late afternoon he washed and changed and went down to dinner. Each guest had his or her individual servant standing behind the chair, which was put in place and lifted away as the guests sat and rose again. On occasion they were served up as many as seven meat dishes, with the best wines, followed by elaborate desserts. Scullions bore away the dirty plates in buckets down to the kitchens one hundred yards distant.

Around five in the afternoon the ladies left the gentlemen to enjoy their port and cigars while they retired to the drawingroom for coffee and tea and gossip. At about six the card tables were brought into the Long Gallery and backgammon and quadrille played, for nominal stakes, until ten o'clock. Elsewhere in the great room the guests played billiards or the piano, read or wrote letters. Just before bed the servants came quietly in and laid a light supper upon small tables. Thus replenished the guests retired to bed, a fire lit in the grate and hot-water bottles warming the four-posters.

At ten next morning breakfast was served in a small parlour where their host and hostess were waiting. A meal consisted of chocolate, honey and breads baked in different colours for variety.

At one infamous meet a stranger rode with the Killing Kildares. No one had remembered him taking a stirrup-cup before they rode off, but it soon became apparent that here was a matchless rider. Tom Conolly jumped everything in sight with the stranger a stride behind; and so it went on all morning, jump for jump, at some of which more cautious huntsmen turned aside. Until they came to an impossible jump at which Tim Conolly drew back and watched amazed as the stranger in ratcatcher on the sweating black stallion sailed over.

Tom Conolly invited him back for dinner at Castletown.

He sat next to Lady Louisa as composed he had sat on his horse, now washed and brushed, with not a splash of mud on him. He joined the gentlemen for cards after and proved to be as good at cards as he was at jumping ditches – until he made the mistake of dropping a card (it was the ace of spades); or perhaps that was in the design too, for else how would he have identified himself, at the heel of the hunt?

'By the way, the name is Satan.'

It was old Nick in full hunting pink.

The blushing young serving-wench from the village stopped to pick up the dropped card, having begged his pardon and curtsied nicely. She reached down her hand and was shocked to see that the guest had removed his riding boots and wore no socks over cloven feet, and had a close whiff of brimstone before she screamed; for what young thing waiting at table would expect to be serving Satan himself between soup and grapes! He touched his sybaritic lips with the serviette and coughed behind his hand, saying politely, 'No more for me thank you, Lady Louisa. I am full to the muzzle. You see before you a lover of beautiful things. I knew your Christ once.'

He gave a short barking laugh as he threw back his head, whereupon the terror-stricken maid crouching at his feet keeled over backwards in a dead faint at this atrocious blasphemy. Nor could the mouldy old Vicar shift him, for he would not budge an inch but sat there, impervious to prayers and insults, grinning mischievously as he drew on a long cigar. He appeared to be in his element.

The portly, red-faced Parish Priest – for *he* had been summoned when all else had failed – having drenched the unwelcome visitor with holy water to no avail, showed the cross on his rosary beads, and with fearful execrations IT vanished in a puff of acrid yellow smoke into a crack in the floor, leaving the shaken priest to 'sweat seven shirts and die', as the Keegans graphically reported, as if they themselves had been present at these strange proceedings. 'As true as God,' Neddy said, blessing himself.

Welcome and unwelcome visitors had come up the front
driveway between the lime trees that turn coppery in
autumn. The heiress Katherine Conolly, daughter of Sir
Albert Conyngham, had been no beauty, and survived her
husband, buried in the preposterous mausoleum on Tea (or
Tay) Lane. She was succeeded at Castletown by William
who married Lady Ann Wentworth, daughter of the Earl of
Stafford. He died two years later, leaving Castletown to his
son Thomas, who married Lady Louisa Lennox, daughter
of the Duke of Richmond, when he was four and twenty
and she was fifteen years of age. She was to survive him by
two score years and more. She was a homely looking lady.
For 'she continued to perpetuate his memory' read: by
threats, overt and sly, she continued to remind her tenants
and dependants on which side their bread was buttered, and
who was buttering it.

As the estate was self-supporting, it required brewers,
bakers, weavers, carpenters, dairymaids, stable boys, gardeners, coachmen and masons in its upkeep. The estate was
run by a land steward and a farm staff of up to five and
twenty men and boys working a six-day week, rising each
morning at six o'clock (her Ladyship rose at eight).

Butlers received remuneration at the rate of thirteen
pounds old currency per annum, cooks twelve, coachmen
eleven, gardeners ten, kitchenmaids and cowkeepers three
pounds to keep body and soul together. They were fed by
her Ladyship. It was ever thus; the heiress graciously
accepted two rich inheritances as her right. It was like that
in those times for those people; the rich had the ball at
their feet.

Castletown House commanded one hundred grand
rooms to accommodate whatever guests were invited. Draw-
ing-rooms and dining-rooms, kitchens, bedrooms and four-
poster beds, a print room, all were there for their pleasure.
The servants' quarters had an army of servants awaiting
their pleasure, for 'the quality' expected only the best.

This stately residence originally had two hundred and

thirty windows but one had been blocked up in deference to Buckingham Palace's two hundred and thirty windows. For three weeks' work in 1783 the window-cleaner's bill came to three pounds ten shillings.

Only the richest and blackest of natural-born Protestants had ever occupied the manse. Peacocks strutted across the gravel and the black rabbits gambolled on the river banks below; above them a flag flew, a sky for the favoured.

The great Palladian manse laid out over extensive acres had been the brainchild of William Conolly, the poor son of a Ballyshannon publican from Donegal. The plans were conceived and carried out with no regard for cost – thanks to the wholesale appropriation of forfeited land in the six counties – by the Italian architect Galilei, as an appropriate country seat for the Speaker of the Irish House of Commons.

Judicious interbreeding had brought revenue but no progeny; Speaker Conolly was to die without a son; Lady Katherine barren as Lady Louisa after her.

Lovell Pearse, designer of the Irish Parliament House, is credited with the details of much of the interior; slate, stone and fine furniture were of Irish manufacture and the silverware from Irish mines. It was said to be the largest eighteenth-century house in Ireland – a veritable Xanadu on the plains of Kildare. The façade was four hundred feet long by sixty feet high in granite cut from Hazelhatch quarry, flanked by curved colonnades and outbuildings, messuages and curtilage assigned to their use. It was this noble pile that met the eye of the rebels on a morning in May 1798 and fairly took their breath away.

Before them an immense granite façade towered up into a cold moonlit sky full of icy stars, massive as a fortress or a grey military barracks for ever braced against them and their puny likes; an impenetrable Protestant breast of iron three feet deep, four hundred feet long and sixty feet tall, with a flag flying brazenly at the masthead and a hundred or so full moons racing and skipping pellmell athwart every window.

16

The Names

Behind any text of any value lurks the subtext. 'Here's I: Sunny Jim.' Old Thady Neales boasted in 1729 that his ancestors had come to Celbridge when it was Kildrought in the reign of the first Elizabeth, about the time the Dongans had acquired (that resonant word) Castletown and all the others had followed, mongrels after the bitch in heat,

    the Dutchman Vanhomrigh*
    the Napiers
    the Clements
    the Prices
    the Baillies
    Thebold Donnolly**
    John Maunsell***
    Chief Justice Marlay
    Fisher the nailer
    Tilbury the glazier

*The agent of General Ginkel, Earl of Athlone and Chief Commissioner for Revenue in Ireland, whose only daughter Esther fell in love with Dean Swift, who repudiated her; whereupon she 'embraced Bacchus'. Took to the bottle.
**who changed the name of Celbridge House to Oakley Park and bought the house and lands from Colonel George Napier.
***who in 1813 purchased the estate for his son Richard so that it remained in Maunsell hands for over a hundred years.

Carberry the brewer
Martin Lacey
Elinor Sadlier
Hinzell
Charles Davis
Annesley
Lumley
Dignam
Finnerty the dyer
Carter
Finey*
Ahern
Cotter
Tyrell
Kane
Stephen Coyle
Kevany
Russell
Rourke
Doyle
Dease
Darlington
Dempsey
Tisdell
Hart
Sutton
Fenaughty, who looked after Tom
Jeremiah Haughton
Clancy
Talbot
Cotter
Hannan
Dunne
L. W. Flowers
Blake
John Wynn the baker
Dr Robert Clayton, Bishop of Clogher
Richard Nelson of Maynooth
Thomas Croker, lawyer of Backweston
Ann Rives, Dr Clayton's niece

*(George) who built Mulligan's House in 1750 on the site of 14 mud cabins along the road to Maynooth.

Arthur Maguire
Louisa Staples, wife of Admiral Packenham
Thomas Conolly of Castletown
Revd Henry Lomax Walsh, Prebend of Swords
Mr Waters, Vicar of St Mochua's
Hugh Hill,
the Fordes of Donashcomper and Simmonstown,
William Kirkpatrick who married Mary Carr in 1809,
Sir Ivone Kirkpatrick who died in 1964,
Mr J. Bruce Bedin of Wilmington, Delaware,

Barry the auctioneers,
Gleeson,
Leslie Young,
Eric Murray,
Van Lonkhuyzen,
J. J. Young, Victualler,
Mr Edward Williams, teacher,
James O'Neill, teacher,
William Gibney, teacher,
Ellen Wall, teacher,
Miss Fennell,
Boylan's Garage,
Londis,
Allen,
McDermott,
W. M. Callender,

to mention only these. In a will made out in 1561, 'all these
lands of his (Sir James Alen of Saint Wolstan's) were the gift
made to him by King Henry VIII of most noble memory,
up to the dissolution of the monastery or priory of Saint
Wolstan's; his principal place by the New bridge in the
Countie of Kildare called Alenscorte, otherwise Saint
Wolstan's.'

The Alens, as likewise their neighbours the Dongans of
Castletown, were Catholic and had fought on the losing side
for King James (James the Shit) in the Jacobite-Williamite
wars. When the Normans arrived in 1170 they had found
much of the land under grass.

My own Family Tree had sent out sprouting roots here

and there down the years. Of those, Aunt Ada (Mrs Frank
Lynch) lived in Dun Laoghaire but ended her days with her
daughter in England. Hilda Boyd (Mrs Perren) lived in
Buenos Aires all her married life. Herbert Boyd and his wife
Nora lived in Dublin. Their son Bill, of whom little is known,
lives somewhere in England. Aubrey Boyd (the detective
manqué) lived in Montreal; his daughter Aideen (Mrs Ron
McKenna) lives in Abbotsford, B.C., sending 'very chatty
letters each Christmas' to Mrs Margaret Moorkens the widow
of Captain Gus, holder of All Ireland High Jump record as
a youth, Captain of Terenure Bridge Club and chairman
of Irish Firearms Dealers at the time of his death; son of
Gustave senior, my parents' go-between.

My Aunts and Uncles are as follows:

1873–1915 Mary Jo. Higgins married Patrick Newman
1881–1936 Margaret Higgins married Peter Newman
1882–1916 Thomas P. Higgins married Ciss Foran
1885–**** Norah Higgins died as a child.
188***** Jack Higgins
1887–1969 Bridie Higgins married Michael Connolly
1888–1963 Molly Higgins married Charles Smith
1889–**** Anna Higgins married Dr Vincent Delany
1891–1970 Bart Higgins married Lilly Boyd
1892–1971 Nora Higgins married Jack Healy
1894–1963 Tess Higgins married Mjr Hugh Stevenson
1897–1987 Gertrude Higgins married Andrew Moore
Grandfather:
1835–1897 John Higgins married Margaret Carroll
Great Grandfather:
c.1810–1879 Patrick Higgins married Hanora Flanagan. Patrick
was a farmer, near Boyle.

May their shadows never grow less.

The Diocese of Kildare appears to have been founded
towards the close of the fifth or the commencement of the
sixth century by St Conleath or Conlaid, who erected
the Cathedral and became first Bishop. The first English

Bishop was Ralph of Bristol, consecrated in 1223. The first
Bishop after the Reformation was William Miagh.

17

A Longford Wedding,
Suicide of Josef Moorkens

I n one of the heavy family albums Joss had drawn the
Angel of Mons in a HB pencil, as good as any you would
find in a magazine; an angel with huge wings kneeling
to offer the bays to a fallen hero, while overleaf Dado in his
best hand had inscribed an elevating thought lifted from
Shakespeare:

> Give thy thoughts no tongue,
> Nor any unproportion'd though his act.
> Be thou familiar, but by no means vulgar.
> The friends thou hast, and their adoption tried,
> Grapple them to thy soul with hoops of steel.

On the verso were protective sheets of semi-transparent
tissue paper so that the angel and the Shakespeare thought
appeared through gauzy veils, and there was Uncle Jack the
roustabout receiving a tin of petrol, now just handed off
the wharf for the *Whoopee* and Auntie Nora belting another
fag on the quayside and Honor and Maeve pulling faces at
the camera, and a commemorative photo of Mumu-to-be
and Dado-to-be posed as bride and groom on the driveway
before Melview soon after their wedding day.

The bride wore a wide-brim hat with a conical crown, a
smart going-away outfit that made her hips flare out, white

calf-length little boots with high heels and pearly buttons down the side; in one hand she held a folded parasol and smiled her sweetest secret smile for the camera, for Batty, as if holding an invisible nosegay.

The groom displayed a manly pair of calves in checkered woollen stockings tucked into plus-fours cut in the loose baggy style made popular by Bobby Jones, and two-tone brogues with pointed toes, a tightly fitted two-piece suit of houndstooth tweed with vent, a bow-tie at a gallant angle, a small curly-brim derby balanced on the crown of his head, with centre parting above a conspiratorial smirk (for who knew what lay ahead?).

The new groom's ever-impatient right hand was about to throw open the little latched side-door of the Hillman; the camera had caught him in the very act of opening it for the new bride to ascend, all scented and smiling and ready for the great journey to begin. The hood was lowered and a large trunk commodious as a wardrobe lashed to the rumble seat. On the side of the trunk facing the camera a careful hand had painted in block white lettering

MR & MRS B. J. HIGGINS
SPRINGFIELD, CELBRIDGE
CO KILDARE

A spare can of petrol was strapped to the runningboard and the newly-weds about to depart to Mulrany for their honeymoon. The crank-shaft hung docile and ready between spoke wheels. My progenitor is probably informing my mother-to-be that he will presently give her (the car) a few darts, to warm her up. He knew nothing of the workings of the internal combustion engine; as ignorant of that as he was of the workings of his own interior, dosed with tea, balls of malt and Epsom salts for a curative. He drove with old-world panache, his jaw out, arms rigid on the steering column. Ahead lay seven anxious barren years. The Dodo was still an angel in Heaven, waiting to be summoned (I was to arrive nine years later).

But the groom's impatient foot is already on the running-board. And off they go to Mulrany. I turned over another gauzy page and saw a sepia print of the pair of them in a jaunting-car with a bit of blood between the shafts. In one gloved hand the triumphant groom holds the reins; from an inside pocket he dramatically withdraws a large service revolver for the sun to shine on the long dangerous barrel and oiled chambers. Lillian Ann straightens her back and her eyes sparkle as Bartholomew James cocks the Browning. Did you ever, he asks waggishly, ever in your life see such a large revolver, Lillian Ann Boyd? Oh no indeed she never had, oh never.

Brandishing the loaded revolver and with whip aloft in its bracket, my ardent father drives the high-stepping pony at a spanking pace down the Battery Road through Longford town. He was deep in one of those daydreams that can overtake even the shallowest of men; akin to being in the midst of the most tumultuous of parties. Lillian Ann is aglow, luminous with happiness.

British Army troops from various regiments had been garrisoned in the cavalry barracks at Longford over the years. But he protects her from the murderous Black and Tans who career about the back roads of Ireland in Crossley Tenders, intent on humiliating and shooting down innocent Irish.

The Sherwood Foresters was a name that kept cropping up whenever Mumu mentioned Longford and Melview and Jamestown or Battery Road. The Sean Conolly Cavalry and Artillery Barracks, Lower and Upper, had been occupied since 1899 by a succession of regiments that began with the 90th Battery Royal Artillery, then came the 6th Battalion Rifle Brigade that saw service in the South African War. Then came the Royal Army Service Corps, maintenance staff only; then the 5th Battalion Royal Irish Regiment that saw the Dardanelles. Then the Sherwood Foresters, cheered

on by Mumu, the King Edward Horse, the Unknowns of
1917–20, before the 9th Lancers and the 13th Hussars. Last
but not least came a Company of the East Yorks who were
to hand over the barracks to the Irish Army.

Another picture is thrown on the magic-lantern screen by a
shaky hand. A line of ashen-faced Tommies in tin helmets
and baggy khaki uniforms, carrying heavy packs on their
backs, go into action with bayonets fixed, having beshat
themselves and risen in absolute silence from a trench deep
as the grave, urged on by their ashen-faced officers, and
begin to cheer – their mouths wide open and not a sound
issuing; they stumble forward for King and Country into the
German gas that drifts in a sinister way slowly towards
the English lines; their weakening cries founder in the toxic
fumes. Poison gas drifts across No Man's Land, creeping
over the barbed-wire entanglements, into the shell craters,
deep into English lungs.
    Josef Moorkens, my uncle by marriage, the brave Belgian
volunteer well under-age, will soon swallow German gas, as
he prepares to go into action with the second wave of
Belgian troops, slapping his pockets, carrying parts of a
machine-gun that will never be used that day. On his long
feet, puttees, polished boots laced up; on his face a dreadful
expression, for he fears that he may be going to his death
that morning. On his head a peculiar potty-shaped helmet
with a ridged backbone down the crown.
    All is silent but for the whirring of Ger Coyle's projector
(for we are watching a private film show in the back lodge
with Miss Coyle serving up buttered water biscuits which I
will not touch).
    But look again!
    Here he is large as life, standing with folded arms, his
legs planted wide on the duckboards, now helmetless (it
rests on a sandbag within easy reach), enjoying a pipe. His
dark eyes stare fixedly out at me. In the sepia background
the Box Brownie has picked up trees with their heads blown

off, shell holes filled with water, a torn-up waterlogged waste-
land: Flanders Fields! On the back of the curling sepia print
a hand (Joss?) has written in faded blue ink: 'view of a
mudshow after bombardment 20–12–1916'.

Speculation about a dead person only begins to be legit-
imate after the ascertainable has been ascertained as far as
possible. Take the death (by his own hand) of my uncle
Josef, the go-between when my parents were courting ('Bart
will follow on bicycle') as a case in point. Mumu, slightly
psychic in her quiet way, for it wasn't all nerves, as she was
slightly hysterical, had in a nightmare seen the corpse of a
naked man laid out on a cold slab in a windowless room
that was very chilly, though the corpse was sweating. She
confided this to me some years later in Doran's snug in
Baggot Street.

The slab had been cold as ice when she touched it. The
corpse was stiff as a stone statue but sweating and she could
not look at the face. Two years later Joss was dead. It had
come about in this way: he was in the construction business
in Dublin where building materials were consistently being
stolen from his building site at night. He took to patrolling
the site after his workmen had left in an effort to catch the
thieves, returning home on the last bus.

On the night he died the last bus could not travel due to
the icy January roads and he had to spend the night in the
relative comfort of the most complete house on the site.
There was no oven connection in this house, but there was
a simple gas burner on which the workmen could boil a
kettle or keep themselves warm. At some stage on that
breezy night in the unfinished house the flame blew out
and Joss died. He had lit a cigarette before he fell asleep and
the burnt-out butt was found between his fingers in the
morning. He could not have opened the gas tap unlit,
the lighted cigarette would have caused an explosion.

His eldest son, another Gustave, the spit and image of his
tall father, had been led by a Civic Guard into the Dublin

Morgue to identify his father. When he stepped into the cold windowless room he had entered my mother's nightmare; for there was the long dead man sweating on the slab; when they pulled back the sheet he recognised his father. Mumu's dream was out.

After the seven barren years she gave birth to the Dodo who was to inherit her hazel-green eyes, her withdrawn and secretive nature, her reserve, her morbidity (was it a morbid shyness? 'Mortified' was a habitual term with her; crushed with mortification, with embarrassment; in her expectation, people rarely if ever came up to scratch).

As to the Dodo, he is a complete puzzle to me, an enigma, as was Mumu's brother Aubrey, whom I had never met. He had followed people about Dublin silently on rubber-soled shoes, unseen and unheard, overheard confidences and indiscretions, taking notes. That was the way of secret natures. I knew little or nothing about the Boyd side of the family, apart from what I had inherited from my mother, her secretive side.

As naturalist Henry Williamson, the Dote's hero, invisible as a poacher by night, crossed No Man's Land and crept close enough to the German lines to hear the Huns talking among themselves beyond the barbed wire entanglements; so Aubrey, so Mumu, so the Dodo.

In the big heavy memorial album interleaved with tissues reposed the pencil sketches of houses in snow and harbour scenes, modelled on the nuns' coy ways with themes and slushy poems and elevated thoughts, all seen through a sort of mist or haze. Brinsley MacNamara, who had famously shared digs in Dublin with Mumu's brother, had inscribed one of his own poems that began:

> Her shoulders shone
> As though polished by the admiration
> Of a thousand eyes . . .

Dado wrote in the same slapdash hand that he had used at the Agricultural College where he had kept notes on sheep drench, yaws, foot-and-mouth disease, crop rotation and stock feed.

Old photos that Time had bleached out, turned sepia, were glued fast onto the thick pages and constituted a faithful record of parents and grandparents posed and arranged as stuffed figures in a waxworks; grave be-whiskered men of substance in stiff cravats that made their jaws protrude. Spats over polished brogues, paunches spanned by half-hunters secure in fob pocket, waistcoats stretched to bursting across the well-filled stomachs of stout paterfamilias. Some casting demented looks, fixed stares (from holding an awkward pose to accommodate the time-exposure) directed at the shutter; frantic-looking ladies in hobble skirts and unbecoming hats, holding fans, umbrellas, parasols in chubby hands, holding themselves rigid and upright as Victorian dolls, squinting.

When Ger Coyle touched a lighted match to the fuses of the long fireworks that hung on the railings in front of the house, they went whooshing up over Springfield to spread themselves out abundantly in the sky like luminous flowers spending themselves with matchless effulgence, for Mumu, enchanted, to cry out, 'Oh isn't it just lovely!'

As indeed it was.

18

Starlings Invade the Nursery

One fine morning in June Dado entered the nursery, barefoot in his pyjamas, the day being already well advanced and the sun well up and shining on the ceiling in thin layers through the reflected slats of the venetian blinds.

He had marched in to inform us that the sun was shining and it was high time to be up and about. Going up to the nearest green venetian blind he remarked, 'It's a bit stuffy in here, lads. I think I'll just throw open a window.' And with that he gave a sudden short pull to the cord that rolled it up and down, and as he did so his pyjama trousers slipped down below his knees. The rear exposure was sensational, something I had never conceived of, the hairy crevice and billygoat's matted danglers and dingleberries, though he had the trousers up about his waist, held with one hand, in a trice. The blind rattled down again as he knotted the cords of his pyjamas, flannel pyjamas striped blue and white like a butcher's apron but faded and bleached with washing, with a great rent or gash in the groin.

Scarcely yet fully awake but alerted to strangeness and abominable effects, I averted my eyes from whatever fresh horrors might be in store as he turned to face me. He drew down the sash window and a stream of fresh air flowed in, and with it a single starling. He moved to the second blind and just as he jerked down the cord a second starling flew in via the open window, followed by a third and fourth. Others came in as the second window was thrown open; there were eight or nine stares flying about the room, knocking against pediment and in a flustered way against the frieze of bathers and donkeys and bathing huts towed into the sea, the repeated motif confusing them even more, though birds cannot see pictures; as if they could make their escape that way, out over the false sea.

They flew about the room, making no cry, just the rustle and flutter of agitated wings like silk rubbed briskly against silk. Until one of them found the second open window and flew out, presently followed by the others, to the great amusement of the Dote who was just waking from a deep sleep. Mumu, in a summer frock, now appeared with fresh orange juice, and was told of the miracle, the four and twenty black birds, which I made much of, attempting to block out what I had inadvertently been privy to, the forbidden fruit which in the years to come (and how soon) would be taboo, the fruit of the loins and the closed bedroom marked:

Strictly Private
Keep Out

and the shameful dossier marked 'Marital Secrets', all of that.

Dado glancing down and perceiving the great opening or tear or rent or gash at his groin and the vision of sunscorched shanks, hurried from the nursery in order to change into his sunbathing outfit immediately. His slashed shorts were the cut-down trousers of a suit; with their fashionably frayed edges they were three decades before their time, when idleness and lolling on beaches became the rage. 'Batty' Higgins, like Albert Einstein, had tried to simplify his life as much as possible; in his case, by doing very little work. With stained rug and linseed oil he was off to the long grass of the orchard for some intense hours of 'getting a colour up'. His skin wouldn't take the sun and he first turned the colour of rhubarb, then the purple of peony rose or the wattles of an enraged turkeycock. Being more or less permanently idle did not fret The Narrow Fellow in the Grass; for idleness suited him, with some light scuffling of gravel. No odder farmer refused to farm in Kildare. Was he a *Waster*? Certainly he had spendthrift ways, sucking the juice from an orange and throwing the rest away, discarding packets of cigarettes (Players No. 3) with a few cigarettes still intact, which had made secret smokers of myself and the Dote. It would have come as a great surprise to him that Kildare land values multiplied; the forfeited lands given away after the Battle of the Boyne would be worth £300 an acre in 1990. Dado was born on a small farm at Newtown-Forbes. Great-uncle Tom, the LA millionaire, had bought Melview and provided for them all. Dado was left it by his grandmother in 1921 and soon sold it to Margaret Newman and moved to Springfield, which he purchased for £3,000, a good price then. It would go for £25,000 less than thirty years later.

(If his animus against 'nancy-boys' was more pronounced than his animus against 'corner-boys', his animus against 'Jewboys' was greater still. He had a strong streak of racial bigotry in his nature, and was not alone in this, in Ireland.)

19

Mistress Mumu & Old Jem Brady

Mumu, sucking a Zube, had many terms of dis-approval for those whom she disliked; 'obnoxious' was one of them, an obnoxious one (a Yahoo) was beyond the Pale. 'Etiquette' was a strong term of approval; it conveyed sound morals, backbone. 'Gone West' meant (of an object) irrecoverable, lost irretrievably. If someone was 'all over you', it meant they were being smarmy and insin-cere; 'insincere' was the most damning of all terms in her high lexicon of disfavour.

'Few and far between' was one of her beady-eyed selective terms for weeding out worth from dross; few and far between (as far as she was concerned) were the rare ones, the hearts of gold. Essy Brady, the dumpy daughter of old Jem, had a heart of gold. When Mumu brought her flowers from Springfield garden, or apples, wasn't little Essy profuse in her thanks. Mumu, it must be admitted, liked nothing better than playing the gracious lady, and old Jem was most defer-ential in her presence, standing hat in hand before her.

Then one spring old Jem Brady began to go queer in the head. Dado told him that there was a colony of rats in the hayshed and old Jem said: 'Of all the birds in the air I do hate a rat,' which was to become a stock phrase in our family. As with the old standbys: 'Is that a dadger I see

forninst me? Tell me this, do you ever open a book at all?
If the blood isn't in first-class condition, out march our
friends the pimples.'

He had a colony of rats in his own head and couldn't get
rid of them. By summer he had become very strange, off
somewhere on his own. Then, early one morning with heavy
dew on Noonan's wheatfield, he resolved to do away with
himself (the Guards traced his footsteps through the morning dew). He threw himself head-first into the quarry, said
to be depthless, and sank like a stone through the lilies.

The Guards dragged the quarry hour after hour; on the
point of giving up they decided on one last trawl before tea,
and let down the grappling irons once more. This time, up
came the drowned man clutching lily pads and weeds, his
eyes and mouth open, filled with mud, his white hair mud-
died too, for he had left his hat on the bank.

The corpse was washed and set in a coffin on trestles at
the rear of the church near the PP's (Fr Hickey) confessional. The Keegan boys told us that he was dressed in a
monk's brown habit, with holy scapulars about his neck and
his rosary beads entwined around his hands. He was buried
in Donycomper cemetery with all the other Bradys and
Coyles and Russels and Mahoneys and Cotters and Aherns
and Tyrrells and the rest.

'Fend for yourself,' Mumu said with a resigned look.
'Charity begins at home. Everyone for themselves.'

Mother Machree was far away.

Thereafter the blue light hovered over the surface of the
quarry depths in wisps of early-morning fog as we tore past
on our bikes for eight o'clock mass. The Keegan boys (our
authority on faith and morals) said his soul was suffering in
Purgatory and would be there for maybe thousands of years,
doing penance for having taken his own life.

20

Because We Are Catholics

Because we are Roman Catholics we eat fish on Friday and attend Mass on Sunday and Church Holidays, whereas Protestants such as Helen O'Connor and old Doctor Charlie O'Connor and their English nephew Derek Chapman do not believe in the Virgin Mary or go to Mass.

They go to a different church with a different outside and an inside that I have never seen and a different spire and different religious ceremonies and a bell that sounds different to ours, and they do not bless themselves or dip their fingers in the holy water font when entering the church and they wear different clothes and speak in a different voice in a different part of their throat and the Protestant complexion is different from the Catholic which can be reddish like baloney or very pale like cheese or yellowish purple like a fungoid growth.

Old Mrs Henry and Bowsy Murray and Lizzy Bolger and Rita Phelan and Grogan the groom and the Darlingtons and the Keegans are all Catholics and go to Mass every Sunday. The Bowsy Murray blesses himself before he eats and when he is finished eating and when he hears the distant sound of the Angelus bell coming on the wind from a mile away in the village he stands up as if in church and draws out his rosary beads from his coat pocket and kisses the cross and begins murmuring his pater nosters with his lips moving and the walrus moustache too, with his eyes closed, and he ends with an arthritic dip of one stiff knee in the sketch of a genuflection and again kisses the cross on his beads but in an absentminded sort of way as though he and God were on familiar terms. And then he opens his eyes again, pocketing his beads, surprised to still find himself standing in Springfield kitchen with old Mrs Henry, as if he had been up in Heaven for a while and come down again.

Old Mrs Henry said that the Bowsy was a very devout man and that if e'er a man will go to Heaven, it will surely be the Bowsy, who attends evening devotions in summer and goes on retreats and is a member of the Men's Sodality.

But those who take their own lives cannot go to Heaven. So my uncle Joss is damned, as is old Jem Brady: a blue light now hovers over the quarry as confirmation that he is indeed damned, or so claim the Keegans.

Dado is both a practising and a non-practising Catholic at the same time; he practises his religion rather as he drives his car, absentmindedly, erratically.

The flowers on the Straffan high altar came as like as not from Springfield garden and as often as not Mumu prepared the floral arrangements. It was her way of attending Mass, *in absentia*, on Saturday when nobody was about.

Calm and impersonal in a dream of sanctity the priest was saying mass and turning back the heavy pages of the missal and joining his hands and genuflecting and murmuring the Latin.

Dado preferred to arrive late and take his place halfway up the choir-loft stairs with the other malingerers, sending us ahead as his representatives. He kept a display handkerchief stiff as a starched serviette in his breast pocket and another in his cuff, which was removed to brush off the wooden step and spread to kneel on, on one knee, hiking up his trousers and putting his face into the palm of his hand in a gesture of symbolic abjectness (Emperor Charles V humbled in the snow), closing his eyes until the little joined sanctus bells rang forth to announce the consecration over. The priest's distant mumbled Latin was virtually inaudible and the sermon listened to with half an ear.

Thus Dado was both attending and not attending, half-present and half-absent, both damned and saved. Although it was probably the fears of eternal damnation rather than the notion of setting us a good example that drove him there in the first place. It was a way of getting up an appetite for lunch.

The sternness of duty did not appeal to him; it was a Proddy virtue unknown to Catholics. It seemed to me that the polychrome Christ in the Stations of the Cross that lined the nave rather resembled the Dodo's figure of Robinson Crusoe baked brown by the sun at Mas-a-tierra (he had come off it 'scarcely articulate', the prototype of all castaways). Christ had lost one leg (or was it one arm?) at the scourging. I saw that as true duty performed well: the scourger laying it on with a will, grunting at each blow; thanne Jhesu sweating biting his lips. Dado, sorry to relate, was a pastmaster at limp performances of duty. He admired bravery and courage in mettlesome men (Uncle Jack riding the Shannon waves in the *Whoopee*, throttle fully open, Major Graham jumping into the Liffey and not able to swim a stroke), because it was something he was deficient in himself. He was a born avoider of responsibility.

He was not the sort of man that could be challenged to a duel; for he would have denied any intention to insult. He could not defend his honour because he had none to defend. For would a true-born gentleman, chivalrous and brave, defend himself with a spade against an opponent squaring up for a gentlemanly bout of fisticuffs, even if footless with the drink? (In later times, with Springfield sublet, subtenant Ball had attacked him while scuffling the front yard.) When he played me at draughts, wrong moves could be taken back.

'I didn't mean that. Take that one back.' Unpalatable reality had somehow to be circumvented.

21

The Bad Smell

Dado could be very dismissive ('cutting' was Mumu's word) and caustic in his references to 'that Jewboy Jack Ellis', disparaging him in company, even though Jack Ellis had sold him a suite of furniture at discount and I suspect lent him money when American funds were slow to arrive. Because that good-hearted man, who happened to be a Jew, helped him when help was needed, Dado had it in for him.

When we heard the priest murmuring the *Laus tibi Christi* we knew that the Mass was ending; soon he would be warning us of the wicked spirits who 'wander through the world for the ruin of souls', and it was time for us to descend the choir-loft stairs and join Dado on the gravel, putting on his cap and motoring gloves and saying, 'Off home with us now.' The car was parked nearby, all the spoke wheels thoroughly baptised by local dogs, who had it in for the Overland.

Dado donated generously at the collection with a wad of folding stuff dropped into the collection plate at High Mass after the sermon in St Patrick's Church. He did not care to make his Easter Duty locally, because the priests 'knew too damn much' about him already; so he made a general confession maybe once a year in the Carmelite Church of St Teresa in Clarendon Street in Dublin, into the accommodating ear of a Carmelite monk who didn't know him from

Adam, behind brown drapes. We sat in the hushed church, with just a handful of the faithful praying by the high altar or doing the Stations, and all the votive candles burning on the stand for all the sins confessed, and we could hear the murmur of the monk shriving Dado and the sound of a harp in Johnston's Court. And then Dado came out of the confession box and went up near the altar to say his penance and then we all went out into Grafton Street and he handed us a half-crown each for presents. After a word with the commissionaire Mr Shakespear outside the Grafton Picture House, he told us to wait on the bench in the foyer and he went round the corner for a ball of malt at the Sign of the Zodiac. And when we had waited maybe an hour an unfrocked clergyman with rotten teeth came in and sat between us and said rotten things in a low but penetrating voice, like a rat whispering dirty which we didn't catch and wouldn't have understood had we caught. Presently he got to his feet and shambled out. As a dog will leave its doggy smell behind in chair or kennel so he left his sinful smell behind. A bad smell.

We sit there meek as mice near the ticket office, a narrow wooden cabin with a small glass window, and talk in whispers. *A Hundred Men and a Girl* is showing with Deanna Durbin and Adolphe Menjou. Mr Shakespear walks up and down and controls the queues, balcony on one side, stalls on the other. One memorable day we saw *The Wizard of Oz* at the Grafton Picture House and then most of *The Thief of Bagdad* (with Conrad Veidt and Sabu) at the Capital, all complimentary tickets. Harris's Music Shop is opposite the Grafton, a dim neon-blue grotto with Hohner mouthorgans laid out on display under glass and a Jewish assistant (who is perhaps the owner), suave and sinister as Conrad Veidt himself.

The blue convalescent neon light of the music shop we dared not enter unaccompanied is repeated in Jack Ellis's underground toilets, where the urinals smell of hospital, and pedestrians can be seen in shadowy form, passing overhead on the thick opaque glass. But that is not all. 'Soon It Will Be Their Turn' hangs there between the Gents and the Ladies. What do they want of me, this speechless company standing huddled together, wringing wormy-veined hands and staring out at me with their afflicted eyes? Behind them immense clouds rear up. Is it a cyclone or duststorm on the way? A bunch of dirt-farmers with no time to read or educate themselves, doomed to poverty. Are they Mormons or Duke-bors or Okies? They stand silent in the depthless pearl-grey atmosphere of oncoming afternoon, mistrustfully eyeing me.

One of Dado's great heroes was the boxer Jack Doyle, who later in his career became the all-in wrestler passing himself off as 'The Gorgeous Gael'. Cartoonist Tom Webster had much fun at his expense, dubbing him 'The Horizontal Heavyweight', because of the number of times he was knocked out in the ring.

It wasn't because he was knocked out so much that made him a hero in Dado's eyes, but because he had married Movita, herself a knockout and stunner who had been in *Mutiny on the Bounty* with Charles Laughton and Clark Gable. Dado was very impressionable where good-looking women were concerned, particularly when associated with wealth, or what looked like wealth. Dado was a puritan affecting to be a swinger, which made him a hypocrite as well. The famous Doyles appeared together at the Theatre Royal with the Royalettes in *Something in the Air.*

Some years later in London, from the upper deck of a double-decker bus bound for Shepherds Bush, I would see the Doyles below me on the footpath outside Mooney's pub at Notting Hill Gate. The Gorgeous Gael now wore a leather eye-patch like Peg-Leg Pete. He had a lowly job as bouncer in Mooney's. Thus had the mighty fallen.

22

Flotsam

Nothing done by Nurse O'Reilly in dusting and airing the bedroom or bed-making and sheet-changes or removal of chamber pots or replacing of jaded flowers or general freshening up could ever quite dispel the stuffy sickroom smells that still clung to pediment and blinds and skirting-board and eiderdown and puffed-up pillows, which smelling salts and 777 sprinkled on the clean sheets or the regular hoovering of threadbare carpet had attempted to banish without success.

The big white chamber pot had been removed and in its place came a sort of portable lav shaped like a footstool in inlaid mahogany which concealed the invalid's potty behind an angled trapdoor and could be closed up when not in use or emptied when full, which now made its appearance with a dreadfully complacent air of permanency at the foot of the bed. The invalid's potty removed from its container and draped with a hand-towel would join Dado's chamber from the middle room where he slept, a chamber generally a third full of startling orange pee, at the head of the stairs, and both pots in due course carted off, emptied and washed in readiness for new stinks.

Mumu's periodic absence in the bath offered an opportunity to freshen up the bedroom. Mumu in kimono and slippers made great ceremony and to-do of an elaborate

long immersion in bath-salts and foam, after the water had
been heated up, and recharged in mid-session with boiling
water carried up by Lizzy and taken by Nurse O'Reilly and
tipped in after much, 'Are you ready now, Mrs Higgins?'
and calling out and banging of doors and sounds of running
feet. During which time the fresh garden flowers were
arranged and the venetian blinds drawn up tight as a drum
and the sash windows thrown open top and bottom, and all
neat as ninepence against the reappearance of the invalid,
scented and pomaded, declaring herself to be a 'new
woman', to climb into bed in her dressing-gown and turn
her face to the wall, the blinds having been drawn again
and Nurse O'Reilly having removed herself, backing out,
closing the door silently, as upon a dead person.

As elsewhere alongside the other beds an upended apple-
crate stood beside the high double bed reared up on its
castors where Mumu slept alone now, Dado having been
relegated to the small middle room above the front porch,
facing out to the distant hills and the Hellfire Club on the
summit.

   The apple-crate did service as a narrow bedside table with
cretonne tacked on and two shelves turned inward to carry
night accessories and invalid stuff required; bromides, Milk
of Magnesia, Milton antiseptic, Eno's Fruit Salts, Macleans,
a comb, a brush with brown hair stuck to it (it was 'coming
out in fistfuls'), a glass of water, a half-peeled orange, polar
bear mints and Vaseline, hair-slides, lipstick, nail file and
buffer, and a fat black novel (its jacket removed) glistening
like a slug, a bookmark protruding midway through.

   I picked up a dogeared page at random and read with a
creepy reawakening of the flesh – a forbidden excitement
returning (as immersed stark naked in the cattle-trough I
fornicated with its mossy side, harkening to the souse of the
sea) – for just then and there in that place (a German hotel)
a man (who was perhaps a soldier on leave or a sailor off a
boat) overheard a couple enter the room next to his and

begin to undress. The man listened and heard the soldier presently say that all he wanted was a big bun, to which the woman responded with a slap and a laugh, saying that she thought she could supply that all right, and after a while 'crowed with pleasure' at whatever the fellow was doing to her, engorged in the woman or vice versa.

It was a novel entitled *Flotsam*, translated from the German, one of the banned books supplied by Helen O'Connor. With blazing face I threw the novel down and fled from the bedroom as if the Jaws of Hell had opened wide, and some of Satan's hellish cohorts were in full cry after me.

(A coalfire stacked with damp slack was roaring up the chimney and black tobacco fumes rising upward clung to the ceiling of the livingroom where Fatty Warnants sprawled in one of the squat leather armchairs (sold at discount by Jack the 'Jewboy' Ellis of the Grafton Picture House in Dublin), wedged in by his own grossness, puffing on a fat cigar; opposite him sat Joss, of whom one could see nothing behind the smokescreen but immense leather gaiters stretched straight out before him in highly polished boots; and the pair of them gargling and gulping and snorting away in Flemish.

So that's what it was to be adult; to smoke like a chimney and stick out your great boots and gaiters and exchange opinions in an incomprehensible tongue. I thought of trenches and dug-outs and Belgian troops mustering on a station platform, awaiting a train that would carry them on leave to their pleasures or to the Front to their deaths, for the entire Belgian Army had been virtually wiped out on the first day of battle. So I turned the heavy pages of the great black album.)

A press of people in winter clothes blocked the main entrance to the GPO under the pillars. Near the bridge sat bloated bronze ladies with sleepy eyes, their nipples punctured with bullet holes from the time of the Troubles. County people were hurrying for the last bus that left from Arran Quay, their children sucking icecream cones and crying. The last bus departed in daylight during summer, after which no more buses ran, for the Emergency left everything in short supply. Dado brought home strange brands of cigarettes – Passing Clouds and Capstan and Balkan Sobranie – kept for him by Dermot Morris his tobacconist who was also his solicitor; as well as Craven A and Gold Flake and Player's No. 3 from Miss Nairn at the Grafton Picture House, in exchange for apples and plums from Springfield. The Dote and I were given pocket money for sketchbooks and Windsor & Newton watercolour paints and Dado bought us two Hopalong Cassidy novels from Combridges. Sitting with his back to the balusters of O'Connell Bridge, a legless beggarman played 'The Isle of Capri' – my tune – on his harmonica, vamping. We had saved up to buy new mouthorgans at Harris's Music Shop and Dado had embarrassed us by talking of crops and the weather like a true-born countryman to the posh Jewish salesman. For Dado spoke to all men as if they too were farmers; as he spoke in a special knowing way to all women and embarrassed us again before Miss Nairn in the Grafton café by asking what was there to eat, for the lads; and when Miss Nairn had replied, 'We have nice ham,' Dado had said, very well then, we would all have the nice ham.

On the Liffey embankment a rebel hand had painted in white capital letters that dribbled 'DOWN WITH THE IRISH RULING CLASS, LACKEYS & GOMBEENS OF ENGLISH IMPERIALISM!'

The neon Bovril sign still bled all over College Green.

Gulls flew over the bridge, letting loose their plaintively sad gull-cry *Woe! Woe!!* in a stink of diarrhoea.

It was Spring as we set off for home again with the two new Clarence E. Mulford's in our bags, wrapped up by John Sibley himself, and were we not happy as the day is long? Oh that Mesquite Jenkins, that sprinting and deadly nakedness!

Maria Montez's eyes had flashed dangerously; she wore a transparent dress and her dander was up. Sabu had curly lips and rode on an elephant. A trapdoor opened. Below, sewers, rats, nameless filth, where a hideous fate awaits. Streets are obscured in ground-fog and an old Italian plays a violin. Two fellows listen, one says, 'Luigi has found it!' Luigi is blind. I try not to cry but feel sick in my stomach (the icecream in Woolworths, the hair stiffener at Maison Prost, the smells of the city) as melancholy overwhelms me.

'Any excuse for swigging in bars,' Mumu said.

She refers scathingly to 'lounge-bar lizards', and I see Dado drinking whiskey with a curious scaly creature who wears a midnight-blue suit, the trousers with razor-sharp creases, black silk socks and black patent-leather shoes that you could see yourself in. They sip some green concoction from long-stemmed glasses, sitting with legs crossed on tall bar-stools in the Royal Hibernian Hotel. The LBL is smoking a cigarette in a long amber holder while eyeing my father through the smoke with slitty dark eyes and I wonder can it be the 'Jewboy' from Harris's Music Shop.

I loathed my skinny feet, detested the sandals worn out of shape, drank chilled wellwater from the ring-pump like a cowboy, cupped hands dipped as a bowl, a dipper. I saw the Overland leaving the front yard, going down the back avenue. A courting couple had come a short way up the front avenue to disappear into the plantation. I thought to tell Grogan but remembered that I was not a sneak, not one to snitch.

Old Mrs Henry (who is not my friend) spreads my favourite homemade blackcurrant jam on hot soda bread and silently offers it to me, and I as silently refuse it. I write on the drawing wall: 'The man was smoking on the beach.' I draw him smoking. Then I wrote: 'The sun comes up with colours and the man wakes up.'

I asked Mumu at table what 'flotsam' meant? Was it like

loathsome? Well not quite, she said, and fiddled with her napkin. What was it then? Mumu said it was a mess, something spilled out, sort of floating away, that sort of thing.

But this made it no clearer to me.

'Why do you ask? Have you been reading it?'

'Some of it,' I admitted.

Why did the soldier ask the strange woman for a fat bun? did he not get enough to eat in the barracks? Was it because he was hungry? Was that it?? These were questions I could not put to Mumu.

Mumu had gone very red and said it was quite unsuitable reading for a chissler and would I please stop reading her books. It wasn't appropriate, she said in a frosty way that made it plain to me that the subject of 'flotsam' was closed.

The hungry soldier had said to the unseen woman: 'All I require is a big fat bum.' The words lit up in neon lights, tantalising, riveting, fishy.

The unseen woman responded, 'I think I can supply that all right,' and had 'crowed with laughter'.

23

The Bracing Air of Sodom

Aeterna Non Caduca

Sunday was visiting day at CWC and the cars of the doting parents began to converge soon after lunch. Castle servants were sent out into the playing fields to inform the Line Prefect of a call for Higgins. It was on formal occasions like these that the more theatrical of the Jays came into their own.

The flamboyant became more flamboyant, the eccentric more eccentric (hands folded into the wings of the soutane, a fixed smile on the pale face), the twittery ones became more twittery, the flaky ones flakier, the ingratiating ones more ingratiating, the serious ones more serious, the dancy ones more dancy, as gnu astray amid a herd of exotic gazelle, so 'The Dog' McGlade and 'The Frog' McCarron and 'Lugs' Hurley and 'The Razz' O'Byrne strolled amid the school blazers and the frocks and high heels and demi-veils and the serious pipe-smoking fathers of lawyers and barristers and architects to be; with some of the lay teachers such as 'Horny' Ward (Physics & Science) and Mr Cullen (History & Geography) dressed in hairy tweeds, with 'The Dandy' (the handsome French teacher, reputed to have 'laid' Nurse Redmond behind the bicycle shed) or 'Bats' Brannigan the Arts Master in paper-bag brown overalls such as worn by storeman or car-park attendant – all these exotic creatures were disembarking from the Ark.

There would be the three Line Prefects, the Spiritual Father, Father Minister and the Rector himself, perambulat-

ing through the Pleasure Grounds and by the First XI pavilion or taking tea in the Castle with the ever-loving mothers;
the mothers and sisters in their finery lending a welcome
unfamiliar feminine touch to the proceedings of an institution resolutely male as Artane or Mountjoy. This casual
parade of prosperity and wealth, with Bentleys and Over-
lands and Rileys and Buicks parked bumper to bumper on
the driveway before the castle where the CWC flag flew, was
a reassuring sight for all concerned, to be sure, there by the
Gollimockey stream.

The visiting hours were as ritualised as the older forms of
Jesuit punishment dating back to the Inquisition and torture
and execution at the garrotte in a public square. Or the
victim put to the question in private torture apartments and
brought forth to be executed in public with a great show of
pomp and circumstance to drum-taps and hooded processions in the days of the *autos da fé* in Murcia, Oviedo,
Sevilla, Cartagena or Cadiz. For they (the Jesuit Fathers)
'had not got where they were by hiding their lights under a
bush,' Dado said with a dismissive sniff.

The penal docket issued in class was in Latin, the number
of pandies (usually four to six on alternative hand) specified
by the Jesuit Father or lay teacher, folded and handed to
the offender who took it to the office of one of three Line
Prefects situated far apart in different quarters, each of them
known by reputation for varying degrees of leniency or
severity, gentleness or sadism.

The procedure was that you knocked on the door and
were called in, presented the docket, watched the pandy bat
(some were slim, some fat) being removed from a drawer
or inside the soutane. You took your punishment on either
hand, thanked the priest and withdrew. Some pandied heavily, breathing hard; others lightly, going through a formality.
In winter you warmed your hands on the radiators. There
was no horseplay.

The pandybat was a sort of *sjambok* slick as a spatula that
imparted sudden deadening pain, felt in the head as in

either hand, turn and turn about, pain travelling through the nervous system.

In order to reach the Line Prefect known for soft punishment beyond the baths and the whirlpools of Charybdis it was necessary to pass the lair of Scylla, namely, the Prefect of Studies, a notorious flogger of boys whose door was always threateningly wide open and himself inside on the q.v. for fellows tiptoeing by with punishment dockets in their hands, holding their breaths. You were likely to be called in and punished on the spot.

Stout Tom (he of the florid complexion) roamed the corridors to punish any boys found outside classrooms, waiting in a sort of intermediary zone between punishments not yet formulated or for the master within to cool off and summon the culprit back in. If caught by the Prefect of Studies, your fate was decided there and then; Father Tom decided what was the apposite punishment and began laying in without a word spoken. Those habitually sent out to cool their heels outside a classroom were dealt with in the appropriate way – the choleric Prefect of Studies rising on his toes when pandying, really laying into it. Woe betide you if he found you on one of his bad days. His choleric nature was to get the better of him in the end; watching CWC defeat Belvedere in the Senior School's Cup proved too much for his ticker and he keeled over at Donnybrook and was dead before the ambulance arrived. I was in the infirmary when the news came.

The bracing climate of the institute of higher learning that was the great Jesuit monolith CWC set down on the plains of Kildare – where the wind seldom abated but was always busily blowing around the old turreted castle of the Wogan-Brownes – plus the more or less constant supervision that was *de rigueur* with the Jesuit Fathers (some of whom now teaching had after all been model boys themselves and must have had some inkling of what might be going on there under their noses) had produced a simmeringly overwrought tumid atmosphere that was a cross between racing-stable and bordello, in the tumult of indoctrination and inter-disciplinary pursuits as laid down by the blessed Ignatius Loyola.

But hormones were hormones, that was not to be gainsaid, and boys would be boys, more's the pity, and required sharp watching all the time.

After two years of Killashee and the neurotic nuns, we had gone there at reduced fees, the Dote and I; from 1942 to 1946 I passed painfully through successive grades of Grammar, Syntax, Poetry and Rhetoric, having arrived too late (too old) for Rudiments; enduring a boredom that was acute.

CWC: Hothouse of Frustrated Desires.

The tall handsome Higher Line tack (Prefect-in-the-making) Phillipa lusted after Mitch of the Lower Line, who pined in turn for Conny the exquisite soprano in the Third Line who sang a heartrending *Veni Creator* from the choir loft at Benediction.

To avoid detection and ridicule, the Black Sow (who was much admired) lay supine on the floor of a deserted classroom (it was 2nd Syntax, where I had often suffered) during all-out after breakfast, to practise on her French horn; emitting vulgar fortissimo farts and what sounded like the doleful mooing of cattle en route to the abattoir.

CWC on its lush acreage of good arable land was divided, as was ancient Gaul, into three parts, in an ascending scale of learning: viz., the Third Line for ages 12–14, the Lower Line for ages 14–16, and Higher Line for ages 16 to 18 or 19; each Line or House taking in around a hundred Catholic boys.

Myths and legends, as in prison, were rife. Was it the bracing climate, hormonal eruptions, the temptations of the flesh or the strictness of the Jesuit regimen – the niceness of an overt jurisdiction which afforded every freedom, and none at all? We were in permanent distress in a cage of our own devising.

The Dodo (OC 1931–37) was still remembered! He too had become part of a legend. Like 'Spike' O'Donnell (thought to be murderous in his ungovernable rages), the 'Baa' Keegan and the indomitable Fahy, small but fierce, who when crossed in love fought a hated rival in a duel with hatchets behind the Lower Line pavilion, all for the love of a Sow. Fahy was fierce as Finn MacCool, so the legend ran, with his dander up.

It was said of the Dodo that the subjects that failed to interest him – Irish, Mathematics and Science – he refused to study. And special rules had to be made for him; he was exempted from all rough games and punishment; and this, mark you, in an institution that believed in both – games in the bracing cold to curb the rebellious young Adam; frequent punishment to curb the wills of demons – working on the assumption that a good beating never harmed any boy, always a debatable point when dealing with out-and-out neurotics.

Under immediate threat, the docket in his hand specifying the punishment to be administered by a Line Prefect far away on duty, the Dodo had fainted.

Exposed to the permanently drenched and windswept playing fields he had promptly caught pneumonia; when the echoing corridors resounded to the busy pandy bat at work (Father Tom with a scowl on his face was doing the rounds) the Dodo would be safely tucked up in bed in the infirmary, a coal-fire burning in the grate and matron on her way with Horlicks and buttered biscuits.

Fearfully I crouched at stool like a madman in Katanga awaiting revelation, for the jax roof to be removed and God speak to me direct! On the inner door of my box a wit had written in pencil:' 'A man without a woman is like a fish without a bicycle,' and I thought of the wooden cleats of rugger boots that resounded like drum-taps on the parquet floor of the changingroom (or a chorus girl's high heels) when Dog's Hole ran out for play-up in scandalously brief shorts (her daringly raised skirt): the earthy stains of contact sport suggested venery.

A thick gob of semen the size of a sheep's eye was stuck fast to the door; it began to slide downward as I watched. A naked male figure with arms outflung and widespread legs showed off the balls of a stallion and a careful hand had pencilled below: TB AMAT BF and I guessed who they were, lurking in the darkness.

The love-notes arrived by circuitous routes and in curious forms in the long term when resistance was low and whole classes dreamed of the bared thighs of boys who had become girls overnight, the sows. (There were two in 2nd Grammar.) The girl was the good-looking boy made up in the December play who had become a real boy in the dormitory again; an easy lay, a good ride. Shower-nights were electric with promise. The short towels were tulle skirts thrown over the shower stall; the gush of steam suggestive of sauna and Roman orgy. Cold fumbles in the scrum were reenacted by gingery Doorley against the tittery Black Sow under her towel as she ran for bed, when the Line Prefect's back was turned, more interested in young McLoughlin who had strained a thigh at play-up and needed massage.

Looking out of the Lower Line library one dreary afternoon when shop had closed and rain had made play-up impossible, whom did I espy but the same pretty Dog's Hole followed by the Black Sow (two much-desired blondes who apparently fancied each other) emerging from the storeroom opposite where pingpong tables were stacked, where they had been comparing vaccination marks.

Certain Lower Line tacks had dry-bangs (a ride without the trousers removed) with passing Third Line sows pulled into the deserted library while the chapel filled for evening devotions. The two lines moved slowly by either wall, coming from the Third Line quarters, and spies were out to watch who was coming.

When full the school chapel held three hundred or more and the Higher Line Prefect knelt behind on a small rostrum, leading the prayers. The Stations of the Cross ended with a prayer for peace.

The persistent drill of prayer combined with the iconography of bared flesh and bleeding wounds, the insistence on abstinence and suffering, had become an aphrodisiac itself; the long hours spent in religious devotions from an early call (6.50 a.m.) to late prayers, sapped resistance, patience, willpower, sapped us. Catching tantalising glimpses of sows and the favoured ones secretly desired and ignorant of such adoration, wedged between rows in chapel, now kneeling, now standing, now singing, now silent, now devout, now half-smiling, now definitely tartish (notes were being passed) or thoughtfully picking her nose, did nothing to help; nor did the sudden vision at study, six rows in front, of Holland perched whorishly back from the seat of her desk, the Lady on the Swing.

Third Liners with high unbroken voices were lusted after by lusty Lower Liners with their contraltos and tenors, who were in turn lusted after by mature Higher Liners with their baritones and basses announcing in no uncertain manner that soon they would be out in the world and free to impregnate real girls if they so wished.

All joined together to sing 'Daily, Daily, Sing to Mary', and Paddy Courtney and Bot O'Toole (who was English) were smirking behind their Westminster Hymnals at Pierre Daly, the tall prefect standing in the front row of the Higher Line pews. For his ears alone they sang loud and lewd 'Daly, Daly, sing to Mary!' watching the quiet wing threequarter with the long spidery legs who was so hard to bring down in a tackle. Was Mary one of the laundry slovens who did the beds, finding a note under Pierre's pillow ('I'd love to ride you'), signed Pierre Daly? They might just as well have sung 'Eskimo Nell' or 'Roll Me Over in the Clover', they sang with such gusto and *élan.*

The cubicles in the square were often defaced with drawings and graffiti, to be whitewashed away by lavatory attendants who were rarely seen, to be defaced again, for it was natural (at Declamation Father Kelly declared that it happened in Pompeii).

Strands of barbed wire stretched above the high wall as if we were indeed in prison, though half the Higher Line had once done a bunk under it and decamped to the Liffey in preference to a dull debate held in the gym.

Entwined initials and hearts oozing blood and pierced by daggers were whitewashed out over and over again, as were coded solicitings in chalk and pencil. Many generations of adolescent youths had ejaculated and slashed against these slates. The college was old, but those Graeco-Roman practices were still older.

To slash (to piss), to take a box (to crap), to spoon (to court), to sow (to love), to sigh, to sin-o; it was nature, as was tossing off, pulling one's wire, getting one's hole, going out with, getting a horn, getting into; and the graffiti, the epistolary flourishes, but the capricious synonyms adopted to lull suspicions and conceal whatever flutterings and hankerings might be festering in the breasts of some three hundred adolescent boys over a period of five years in the long ferment endured and suffered through three months of isolation in the long term in the depths of County Kildare away from the refreshing if disturbing company of any females and obliged to make do with these pseudo-girls with names like 'Titch'. It was the little language of lovers, qua Swift's *Journal to Stella*. All was temptation in flowery dells, in term-time, as in a penitentiary.

Meanwhile one day in the stinking gym, didn't Handle-bars Hastings go and treat us to a regular tirade of abuse, twirling his waxed moustache and pacing up and down as if on the parade ground. His grown son helped laggards over the wooden horse and attempted to pacify the old man, an ex-British Army drill sergeant shell-shocked and irascible. He went for a lad called Billy Roche. Roche complained to the Rector and a token apology was offered: he had been thinking of a different Roche altogether.

Redhead McGivern inscribed Fairy Moore's name (Michael) in lovingly elaborate Gothic script on the fly-leaf of Fairy's missal and surreptitiously passed it back as the

Third Liners filed past the Lower Line tables in the refectory under the wooden rostrum where Father Minister (it was little Micky Kelly) presided over the tables with a twinkle in his eye that could be seen at the far end of the refectory.

The Dodo had opened the batting for the CWC XI. Once dug in – and his remorseless strategy was one long patient process of digging in – he was extremely difficult to remove, scoring nothing but staying on and on, blunting any attack, until all the other batsmen had departed and only the Dodo remained, walking in slowly, carrying his bat through a whole innings.

He became such a fixture at the crease that the attack wavered before such obduracy and gave way, no bowler was able to remove him. But he refused to score runs, take chances, and partners were run out halfway down the pitch. The Dodo refused to budge, raising a batting glove, Wait! No run, partner!

He played a ghastly game, making up his own rules, slowing it down to a dreamlike pace; collar about his chin, white CWC cap down over his nose, glaring at the bowler as if through a visor in a suit of armour. Jabbing and poking, levelling the crease about him with the tip of his bat, picking up straws, rearranging pads and gloves, studying the field placements, leaving his crease as the bowler ran in – Wait! a mote in the eye? The umpire (Harrison of Notts, the school coach) eventually gave him out in order to see the last of him. It was not a joyful performance.

'Iggings,' Harrison marvelled, scratching his head, 'blimey wot a blightah!'

Fidgeting and scraping at the crease, 'gardening', ever and anon taking fresh guard, continuously adjusting his batting-gloves, the peak of the white cap, the shirt collar up about the bridge of the aquiline nose; surreptitiously fixing his protective box, the Dodo stood his ground, implacable. With sly Ranjilike leg-glances and glides he wore down the attack, tickling it into submission long before stumps were drawn. An explorer poring over a map of unknown terrain would have hardly applied himself so assiduously, so tenaciously, 'coldly heroic'.

He kept judicious records of the time spent at the crease, in default of scoring runs, holding up the game until the opposition capitulated, noting questionable or 'wrong' decisions; for 'Wrong decision' appeared often in these private Wisdens of his. Crouched at the edge of the white mark, at the edge of the dream, after taking a guard of middle-and-leg, tapping the white line with the tip of his bat as the bowler ran in to deliver a bouncer.

The fast delivery sang past his ear.

Then the affronted stare, the careful re-examination of the field placing, the resumption of preliminary tactics of preparation, the fiddling, the digging in, the tap-tap and nervous back-lift of bat, bracing himself visibly for the next delivery, for all this would go down in the book: 'Received two bouncers'.

When finally removed by some phenomenal 'shooter' he waddled very slowly back to the pavilion, unpeeling his batting-gloves as he went, ignoring the incoming batsman for whom he had no word of advice, approaching the silent crowd as though a wrong had been done him and for whom applause was somehow superfluous.

D. J. B. Higgins c. Hayden-Guest, b. Blood-Smith . . . 4 was set down in the score card. The Dodo, having removed pads and protective box, donned his First XI purple blazer and cravat, washed his face and hands, combed his hair, and sauntered into the score-box to gaze down sadly at the action on the pitch below, Blood-Smith high-stepping into his next torturous delivery.

When questioned about his dismissal he would open his hands, raising a 'quizzical' eyebrow, then the hands together again in a limp silent gesture more expressive than words, a mime that can only be described as liturgical. Words failed him; he had run out of patience.

His strategies for survival were all negative.

He had fainted away when about to receive pandies – the

leaded leather disciplinary strap – and thereafter was excused
punishment by Father Minister and wrote lines instead, as
though he were an English schoolboy – a unique dispensation in CWC. He spent much time indisposed in the infirmary, well muffled up, just his nose showing. A model pupil in
most respects, he was quick to pick up a virus. No one bullied
him; he did not put on the gloves in the gym or wrestle on
the mat, he was beyond all that, it was not his field.

One Sunday at visiting time Dado arrived in the Overland
well stocked with food for our hamper and we walked in the
Pleasure Grounds with the Razz O'Byrne. As behoved an
absent-minded genius – for he was a Greek classical scholar
of distinction – the Razz's black soutane was liberally smeared with chalk-marks where he had wiped his hands when
grappling with difficult Greek on the blackboard. The oily
eyes of a bullock peered from behind his small bifocals. He
clasped his hands behind his back, folding the wings of the
soutane and walked along wrapped in thought. Other Jesuit
Fathers walked there by rhododendrons just coming into
bloom, in the company of parents whose boys were under
their care. Our parents had known the O'Byrnes in Longford and had the utmost respect for the Razz who had famously knocked the stuffing out of an anti-Christ Spanish
Nationalist when he cursed him and spat on his cassock.
(The Razz had been a novice in Salamanca, a *novillero* in the
great Bullring in the Sky.) Whereupon the Razz (so ran
the CWC legend) had torn off his dog-collar, spat on his
hands, squared up to the impertinent anti-Christ, spat on the
ground at his feet, and said, 'Nobody spits on me! Come on,
you pup, you're up against Gerry O'Byrne!' and laid the
fellow out with an almighty haymaker in the breadbasket.

One Missionary Night the Razz had shown his long-prom-
ised footage of the Spanish Civil War in a small room behind
the gym, packed for the occasion. A rooster crowed silently
and flapped its wings and then soldiers in forage-caps were
brandishing rifles and stumbling up a hill, giving the

clenched-fist salute, and the great stone cross was slowly
falling from a church dome in slow motion and a long line
of refugees with their children and possessions were making
their way along an endless road and fingers were pointing
to a clear sky out of which the bombers would come in
formation and in Madrid on a balcony draped in flags General Franco was haranguing a silently cheering crowd below.

The Razz had been on the side of Franco, because Franco
was against the Reds and so must be on the side of God
(and the Pope agreed). He had confidently identified a
Republican corpse on the battlefield, a close-up of the dead
face covered in flies, projected on the sheet, as a mountain
range near Malaga.

Father Gerry O'Byrne, S.J., was a scream.

Dado spoke to him familiarly as though to an old friend
who had shown up again. The Razz spoke of atrocities in
Spain, the violation of nuns and the torture and murder of
priests by those forces on the side of Satan.

He said he had no objection in the wide world to CWC
playing cricket matches against Protestant, Presbyterian,
Methodist or even Masonic schools, but disapproved of the
game on principle. 'It's a garrison game, Batty – an English
fancy, and we should have nothing to do with it. We have
our own games.'

Here spoke the hurler on the ditch.

Dado must understand, the Razz urged with some warmth,
clutching his arm, that 'all those fellows with double-barrel
names' (Gifford-Clark, opener; Blood-Smith, medium-pace
offbreaks) were nothing but the illegitimate offspring of
titled English families who had discarded them and sent
them over to Ireland to be brought up as Masons and Metho-
dists. 'You had only to look at those fellows to know that.'

Dado nodded his head sagely, being as big a bigot as the
Razz himself.

That very evening we had a treat in store.

The Dog McGlade was giving the spiff! When the Dog

climbed into the pulpit he was frequently carried away by his own rhetoric; and the longer the sermon the shorter the study time. Dado said that he would certainly stay to hear the Dog; he would sit in the back of the chapel where he would not be noticed. Anew McMaster in his prime could scarcely hold a candle to the Dog McGlade at sermon time!

The sacristy door swung open and out came two gorgeous altar boys followed by the Dog scowling down at his boots. Dipping one knee and pressing it down with both hands he genuflected as one long-accustomed to genuflecting, moved to the pulpit, adjusting his surplice, black highly polished boots visible beneath the cassock. Firmly grasping the white marble balustrade he pulled himself up Father Mappelwise; the noble head presently appeared over the lectern. He laid aside his missal, set out his notes, unstrapped and discarded his wristwatch (a flurry of excitement here, time was to be of no consequence), hoicked up his surplice, cleared his throat and prepared to launch himself like a high-diver into yet another of his justly famous Sea Sermons. For the Dog was obsessed with the sea.

Combers were surging onwards towards a distant shore, pounding the boulders to smithereens where gulls were tossed by the wind (the Dog was off!), seacoasts threatened by a storm, mariners imperilled by raging billows, the valiant helmsman notwithstanding. The long watches, wind-shifts, swelling surges, torn sheets, tidal stinks at moonrise (no heaving embonpoint, for women never appeared during the ecstatic course of these spiffs; they knew their place and remained indoors out of sight), and the packed chapel shuddered to its foundations, to the very rafters, to the fine oaken beams, to the Evie Hone stained-glass windows above the high altar; observed by half-naked he-men in skimpy togas – the Apostles – and a Saviour in a loin-cloth brief as decency would permit, as rendered in oils by Sean Keating (RHA). Judas Iscariot was said to be based upon one of his (Sean's) deadly enemies.

Holding onto the pulpit now drenched with spume, aghast at what he had stirred up, and as if standing on the very poopdeck, tilting and heaving into a raging tempest or Force Twelve gale, the Dog, swaying with the movement of the ship, indomitable, wind-whipped, chap-lipped, drenched in salty spray, hair on end, took the chapel by storm. He invoked wrath, wrack, sea-bladder (sniggers here), cross-winds, monstrous tides, *more* onrushing combers (his flash word), muscles strained to the limit and beyond, fortitude tested to breaking point, as his oratory rose to new heights of theatrical panache, arms thrown wide.

And then slowly subsiding, modifying his address, bringing us back to reality, the hands now joined, then a delicate blowing of the nose and handkerchief replaced in sleeve; leaning forward he stared piercingly into the body of the church. He was finished.

The whole school, cowed, knelt now with eyes closed and heads bowed, prayed for succour, for the success of the forces of Christ in Europe where the war still raged on. The silent congregation was drenched in spume, by spent combers, awaiting their deliverance (Dado having dipped one knee in token genuflection and quietly departed before the Dog had gotten into his stride).

The Dog McGlade never gave anything less than his best. His oratory had the formal majesty of an organ voluntary.

It was a raw winter's day at the end of a wet week towards the latter end of a wet year; term-time in mid-November, another Sunday, visitors' day again at CWC, and we were expecting Dado.

He arrived in the Overland at the hour he had promised.

We had sat a Latin exam and partaken of a soggy lunch. Now we sat in the back seat of the Overland, parked facing in to the moat, the Gollimockey stream, eating blackberry tarts and drinking Bulmer's cider. With curtains drawn we were in a sort of tent, looking through the cuttings from newspapers that Dado had brought us. Mutt and Jeff in the

Evening Herald, Mandrake the Magician in the *Evening Mail,* Cruiskeen Lawn in the *Irish Times,* with miscellaneous news items that had caught Dado's fancy. The pincer movements of Panzers in Russia, an American airman kneeling to be decapitated in Japan.

Dado had come early as promised; the Overland was stocked up with provisions for our tuck-box, homemade cakes and apples from the orchard. Dado smoked a cigarette and questioned us about the exam.

Thornley sat beside me in class. He had an unclean mind, and could make his tool stand up at will, a ferret stirring in a sack. The General was casting our theme-books around and Thornley whispered, 'Star in the east', glancing down at my fly-buttons undone. 'Playing pocket-billiards again, old son? Pulling the old wire, eh?' he gave me a nudge.

'My son,' whispered Father Perrott, with drawn face white as a sheet, through the wire lattice from the darkness of the confessional, wrung from the depths of his compassion.

A white figure dressed for rugby in the briefest of white shorts flitted by on high studded boots over the gravel to where a cutting wind whipped around the castle walls.

'Looking shagged,' murmured Thornley in my ear (my bad angel), his bitten grubby fingers pointed to where the loved one was shivering in thin rugby togs, sulkily avoiding all bodily contact far away. 'Little balls of fire'.

Father Kelly was everywhere at once. He had come to CWC after years in Australia, with advanced theories on coaching; the College XV and subs were to be given chops at supper, fed up like a hunting pack. And with good results; the historic day was about to arrive when CWC would finally defeat their old rivals Blackrock College (Dado's alma mater), thanks to Father Kelly's coaching.

Father Kelly was running alongside the attacking backs, threading his way through the forwards, digging the heel of his rugger boot into the ground, pointing, blowing his referee's whistle, scrum-down! He was taking no chances. The team was trained to a hair.

'Soul of my Saviour,' I sang feebly with the rest, not feeling pious but a perfect hypocrite, 'sanctify my breast.'

'Little gains,' our Spiritual Father (Father Adare) intoned creepily, 'little gains, little losses.' He had encouraged the whole School Sodality to even *earlier* rising; up at crack of dawn in winter was not enough for the brave soldiers of Christ, who were now required to rise at 6.00 and wash in cold water, to be in the Sodality Chapel not later than 6.50 a.m.

'To seek,' prayed Father Adare unctuously, 'to strive, to gain, and not to yield,' making a deep obeisance before the open tabernacle. A voice of manifold reason, though other baser promptings might still prevail.

It was rumoured that the Black Sow had shown her tool to Marshall, her Lower Line lover, on the Castle stairs.

Early Mass in the Sodality Chapel in the Castle tended to be a cosy affair. Father Adare made religion sound warm and tame; piety piled upon piety sounded safe, if also dull as botany.

A small toadlike bald visiting priest made it sound dangerous as a lobotomy, and put the wind up all his hearers at the Annual Retreat, three days of silence and meditation. No love-notes were passed in chapel now. The retreat wore on, from which Third Liners were being excused. Thornley, the ferret in the sack, my bad angel, no longer engaged in piggyback rides in the empty Lower Line library with desirable Third Line sows dragged in off the corridor and submitted to a quick dry bang with trousers on; he had had no emission stains on his flies to cover with a book while dipping a quick genuflection and leaving chapel with eyes modestly lowered. As a Tack he had come in last and it was his privilege to leave first. He spoke of nothing but screwing, getting his hole.

Now the confessions were full.

Spooning, sowing (Dutch *zog*, German *sau*, Latin *sus*, Greek *hus*, *sus*, female pig; sodomy), making sheep's eyes, passing notes, feel-ups in the scrum, 'bad' thoughts and attendant surreptitious acts were definitely 'out'. Unseen, aloft behind us in the choir stalls by the great organ, the tenor Waldron with a broken arm sang 'Stabat Mater'. The clear voice was an asphodel in the wind, pollen blown, intractable amber; it came on a joyful wave-frequency of incorruptible uncompromising (it was a dead language and couldn't change) uncontaminated Latin. The voice, still ascending, seemed to drift from afar.

> . . . *mater dolorosa, juxta crucem lachrimosa* . . .

Father Perrott, ghostly pale, clutching the wings of his soutane, glided into the confessional and took his seat, drew the curtains, pushed open the Judas, prepared to hear the worst.

'Now, my son,' he whispered, 'what have you to confess?'

Give or take, let all slide; all turned to impurities in the end.

* *

Captain and crew of the good ship *Loyola* were Rector, slim Father Jim; Perfect of Studies, stout Father Tom; Father Minister, little Mickey Kelley; and the three Line Prefects, Father Weft, Woofe, and weeshy Father Ween. Trim Father Adare was Spiritual Father of College and Community.

Among the latter were Warrandance, Fr Warranty, Fr Colloney, Kilfenora, Tooey, S. Pettigoe, Errigal and the venerable Fr Durance, who was as old as the hills. The lay Brothers Boyce and Stack were in charge of refectory and toilets.

24

The Price of Land,
the Great Lord,
the Gollimockey Stream

Included in the old parish of *Donaghcomper* were the town-
lands of Rinnawad, Ballyoulster, Commons, Coneyburo,
Coolfitch, Elm Hall, Loughlinstown, Newtown, Reeves,
Straleek and St Wolstans.

The original parish of *Kildrought* (Celbridge) contained
the present townlands of Aghards, Castletown, Celbridge
Abbey, Crodaun, Kilwogan, Moortown, Oldtown, Thornhill
and Oakley Park.

Many miles of rough-hewn limestone walls standing over ten
feet high and three and a half feet thick at the base and
twenty inches at the top and surmounted with broken bottle
shards, not infrequently green Guinness bottles set into
cement, built by Catholic labour to hide the prosperous
owners who had paid out the lordly sum of a half-crown per
perch to protect their Protestant privacy, are a feature of
County Kildare as distinct as its towers and follies, as also
found around the grand estates in County Kilkenny.

In the time of Ludlow and Orrery the forfeited lands had
been portioned out to Cromwell's officers and soldiers who
had signed up to fight on credit and would have to commute
arrears in pay in exchange for land and property; they and
their descendants would have all of that, the good weal in
perpetuity. One million acres had been set aside to meet the

Adventurers' claims, three-quarters of the prize was theirs by bailiwick. By May of 1652 Ireland lay prostrate before its foes; the Statutes of Kilkenny would deliver the *coup de grâce*. The extreme misery of the Irish race was pressed down hard and running over. (An artificial drain – quite erroneously called the Gollimockey by generations of inkstained CWC boys – had been laid down by the Wogan-Brownes to feed into the moat; whereas the little Gollimockey stream, a small meandering tributary of the Liffey, flowed close to the left of the back avenue or what the English prefer to call 'drive'.)

After the Boyne bloodbath the Unprofitable Land ('Mountain & Bogg') went for a penny an acre or was given away; profitable land went for four shillings an acre.

Rent per plantation acre, in pence

c. 1660	30
1683	40
1725/6	53
1752/3	67
1755/6	200
1815	360

The Napoleonic Wars may have inadvertently contributed to the 1815 increase.

With uniformed outriders and postillions the Great Lord rode out with the utmost elegance in his splendid vermilion-and-gold state coach (a plushy parlour in cloth of gold and coral, a musky travelling chamber), down from his town residence in Capel Street onto the northern quays, and on out via Ormond Quay, Wolfe Tone Quay, Parkgate Street and the Department of Defence, and so on to Chapelizod. The spanking greys and the golden coach more an object of bewilderment and wonderment to labourers who uncovered, and to passing gentry who formally saluted the Lord Justice (one of three), the foremost man of his time. Awed (the gentry) by the £25,000 per annum income, the high style, the panache (was he not the son of a poor

Ballyshannon publican in County Donegal? an upstart who
had made good?). He was his own man.

Dado must have inherited some of grand-uncle Tom's
nature, for he liked nothing better than to dispense largesse;
a gold ring for a grandchild, the head chef from the Shelbourne Hotel hired when he entertained lavishly at Springfield. Mumu, with a hangover, read Ethel Mannin (*Too Late
Have I Loved Thee*), the liniment and smelling-salts by the
bed, Eno's, Milton, Negley Farson's *The Way of a Transgressor.*

Mumu had an unforgiving nature. 'I *detest . . .*'

She had a repertoire of disparaging terms. 'A right
common little article, that one. Common as dishwater.' By
her high bed on the upturned apple crate, a powder puff,
lipstick, nail scissors, hair-pins, the articles of her toilette.

The Boyds did not know where Auntie Ada had come
from (she had married a man called Lynch by whom she
had three children); her appearance (wistful, peakily pretty)
was unlike any of the other Boyds. She introduced herself
apologetically: 'You see I am the common one of the family.'

'Sod that for a lark!' burst out brother Bun, pal of buck
privates and the common man.

'A little bird told me,' Mumu said mysteriously.

Well, that was the mysterious Aunt Ada; a wistful, pretty
little wren's face under peek-a-boo dark hair, anxious eyes.
She watched the Dodo batting in the nets at Springfield,
old Keegan in hobnail boots, belt and braces, in his shirt
sleeves, bowling long hops.

As batsman (stone-wall opener for the College XI) the
Dodo had a composite model in mind; the dour
unemotional Douglas Jardine whom no attack could
trouble, and Ranjitsinhji with shirt billowing like a sail. He
and brother Bun (who kept wicket) were on the College
XI and on vacation time were picked to play for North
Kildare CC near Kilcock, turning out with old Jack Wallace
(phenomenally slow twisters), young Wallace (fast and
erratic), Barney Parr and the Pig Menton whose big brother
Brendan could clout sixes into the Grand Canal.

The Menton brothers too had been to CWC, and all knew the slang which did not change from generation to generation; in the generations before us, in those endless terms, they learnt it all.

Now touching the matter of floating a debased currency, Swift in his *Drapier Letters* said that if Wood's halfpence ever became currency, it would take 240 horses to bring Mr Conolly's half-year's rent from Dublin to Castletown and require two or three great cellars for storage.

'Whatever you undertake,' wrote a kowtowing petitioner, 'God prospers.' Parents took to naming their children after him or his lady, hoping to inherit some of that luck, if nothing else. The birth registers record William Conolly Conyngham, William Conolly Coan, William Conolly McCauseland. To ensure a twofold patronage his man Finey christened his daughter Williamina Katherina.

The records of Springfield can be traced back to 1734, five years after the death of the Great Lord of Celbridge. In those days the North Salt holding belonged to Castletown, as did most of Celbridge, all prosperity emanating from the Great Lord. Springfield remained in the Castletown books, leased out to various families until the 1840s when it was purchased by the Earls of Leitrim (the Clements family), owners of Killadoon estate, who continued to lease out Springfield until 1906 when a Major Hamilton bought the house and seventy-five acres of grazing land. From then until the present day there have been a series of owners but it is in the same place marked 'Springfield' on the map of County Kildare drawn by Lieutenant Alexander Taylor of His Majesty's 81st Foot Regiment in 1783.

Back in 1734 it had been first leased by Speaker Conolly to his agent George Finey – 'for the lives of John Finey,' Christina & Williamina Katherine Finey daughter – all that part of Ballymakealy, Saltstoun & Tikkow 111 acres.'

In 1763, 'Lease renewed to John Clarke, husband of

Christina Finey for the life of the said Christina, Williamina
Katherina Baillie (née Finey) and John Finey.'

In 1763, 'John Clarke of Dublin to John Franklin of
Springfield – all parts of the lands of Ballymakealy, Saltstoun & Tikkow.'

In 1763 (1773?), 'John Franklin to Lieutenant Richard
Phillips 2nd Regiment of Foot – for £284.7.6. lands as
above.'

In 1780, Richard Phillips of Springfield married Dorcas
Shepherd, daughter of the Revd Sam Shepherd, Vicar of
Kildrought 1735–85.

In 1782, Richard Phillips to Richard Baldwin Thomas,
gent, lands as above.

1786, Lands as above to Nicholas Archdale Esq.

1789–95, Leased to Thomas Long Esq, the famous Dublin
coachmakers.

1801, 'Thomas Long released unto James Langrishe &
his heirs.'

1806, Revd James Langrishe Archdeacon of Glendalough
to Francis Walker of Elm Hall, Celbridge.

1817–26, Leased to John Bradshaw & Arebella his wife.

1833–45, John Bradshaw to James Williams, lands as
above.

1845–54, Leased to John Haughton and Margueretta his
wife.

In 1850 they held the house, offices and lands (52 acres)
from the Earl of Leitrim, who had bought Springfield from
the Castletown estates in the 1840s. John Haughton was the
owner of the Celbridge woollen and flour mills.

1868–1906, John Langrishe leased the property and the
family remained at Springfield until 1906.

1906, Springfield and 75 acres bought by Major Hamilton. Major Hamilton sold to Captain Mitchell who sold to
Captain Richard (Dick) Warren nephew of Major Darling of
Sallins who sold to my father Batty Higgins for a rumoured
£3,000, house and three lodges with 72 acres of prime land;
this must have been soon after the end of the 1914–18 war.

Top left
1. Mumu and Dado at
the time of their
marriage.

Top right
2. Aunt Sissy, reputed to
be able 'to drink Lough
Erne dry'.

Left
3. Mumu in the rockery
at Springfield.

4. Mumu with brother Bun; the Dodo in the background.

Left 5. Author's first day at Springfield, with Nurse O'Reilly, the Dodo and brother Bun, in the days when being photographed was an ordeal akin to visiting the dentist, 3 March 1927.

Right 6. Mumu and author in Springfield garden, summer 1931.

7. Aunt Ada and the Dodo.

8. Dodo, brother Bun, Dado and an unidentified sporty aunt
at Springfield, winter 1928.
Nursery wing in the background

11. Dado, Dodo, brother Bun, author and the Dote at Springfield, 1931.

12. Author, brother Bun, Gustave Moorkens and Dodo in Springfield garden.

13. Mumu with the Dote, author, Dodo (standing), and brother Bun (kneeling), circa 1930.

14. Dote and author with first pipe.

15. Dote and author with first bike, Springfield, 1931.

16. Dodo, brother Bun, Dote, author and maternal grandfather, Peace Commissioner of Longford.

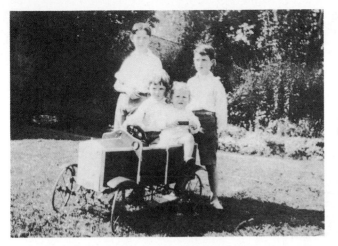

17. Dodo and brother Bun standing; author and Dote in pedal-car, summer 1930.

18. Author, aged three, at Springfield, summer 1930.

19. Clongowes Wood College from the northeast.

20. Springfield, summer 1941.

Some three-score years on, following the birth and upbringing of four sons, Dado sold out to Matt Dempsey the popular horsebreeder of Griffin Rath who fathered nine children there, for a rumoured £5,000, the house and lands with two lodges. Two score years later Dempsey sold out to Alistair Campbell, an Aer Lingus airline pilot, for a rumoured £14,000, house and 12 acres. Alistair Campbell had two daughters reared before he sold out to a Dr Anthony Walsh, a gynaecologist, who converted the old kitchen into a surgery. Dr Anthony was the pale gynaecologist who had practised in a private hospital in Clane but dearly wanted to set up at Springfield on his own, having made his fortune in a Baghdad hospital seemingly staffed exclusively from Dublin, performing kidney transplants during the Iran-Iraq war.

The Iraquis had an anti-personnel bomb that burst twenty feet up, causing fearsome back injuries to troops who had thrown themselves flat.

If a doctor got one kidney operation in six weeks in Ireland he would be lucky; but in Baghdad Dr Tony was getting four or five a week. When he found that the Iraquis were removing the kidneys of Iranian POWs he swiftly removed himself from Iraq. Know your friends.

The house and lands now changed hands for £150,000. The Campbells moved to Bath. An electric blanket ignited and the house caught fire. It was believed locally that the Bank repossessed.

A misfortune far worse than fire was to follow.

Young Morgan Sheehy, Managing Director of Ove Arup consulting engineers, the largest in the land, had his eye on it, and soon had bought it for his Texan wife Libby to do as she pleased. Texan gigantism was given a free hand. Sunken garden, power showers and Filipino servants were installed, a stand of old trees cut down to open up the view and the inner harmony destroyed. The character of the changes – such drastic surgery – was to disfigure what had been there before. By raising 'internal specifications to an exceptionally

high degree' – in the orotund jargon of the selling agents
Palmer McCormack – the character of the house had been
too drastically altered and disfigured; the hasty over-liberal
hand had done its work. By 1993, Ove Arup & Partners
were seeking substantial reimbursement for work done on
Springfield that had been charged to the firm. Morgan
Sheehy died of a heart attack, aged forty-two; his widow flew
her six children back to America.

Offers in the region of one million punts were being
sought for the 'lavishly refurbished' Georgian mansion outside Celbridge.

Refinement and good taste are hard to come by; a heavy
price must be paid for improvements, in one way or another.
When overwhelmed by the sheer weight and preponderance
of vulgarity, thick as buttermilk, newly on display in a plug-
ugly modern state, the pet-food manufacturer's land of
doped lifestock, winter fields reeling with slurry, high choles-
terol counts and human cardiac cases who had brought such
misfortune on themselves by overfeeding; not to mention
FF forcing-beds, Cokes and over-chilled Budweiser, pie-in-
the-sky, and all Irish citizens now fairly bursting out of
their sausage skins with newfound prosperity and consumer
insanity at Crazy Prices shopping mall in grey Portlaoise,
well – something must give. Enjoy your day!

So in a sense all had come full circle.

American money had found the place and American
money had lost it. As Arizona copper in Old Bisbee near
the Mexican border had made it possible in the first instance
for my improvident begetter to buy Springfield and its grazing land, so in the latter stages of give and take had Texan
push and persuasive collateral helped to mar its Georgian
charms – fragile enough perhaps – and even more so than
Dado's wasteful ways.

The grandiose improvements – a new (and superfluous)
entrance gate by the East Lodge with monumental granite
piers alongside the former front gate, the sunken garden,

the seven bedrooms with en suite bathrooms and power shower cubicles, the golden taps, the Filipino servants, the large adjoining glass conservatory – had done nothing much to improve anything, rather the contrary. The foolhardy attempts to convert Springfield into a minor Dallas mansion had not come off. William Conolly, the son of a Ballyshannon publican, who had raised himself up by the straps of his boots, would have been rightly appalled.

Just prior to 1990 agricultural land in County Kildare fetched £1,500 an acre, whereas building sites near services in sought after areas fetched £15,000 an acre; at present building sites near services fetch over £30,000 an acre in the Clane area, probably more in Celbridge and Leixlip.

Bisbee (94 miles southwest of Tucson via Interstate 10 and State Route 80) was named for the San Francisco Judge DeWitt Bisbee, an investor who never laid eyes on the place, there under Mule Mountain where the Arizona lode had yielded eight billion pounds of copper when it closed for good in December 1974. A population of 35,000 in its heyday, much prostrated by summer heat, periodically raided by fierce Apache. Today it has shrunken to 8,500, raided not by Redmen but by pale tourists and 'retirees', the lost people who traipse about USA in air-conditioned coaches.

25

The Dodo, his Habitat

Time stood still in the stable yard at Springfield; time stood still in the garden where the pediment of the sundial was cracked. Dr Charlie O'Connor was a regular visitor; he wore a fur coat down to his ankles and was seldom sober, driving about the country roads at ten miles an hour.

Dado continued to play golf at Lucan and Hermitage, the fees would somehow be found. My improvident parents dined and wined well at the Spa Hotel but had begun (however unobtrusively) to live in elegant poverty. It was a matter of honour to keep up appearances; the four daily papers continued to arrive as did the seven Sundays, the Bowsy brought Young's side of beef each Saturday as usual, Findlater's men continued to arrive. My father remained calm; my mother held her own counsel.

Then one terrible night he woke her to announce that all their money was gone. 'It's all gone, Lil,' he groaned, and turned his face to the wall. The third-born (me) and the fourth-born (the Dote) could not go to Clongowes after all.

'Oh that bloody fool!'

Springfield was sold and we moved to Greystones in County Wicklow by the sea, where we were not known at all.

On the instructions of the owner
FOR AUCTION
SPRINGFIELD PERIOD RESIDENCE
CELBRIDGE
Suitable for Stud Farm
Ideal Hunting Box or Small Racing
Establishment
Inner yard with stabling for 9
Cattle yard with Dutch Barn &
ties for 40 Cattle. Attractive
flower and vegetable gardens.
Fee simple. Rateable Valuation
on Buildings.
SEEN ONLY BY PREVIOUS APPOINTMENT.

Both Mumu and the Dodo had nervous breakdowns.

The weakest ones seemed destined to go to the wall, be afflicted with every ill that flesh is heir to; and for such unfortunates, so numerous, Dado had a dreary formula of invocation as tried and tested as the Litany of Loredo:

'Not looking well . . .'
'Not looking at all well . . .'
'Looking bad a month ago . . .'
'Shocking-looking a month ago . . .'
'Now looking really bad . . .'
'Looking terrible the other day . . .'
'Not looking herself (himself) at all recently . . .'
'NEVER LOOKED WORSE!'

This miserable antiphony of dire forebodings rang constantly in my ears and coloured even the alternative viewpoint, the response always less insistently stated, as the short uncertain summer precedes the long killing winter:

'In *powerful* form the other day!'

'Looking great!'
'Never looked better!'

Temporary states of wellbeing were merely aberrant lapses from the norm (why does it seem so Irish?) of illhealth and never to be trusted on any account; weak as flies in winter the people crawled about, burdened with life.

Sudden let-downs and chapters of disappointment led inevitably to nervous breakdowns, coming in various forms and when least expected – again maladies peculiarly Irish. The condition of one's interior and the conditions of the air were discussed incessantly with a sort of rapt interest and intensity. Whoever heard of an island people stuck with such a vile climate go on about it so incessantly? Do the Eskimos speak of snow and ice? Do the Bedouin complain of heat and desert? No, not them.

The Dodo was set in ritual.

The ritual poke at the fire at specific times, the ritual heavy sigh, the staring fixedly at a stain on the tiles where milk had boiled over and left a hardened scum, all was ritual. For a nightcap (which he made for himself, Mumu long abed) he liked a glass of hot Ovaltine, set on its saucer before the fire; more ritual.

He liked to stay up late, listening to AFN with Hope and Benny wisecracking; this was his sole participation in any human communication. His laugh (a snigger) was a donkey braying far off, choking on it, indistinctly heard.

Gassy smoke spat and was sucked up the chimney in the updraught, to be dispersed in the darkness. A sudden viridian jet came at right angles, aimed at Dodo's fat ankles. He did not yield, but crouched as close as he could get to the flames. All was in order: the pot of tea warming at his feet, the jar of homemade jam, the wireless knob within easy reach of his soft prehensile hand. He liked to work to the distant throb of subdued dance music: Sinatra singing the ineffably mournful 'Moonlight in Vermont', Hoagy Carmichael's 'Star Dust', Perry Como warbling 'It's Impossible'.

His favourite programme was *Hi, Gang!* with Ben Lyons (plumply unctuous), Bebe Daniels (sprightly sexy) with Vic Oliver (plummy Jewish, a gad-about-town) serenading the Marshall Plan in close harmony:

> Gee, Mr RoozyFelt, it's swell of you,
> The-way-yore-helpin'-us-taw-windewãaaar!

He liked the American Armed Forces Network of news and entertainment programmes, relayed like a game of baseball or American football, split up into playing periods, the rapid-fire crosstalk of rivals on the air. The fast wit induced a snigger now and then. The wide-open vowels of the news-readers suggested the wheatlands and prairies of the Land of the Free. The vowel-sounds were assertively open – NŌWOW for 'now', ŌWWER for 'hour'. From six to mid-night the Dodo was glued to the wireless, buffeting it when the reception was poor (a storm on the Irish Sea). On weekends he monopolised the set. Mumu would not dream of interfering; she listened only to *Mrs Dale's Diary* when the Dodo was away at work.

The Dodo was mean to Mumu, cruel like a lover; excused and forgiven like a lover. Smirking at his manicured nails he shared a joke, his head wobbled, his shoulders shook. 'He-he-he-he!' went the Dodo.

'He has a lovely smile,' Mumu said, 'when he cares to use it.'

The Dodo used it very sparingly.

If her cooking did not come up to scratch he flung pots and pans about the kitchen, hissing imprecations between his teeth. He had begun to withdraw into himself, to close up.

He never used my Christian name, it was 'Hey, you!' or 'him' or 'That fellow'. Once (after the bite under the tablecloth) I was 'the rat'.

He had no friends in the wide world, confiding only to a

small pocket diary wherein were scrupulously recorded the many wrongs done to him. The Dodo was a card.

It was a rare smile right enough, when the Dodo cared to bring it forth. The head wobbled, the eyes twinkled, the lips curved into a smile of almost beatific coyness; and shaking all over like a fat jelly the Dodo went, 'Heeheehee!'

'Piece of cake,' said the Dodo between compressed lips. With hazel eyes revolving in his head and one ear pressed anxiously to the wood; the Dodo fairly drank in 'Blue Moon', '(Blew Hooo!), I hear you calling'. He was always at his fingernails, trimming and buffing and manicuring.

Now that he wanted to speak, he found it was too late; he couldn't do it, couldn't articulate. He had lost the words; it was years since we had spoken to each other. (We had never spoken to each other.) Living in the same bungalow, eating at the same table, silence had always reigned and been accepted as quite normal, quite natural, if that was what he wished. We would have accepted anything he did (if he wished to sit on top of the wireless that was okay), no matter how peculiar.

The Dodo had grown corpulent, bulky about the hips, taking short womanly strides. That secrecy of his, the rare soprano giggle, the simper were all womanly.

'*Do you hear?*'

I looked over at him; had I heard aright, had he indeed addressed me? He was fixed rigid on the edge of his chair, wringing his hands. His profile told me nothing, gave nothing away. He looked as posed as the jumper on the high parapet, the suicide leaper gazing down into the void; he would not look at me. All his life he had avoided eye-contact and hand-clasps. I strained my ears, waiting for him to speak again. He sat there rigid, his tea untouched, and something pinged in the air between us, faint as the sound of telegraph wires over a ditch. Some alarming message was humming through the wires, over the frozen ditches; somewhere a hesitant hand reached slowly out, lifted a receiver, and an ear heard, a muffled voice spoke.

I did not speak, leaning forward in the same attentive pose as my brother, bookends both, a couple of stone caryatids. He would not look directly at me, I was receiving that oblique glance he had for others. His close attention seemed to be directed at a cone of violet coal-gas that had fired out and curled back through the bars of the grate, turning a vivid green as it emerged, fiercely ejecting a funnel of brilliant white smoke. It spat poison gas.

'*Hear it?*'

Silence but for the spitting gas. It fanned out, sucked itself back behind the bars again, subsided. Unconsumed slag, eaten with fire from within, fell into the heart of the flames. It was very hot in the livingroom, too hot, our faces glowed.

'Hear what?' I asked him.

For reply the Dodo made an indistinct sound in his throat, heaved himself upright as he pushed back his easy-chair and went in an awkward scurry out of the room. He had taken the red-hot poker with him. I heard him scuffle out, heavy on his feet; there came a cold gust of night air down the chimney, another from the doorway and the Dodo armed with a poker had vanished into the night.

The Dodo and I had been sitting for some hours before the fire, in an unbroken silence; nothing unusual in that, we never spoke to each other, had become virtual strangers. One day he had closed up, and after that all we could get out of him was grunts. He did not seem to approve of us. He had been sitting forward in his easy-chair, staring into the heaped-up fire of slack that burned in the narrow grate.

Cartridge paper had been tacked down on the table behind him and upon it another of his severely perfect designs in a hard pencil; T-square and set-square, ruler and eraser, callipers and marking ink, mapping pens and sharply pointed pencils cut down to a classical third, all were meticulously set out. The drawings would remain there tacked down with drawing pins for as long as the Dodo required his final design; the table was no longer available to the family, as with the wireless after working hours through the week, or all weekend if the Dodo wished.

That seat was his and when he entered the room he claimed it. If he found it occupied he would look astonished and whoever sat in it would defer to him, give him back his place.

The pot of tea and buttered toast, untouched, were still warming in the fireplace. He studied every evening after a day in the quantity surveyor's office on Stephen's Green; working steadily and neatly for his final examination, not tolerating anything short of perfection in himself, and flying into a great rage if his papers were shifted or disturbed in any way. Indications of his displeasure were conveyed to Mumu who passed the message on. She cooked for him, did his washing, mended his socks, ironed his shirts. His life had been arranged in a formally set pattern from which any deviation would be intolerable as we, who feared him, were left in no doubt. At home in Caragh ('Friend' in the Gaelic), a disintegrating summer bungalow on Kinlen Road on the very outer perimeter of the Burnaby in Greystones among Protestants, and fully occupied all the year round, the Dodo spoke only to utter heartfelt curses, spitting out our dear Redeemer's name: JEEeeeezus Christ! The Dodo was of the stuff that your silent psychopathic murderer is made, the one who suddenly takes a hatchet to his frustrations. Oddly enough the terror merchant Hitchcock had lived briefly just down the way in Springmount Cottage on Church Road.

On this particular evening that I speak of, he was not working, but sitting forward in his weekend pullover and leather slippers, staring into the fire, fetching up deep sighs at intervals and studying his hands, appendages that always seemed to fascinate him, judging by the amount of attention he lavished on them, as though they were insured like Betty Grable's legs.

The fire had spluttered again and sent out its licks of

blue flame and my 'Hear what?' was still echoing in the livingroom.

I stayed put.

In a while I heard the Dodo come back in and the catch on the front door clicked to. He came and sat down again, replacing the poker. He was breathing deeply, white in the face, sweating. Silence . . . reigned again. Then the pale hands were extended once more to the flames, the soggy toast, the knobs, to 'Moonlight in Vermont', to 'Star Dust'.

The ever-silent Dodo leaning forward on the crushed cushions of his collapsed easy-chair was a dead ringer for – whom? Where? The sledded Polack on the ice?

He had made himself very remote and austere, like a Great Lord, hardly condescending to see his tenants or hear their grievances. He spent much time in the Godlike occupation of trimming his fingernails and cultivated a haughtily languid manner to impose his will (silently) upon inferiors, foremost among whom were numbered the Dote and myself, coldly subjected to this freezing authority, which I see now as an unconscious parody of Dado's loose paternal control.

The laugh that was suddenly wrung from Mumu was high-pitched and hysterical. Neither she nor the Dodo were given to spontaneous laughter. Of course silence between kith and kin was not uncommon in those days before television, in the country, where you amused yourself as best you could to pass the time. The Dodo's solitary amusements were as sterile as his lonely sports; the distant figure pacing up and down by the irrigation ditch in the gloaming, poking at the rough with an iron in a fruitless search for a lost Dunlop. His patience was phenomenal.

He had some theory about the mastication of food, so many chews per mouthful, the lower jaw moving in a slow lateral manner like a ruminant. And how unnerving when he ceased chewing to glare! If he caught you looking at him he glared at you like a basilisk; you had no right to stare. If he required anything at table he cleared his throat

twice *Err-humm*! with a rising interrogative inflexion, and
pointed with his chin at the object required, water-jug or
butter-pats, salt-cellar or pepper-pot. A treble clearing of the
throat followed by the Err-humm at a more peremptory
pitch that admitted no refusal, meant: May-I-have-your-best-
attention! A heavily ironic Err-H U M! testily signified: Bird-
brain! A pointed and testy AHhem! mean: Cut-it-out! Don't-
try-me-too-far! If our attention could not be gained by these
means (if one flatly refused to look at him), the Dodo was
finally reduced to speech.

'*I say!*'

'What does he want?' Dado asked, looking up and down
the table. But Mumu always knew what he wanted; her
motherly instinct told her, and pepper-pot or mustard was
handed across. Our brother was retiring into silence. One
fine day all communication between us would cease. After
that there would be only the grunts.

In his own home, as in the depths of a burrow, the Dodo
lived his own peculiar life as if it were normal, like some
exotic species of nocturnal beast that is rarely seen and
whose odd habits are not understood. His workroom (the
former schoolroom where our first tutor Mr Barrett had put
the famous question, *What animal with four legs lives in a
stable?* To which the Dote, hardly breathing, stoutly
responded, 'A rat!' to make a show of us, Mumu feared)
smelt pleasantly of turps and oil paint. He was putting the
finishing touches – the lettuce – to a meticulously accurate
copy of 'The Boy with the Rabbit'.

Oh that inexplicable blackout choler of his – what did it
mean? What portend? What did it hide? What hurt conceal?
What greviance long brooded upon? During seven years of
detention in two strict boarding schools he had become
withdrawn, reverting more and more into silence, choler,
accidie. In the family circle he had become dumb, torpid,
and was putting on weight like a Galway hooker clapping
on full sail. Certainly he was no longer the Don Budge of

the Centre Court, as of yore, in the days of Kay Stammers and Alice Marble, in impeccable flannels and headband winding himself up to serve one of his extraordinary complicated services, rigid as a medieval siege engine. The service ball was thrown high in the air, squared at, recaught; the Dodo once more realigned himself, cast up the service ball (two other spares bulging in his pockets), squared at it, recaught it, all aflutter, crying out 'Deuce! . . . Thirty-fifff!! Vantage!!!' In a lather of sweat he disputed the score, retrieving high volleys from the top of the ten-foot high beech hedge, or from the orchard beyond. The Dote and I were reluctant ball-boys, slipping away into the orchard or into the shrubbery when the Dodo's broad back was turned. Mumu sat on the terrace by the summerhouse, knitting, smiling, smoking, waiting for Lizzy to bring out the tea. The missel thrushes sailed down from the beech tree into the yew.

Alone, when all had retired, the Dodo bowled into the cricket net for hours at a stretch, aiming at a single stump, sometimes knocking it out of the ground. Each delivery had to be retrieved, twenty-two paces for the length of the crease and then as far as the rockery wall for the run up, under covert observation from the Dote and I up on our bird-killing platform with Rolos and air-rifles and one of the cats. The Dodo went pounding down the crease below us, his shadow racing after him. Nothing seemed to discourage him. The sun high and the shadows sharp, Voce comes in to bowl. A heavily-built man, he pounds in, propelling himself at the wicket. The batsman (Ponsford of Australia in a baggy green cap) stabs at it, and spectators applaud an easy catch in the slips (where Hammond waits, the safest pair of hands in Gloucestershire) and the Dodo with his shirt out comes running down the pitch with both arms upraised to indicate a virtually unplayable delivery. Ponsford, bat under one arm and cap in hand, shakes his head, begins the long walk pavilionward.

W. H. Ponsford, c. Hammond, b. Higgins. . . . 77

Every evening after work he walked the path by the big beech hedge, a sort of penitential tramping up and down for an hour or so after work; until he had worn the path polished as linoleum. On winter's nights he exercised by moonlight and the path shone under him like a stream.

The Dodo, who had no friends, liked to keep in touch with the old Alma Mater. He had collected piles of CWC Annuals next to *Lilliput*s and *Picture Post*s in his reference library, familiarising himself with the progress of former classmates out in the world at large and photographs of Imperators and teachers who still remained; Mike Clarson (Maths), The General (History & Geography, which for some reason was taught as one subject), Horny Ward (Physics & Science), Brannigan (Art), Father Gerald O'Byrne (Ancient Greek). College, that time of infinite boredom and drudgery for me, is not a time I look back upon with much pleasure; but for the Dodo it was different, for he must have persuaded himself that he had been happy there, in a way, protected from punishment.

One day the hard decision had to be made.

The Dodo submitted himself to a place in the country where he was to spend some time under observation and work on the farm. Hard manual labour would settle his nerves, it was thought; Dr George Sheehan gave it as his considered opinion that this would be the making of him.

Mumu wept for a whole day after agreeing that he should go. On the day of his departure she took to her bed fully clothed in the early afternoon. Or rather she took to *his* bed, in the narrow boxroom between bathroom (where a tap having dripped for months then ran for years) and the bedroom I shared with brother Bun who had become very partial to pints of porter in the pubs of Greystones, for Springfield had been sold to Matthew Dempsey, a farming neighbour who had put in a concealed bid. The Dote was working for the architect Berthold Lubetkin in London.

Mumu patted the place beside her on the blue and white counterpane with its design of poultry that had come from Springfield with us. She wept quietly and miserably as if she intended to weep for a long time, because her heart had been broken, her hair loose and hairpins falling out, her nose and eyes red with crying. She was inconsolable and drew me to her and tried to kiss me, her face on fire, all blubbery and smelly (urine and Baby Power) and weepy, and I held her roasting hand and wished myself far away. She asked, weepingly, what would become of her darling? Would they be hard on him, the rough fellows, was he in good hands, would they understand his needs, his withdrawn nature (she could not bring herself to say his silence), his troubled being? Would the doctors understand? Fondling my hand, would they, would they? And did I understand the humiliations he must endure? He would have to perform hard manual work that perhaps he was not able for, he would have unfamiliar faces about him, rough fare at table, rough horseplay and jokes, and he would have the electro-shock shot into him, and how could he endure that?

Dado had driven him there that morning in the Overland piled high with enough clothes and provisions to take him to the North Pole.

From this ordeal he returned even more taciturn than before, leaving immediately for the officers' cadet course at Cranwell. Not for him the slogging about in the infantry – ignorant buffs all – nor rattling around in a tank, nor sick as a dog in a destroyer, nor even sicker down in a submarine. No, no, it was up in the sky for him, up in the cold air by night, wizard prang in the wild blue yonder – nothing but blue skies for him, 'Stars Fall on Alabama'.

¡El Zopilote Mojado! ¡Contralador de la noche fria! ¡Sereno del aire frio! What is it a sign of when you find a centipede in the bath? A single bat at eventide?

For the mentally disturbed, the room they find themselves in must always be the same room, filled with the identical furniture as recalled by the suffering mind and the all-too-familiar dreaded accessories instantly recognised. The torment, identical as before, is resumed in a new place that is an exact replica of the old, detestably familiar. What takes place there, in the suffering brain, the 'seat of all ideation', occurs and recurs as in the original torture chamber and may not be spoken of by the sufferer, because it is literally indescribable.

So the heated study of a home called Springfield was shifted intact (in the Dodo's troubled head) from a mile outside Celbridge on the wet byroad to Naas and set down intacto in the Burnaby at Greystones less than fifty miles away and now called Caragh on Kinlen Road in the Protestant enclave. So that all his (the Dodo's) torments could begin anew, with not a stick of furniture out of place, not a familiar stink abated, each fire the same fire and furthermore, to lend it the veracity of a true nightmare, the invariably wetted slack thrown on with a hasty and liberal hand by Dado himself without a word.

The study (or library) at Springfield with the heavy curtains drawn and the door closed, two Aladdin paraffin lamps with elongated glass globes lit and the coal fire augmented by wood aglow made all hot as a furnace, hot as Hell. The Dodo crouched forward on the very edge of the commodious but uncomfortable and smelly leather arm-chair (sold at discount from Jack Ellis's warehouse) and extended his soft white hands to the blaze, palms out, then the backs, gently closing the fingers into a fist before opening them again into a fan, in a reflexive manner which with cats, the Dote and I called 'feeling the fires'.

Poor-quality coal would give way to wood as trees were felled and wetted slack give way to damp turf as World War Two (known euphemistically as The Emergency) dragged on. If ww2 was not Ireland's war, not quite real for the Irish, so the Dodo's shift from Springfield to bungalow bliss in the Burnaby at Greystones was equally an illusion. One of his open leatherwork slippers held the front door ajar, which meant that he was off playing golf; *that* was an irrefutable fact. Mumu's 'Would you ever take a look at the door and see if your brother's off golfing?' when decoded, read: 'Is his slipper in the door?'

The so-called livingroom was a low-ceilinged stuffy room smelling of coke and heated leather. A pot of tea and buttered toast warmed at the narrow grate, but of my brother there was no visible sign, apart from these comestibles and the guardian slipper holding the front door off the catch. The slipper-in-the-door prevented it closing and was also a silent order that supper should be on the table in the kitchen when he returned and removed his spiked golfing shoes in the porch to step into one slipper and limp or hop into his cramped bedroom (no room to swing a cat) and step into the second slipper, to make his way into the adjoining bathroom for his ablutions and to take the nailbrush to his nails.

The Dodo playing cricket, even opening the batting for CWC, seemed always to be at practice. Similiarly on his lonely forays over the outer nine at GGC, he was at practice again.

Now he made his way resolutely across the untended garden and the path he had worn by the vegetable patch; moving with short rapid mincing steps, hips and shoulders going, an odd galvanised way of progressing. A limp canvas bag (bought from stout Scuffle in the hut by the railway station) held a miscellaneous set of mismatched hickory-shafted clubs, wielded most incompetently by my brother.

He played alone over the deserted outer nine, away from the clubhouse, lifting his head, splaying his shots, cutting great divots, hurling clubs about, cursing his Maker.

The Dodo's golf was all practice: six or more practice swings followed as like as not by fresh-air shots, wild shanks followed by even more atrocious language; the Dodo played a very blue game of golf designed for himself alone. A distant misshapen figure with arms locked rigid, stuck at the summit of a cranked swing, unable to bring the club-head down. The Dodo was carving his way up the long eight.

Once, in a snow-fight near the ring-pump, I, having had the affrontery to throw a snowball that had caught him below the knee and filled the turn-ups of his grey trousers, stood my ground in the ditch below him and received a coldly dismissive glare from angry hazel eyes.

'Take that out, at once!'

I had cravenly obeyed, the Dodo towering forbiddingly above me with folded arms, Montgomery of Alamein.

Once the Dote and I had filled a biscuit tin with field mice and put it in his bed by the hot-water bottle; he would let them loose when he turned back the sheets. But this affront to his dignity he kept to himself, at least there were no repercussions.

Silent, torpid, crouching over the fire, he drew out a clean linen hankerchief from his trouser pocket, trumpeted into it thrice, studied the results (prone to nosebleeds), folded it and put it away. I suspect that he could bring on heavy nosebleeding at will; it was one of his tricks for getting into the infirmary. A regular splashing in the back of the classroom announced that Higgins senior was having another nosebleed, and should take himself across to Matron.

The wireless knob was within easy reach.

The reception was poor, the batteries dying. Uttering low heartfelf imprecations the Dodo fetched it a buffet, it was not going to best him. On 3rd September 1939 he had strolled in flannels into the kitchen to find the Dote and myself with old Mrs Henry sitting before a roaring fire and had coolly informed us that Chamberlain had just declared war, and sauntered out again. Old Mrs Henry blessed herself and said, 'God save us all then!'

Presently the nagging jeery voice of Lord Haw-Haw came from Berlin, the BBC news jammed with accounts of deaths and bombings, information from spies working in Britain.

The Dodo began to study Morse code at the Atlantic College in Dublin, taking a room in Mespil Road. He had volunteered for the RAF, for nightfighters; the Dodo was above all earthly things and on the side of Gubby Allen and Lord Burghley, Don Budge and Hammond, against Lili Marlene and Goering and Eva Braun and Goebbels and Julius Streicher and Alfred Rosenberg and von Ribbentrop.

'That's what he's set his heart on apparently,' said Mumu. Von Ribbentrop was only a champagne salesman, she told me in her most withering and dismissive manner. She preferred Anthony Eden who was a real gentleman.

The Dodo waited for his call-up papers.

He went off to Cranwell Cadet School, walked through blitzed London in the blackout, saw Pat Kirkwood's long legs and wide smile on the stage when she sang to the troops, 'Oh Johnny, oh Johnny, how you can love!' He sat in the stalls in his RAF officer's uniform at Rattigan's *Flare Path*. For if Mumu loved English royalty, the Dodo loved England, home of Hobbs. When questioned about night-flying he had this to report: 'It's a worrying sort of activity, actually. You are always conscious of the need to get home.' This was a long speech for him, stating the terms of survival.

Of the war itself, which left so many million dead, many of them non-combatants, I recall only the bombs dropped on Dublin by one Dornier or Heinkel that had been chased from the English coast or had strayed over the Irish Sea, rather as a hen menaced by dogs will lay eggs in out-of-the-way places; the shock-waves travelled down the Liffey and through Killadoon Wood to wake all the pheasants and set them shrieking, seconds before Springfield's nursery windows rattled in their frames. Thirteen miles to the west the blast had demolished houses on the North Strand in a trench a thousand yards long. Diplomatic notes flew but to little avail. The status quo remained the same for German combatant and Irish non-participant. Both knew well enough how the wind blew. Dev had been stubborn about the ports, dug his heels in, would not let them go.

If on looking back I (too young to know) could remember only the beginning, the Dodo's dramatic announcement, then he himself (non-participant extraordinaire) had perhaps mislaid it. For the war had ended before he could take off on a mission into the black night.

When he came home on leave, Mumu (whose nerves had gone against her and who was to pass the war in bed) bravely rose up and washed and dressed herself in fur coat and demi-veil to perch on the edge of a wheelbarrow, the Dodo in his RAF pilot's uniform and daredevil forage cap angled on the wobbling head, one hand resting on her shoulder; and on the prudish lips of both (so alike!) the *ghosts of smiles.*

When his leave expired Mumu resumed her life in bed, for an existence without him wasn't for her any life at all. She would prefer to be dead, did not wish to live. Her voice had become fainter, pitched higher; she was becoming him.

On Monday, June 2nd, 1941, the *Irish Times* (price 2d. Saturdays 3d.) headlines were dramatic:

GERMAN BOMBS WERE DROPPED ON DUBLIN

GOVERNMENT PROTEST TO BE MADE
IN BERLIN

DEAD NUMBER 30;
INJURED OVER 80

Investigations having shown that the bombs dropped were of German origin, the Chargé d'Affaires in Berlin is being directed to protest, in the strongest terms, to the German Government against the violation of Irish territory, and to claim compensation and reparation for the loss of life, the injuries suffered, and the damage to property. He is further directed to ask for definite assurances that the strictest instructions will be given to prevent the flight of aircraft over Irish territory and territorial waters.

The four bombs were dropped in the Ballybough and North Strand areas and twenty houses completely demolished. A further bomb was dropped near Arklow on Sunday morning, but no lives were lost.

From within the relatively secure confines of the Vatican City, Pope Pius XII sent out Whitsuntide greetings to the world in a deeply ambiguous message of goodwill and mixed metaphors – a gloss on Pope Leo XIII's encyclical, *Rerum Novarum* ('the Magna Carta of a Christian social endeavour'). His Holiness spoke of deep furrows and grievous disturbances, both in nations and in society, 'until the years finally poured their dark and turbulent waters into the sea of war, whose unforeseen currents may effect our economy and society'.

Goods were created by God for all men and the natural right to the use of material goods provides man with a secure basis of the highest import on which to rise with reasonable liberty (sic), 'to the fulfilment of his moral duties'.

The Pope urged the need for the cooperation of all.

Failure (common to all human activity) should not make mankind forget the inspiring message of the *Rerum Novarum* (issued in 1891 by Pope Leo XIII) which 'tomorrow, when the ruins of this world hurricane is cleared, may be the outset of a reconception of a new social order worthy of God and man and will keep living the noble flame of a brotherly social spirit. Nourish it; keep it burning, even more brightly; carry it wherever a cry of pain reaches you,' the Pope concluded.

The war in Iraq had ended; Crete fell to a German air armada. The British cruiser *Sheffield* entered Gibraltar in a damaged condition; the destroyer *Kelly* went down carrying with her Lieutenant Commander Lord Hugh Beresford, to the inexpressible grief of his mother the Duchess of St Albans and the sister-in-law, the Marchioness of Waterford.

It was a busy Whit.

Between 12.30 and 1.30 a.m. on Sunday, the day after the *Luftwaffe* had bombed the North Strand, unknown

planes were heard passing over Dun Laoghaire, proceeding
in a northerly direction. 'Searchlights were observed.'

Later that morning, shortly after 10 a.m., two tenement
houses collapsed in Old Bride Street, Dublin, killing three
persons and injuring fifteen others. Among the dead were
Mrs Brigid Lynskey (30) and her five-month-old baby, Noel,
and Samuel O'Brien (72), a pensioner of Messrs Guinness.

The precise cause of the collapse was not known; it was
believed to be due to a combination of factors – the old
tenement houses were shaken when the bombs fell on
Dublin on Saturday morning, and a heavy lorry had passed
the building shortly before the collapse.

My mother stayed in bed for two years.

She became obese, inventing a nervous disorder that
would keep her with the too-much-loved eldest son: claustrophobia. She had *claustrophobia* and could not attend Mass
any more; crowded places did not suit her, crowds distressed
her; no place where she had been happy could be visited
again. Her few friends were reduced to an irreducible mini-
mum. The house was a 'disgrace', she was ashamed of it,
the housework was beyond her. Her manner became distant;
she spent hours staring out the window at the clouds. A
priest came once a year to give her Holy Communion.

Dr George Sheehan, a good family friend of long standing, came with his black bag and a heavy old panting labra-
dor. The animal came wheezing into the bedroom after
his master and collapsed on the threadbare rug, its design
(peacocks) worn off by time. The collapsing dog shook the
room, the grey-haired Dr Sheehan reached out his hand for
the patient's fluttering pulse and asked, 'What seems to be
the matter, Lily?'

He examined her but could find nothing wrong and
retired, baffled. The war raged on to the tune of Melachri-
no's strings, *Forces Favourites, Hi, Gang!* and the rhumbas of
Edmundo Ross.

My mother stayed in bed.

My father tolerated it. This was her choice, he could not gainsay it. She was happy in her own way, he said. From her sickbed she dominated him and the household where little housework was attempted any more. Her voice became fainter and fainter. Dado had an offhand way with the bills, impaling them on a wire skewer and forgetting them. Creditors called and were palmed off with farfetched promises of sudden wealth, debts cleared. Then for six months my father dreamed winners. He broke the local turf accountant who called and begged for time to pay. In his experience the bookie had never known of such horses winning at such long odds.

The war, which would come to an end before the Dodo could go into action, continued to rage on.

There was nothing *organically* wrong with Mumu, Dr Sheehan said; her nerves had gone against her, that was all. To be well again she must rise out of bed, get on her own two feet, find outside interests.

One bright day in spring towards the end of the war, my father, urged on by no fewer than three doctors – a nerve specialist had been summoned from Dublin – persuaded Mumu to get out of bed, with much coaxing and promises of a table booked for dinner at a nice hotel by the sea.

'All right,' she said, doubtful but resigned, 'all right then . . .'

None of her clothes fitted; a suitable ensemble had to be let out and a day wasted.

'She's perking up again,' Dado said, glad to see any sign of improvement.

'She'll be right as rain,' said old Mrs Henry.

'Now Ma'am,' said Rita.

She left her bed, seemingly excited by the prospect of an outing. A hired car called. She was weak on her pins, could barely walk, being very obese and short of breath, but managed to get outside the house, marvelling at the bright colours of spring, the birdsong, the refreshing breeze. All teeming life lay without.

But when she saw the sea she flatly refused to go on. Dado coaxed and promised but Mumu would not listen to reason. On she would not go for all the tea in China; no argument could shift her. My father had to tell the taximan to turn around. Mumu went back to bed.

A week later she confessed to me: 'I just couldn't go on, Aidan. Something stopped me. It was the sea that separated me from the Dodo. Do you understand?'

Then followed that numb slow time when my mother refused to leave her bed, refused to be cheered up or even to read, her spirits sunk, her voice gone, sleeping away the days, a resentful unconscious deep-breathing inert apathetic living mound.

What did she want?

What did she think or see? Wings tipping over the waves, the sun in splendour on the water, the tide flowing in and all grief forgotten, the Dodo in his nightfighter giving the thumbs-up from the shining cockpit, saying it was a piece of cake and performing the Victory Roll for her?

She saw only the angel in the Dodo. Bed offered no comfort or rest.

'I'm dead tired,' she often said. 'I'm really tired out ... exhausted now.'

In that sluggish time, when my mother had ample opportunity to sleep and dream away the days, dream away her life, she had a nightmare of Joss dead.

He had been the go-between from Belgium when she and my father had conducted their courting; and had himself married the next youngest of six – was it? – sisters.

Mumu celebrated the end of the war in her own way, by rising up out of bed. The Dodo was in Scotland, now studying to be a Land Surveyor. My parents moved from Greystones to Dalkey, a change before death.

26

The Course Record

	NAMES	H'Cap	Strokes
A	A.C. HIGGINS	3	—
B	G M ROWE	8	—

CARD No 10   DATE 15th JUNE 1950

COMPETITION GRAND HOTEL CUP

100 METRES = 110 YARDS (Approx.)

STROKES

OUT	30
IN	36
GROSS	66
H'CAP	3
NETT	63

Hole	Title	Metres			Par	Index	Score		+ − 0
		Medal	Forward	Winter			A	B	
1	Burnaby	277	254	263	4	18	3		
2	Garden	455	446	431	5	8	4		
3	Ridge	400	393	393	4	1	3		
4	Oozler	160	151	141	3	10	3		
5	Spinney	374	360	346	4	3	4		
6	Narrows	321	315	308	4	5	3		
7	Dolly	148	128	112	3	16	3		
8	Mill	449	437	449	5	12	4		
9	Rookery	127	125	121	3	17	3		
	Out	2711	2609	2562	35	Out	30		
10	Big Tree	364	362	315	4	2	4		
11	Farm	327	263	312	4	14	4		
12	Pigs Hollow	177	168	151	3	9	5		
13	Campbell's	286	284	255	4	15	4		
14	Sugar Loaf	377	366	325	4	6	4		
15	Crow Abbey	339	334	318	4	7	4		
16	The Bell	202	194	190	3	11	3		
17	View Rock	284	276	279	4	4	4		
18	La Touche	334	329	320	4	13	4		
	In	2690	2586	2465	34	In	36		
	TOTAL	5401	5175	5027	69				
	S.S.S.	68	67	67					

STABLEFORD

POINTS	

PAR

WINS	
LOSSES	
NETT	

FOR OFFICE USE ONLY

BACK NINE	
LAST SIX	
LAST THREE	
LAST TWO	
LAST ONE	

Please repair pitch marks on greens and replace all divots

Competitor's Signature .... ac Higgins

Marker's Signature .... G.M.Rowe

ALTERATIONS TO SCORES MUST BE INITIALLED

It was a lovely summer's morning when Geoffrey Rowe and I played in the Grand Hotel Cup. Dado appeared beside the eleventh fairway to ask how the lad was doing. Out in thirty and five under, going strong. I four-putted the next green, which had been enlarged by running a hand-mower over the fairway and the pin placed in it. Thirty-six home gave a gross sixty-six that could have been two or three shots better. It won best gross.

27

On the Isle of Man

On Christmas Day 1951, my first Christmas away from home, a colourless, windless, sunless grey Manx day at the tail-end of an idle year, I found myself sharing a Christmas goose with a stone-deaf glutton in a boarding house on the Isle of Man.

The choleric grunty feeder with perspiration starting from every pore, uttering the deep heartfelt groans of a sated carnivore, was none other than my old Barton Cup team-mate, J. D. Parsons, the Plantigrade Shuffler in person. We had teamed up as an unbeaten foursome combination of flair and lively opportunism, the Shuffler ever in storms of coughing and pipe-drill, rolling in putts from all angles across sloping greens. One of our foursome opponents had been a one-armed Dublin golfer by the name of Hamlet, from Stillorgan, with a stout sweating partner from Galloping Green, a pair defeated one summer's day at Foxrock.

We ate in silence but for the grunting and chewing of bones in Beverley Mount boarding house on Woodbourne Road where my destiny had now taken me; to this salubrious watering-hole in the middle of the Irish Sea, a resort popular with workers from the Midlands and the North of England. A tall monkey-puzzle tree in the narrow front garden blocked out the light. The summer cruise in the Indian Ocean had proved impractical, or perhaps my employer-to-

be had totted up the cost. Suffering from obesity and 'incipient alcoholism', delicately phrased, he had chanced upon
The Fallacy of the Hopeless Case by Dr Alexander Howitzer and
was putting himself into Dr Howitzer's hands in a sanatorium for sad cases near Douglas. The cure went on behind
high stone walls, with a gate-lodge and keepers; straitjackets
and sedation supplied on request. A barren Indian woman
was trying to have a child, a fellow with curvature of the
spine was trying to walk straight; Dr A. Howitzer took them
all in; succour was his forte. Malingering would not be tolerated; the treatment would take ten weeks, fees a hundred
pounds a week with a down-payment of fifty on signing.

The heavy Xmas fare proved too much for me, after a
vegetarian diet of Galtee cheese, eggs and milk. The next
day, with profuse apologies to landlady Mrs Crowe for hardly
touching her goose, stuffed, roasted and basted to a succu-
lent brown, I resumed my ordinary of vegetarian omelettes.

The Plantigrade Shuffler had gone to Trinity College
where he had graduated as an architect. Brother Danny
had lost a leg on Anzio Beach, emigrated to New Zealand,
practised as a doctor, visiting the islands, until lost at sea
(the missing ketch *Joyita*, an unsolved marine mystery), possibly eaten by cannibals, the Shuffler thought. As the eldest
son he was obliged to take over the running of the family
business – a footwear factory in Athlone in the dead centre
of Ireland – and be answerable to his martinet of a father,
old Parsons, a bigoted old Protestant gent who was down
on alcohol (to which both his sons were addicted) and
Roman Catholics ('No truck with Papists!'), few of whom
owned property in the Burnaby, an enclave within an enclave
in the Greystones population of out-and-out Protestants. 'Up
King Billy!' was the blazon on his banner.

One morning the flag of Greystones Golf Club stood at
halfmast to signal the passing of old Parsons and the course
was closed until lunchtime, though the bar was open. The
will was in the hands of the trustees; the home in the Burnaby and the footwear factory in Athlone, with £66,000, was

the Shuffler's *if* he remained on the wagon for a year, test-ified to by a reliable witness. It was a stipulation with which he could not comply; in practice it was impossible.

Thrice a week he drove to Athlone in his Morris; then home, rattling over the cattle-trap under the arched entrance of *Greystones Golf Club (Members Only)* that was a sign for the favoured, by the eighteenth green and up the ramp by the Pro's hut (old Martin), over the moat and under the lowered drawbridge and into the castle yard, the bawn, to the merry sound of bells ringing and bugles calling and a flag flying to announce the safe arrival of the inheritor, and old Mrs Martin (quick to move her hand from the till) opening the first chilled Dutch lager of the day and the members telling each other 'The Shuffler's back!' As the thirsty *castellanus* returning from the wars.

He was a card, deaf as a post but merry as a grig. He dined in the Grand Hotel, the Railway Hotel, the Clyda, The Horse and Hounds in Delgany, making great depredations among the stocks of Dutch lager. Coming and going like the wind, no sooner gone than back for another one; no sooner that drink finished than off with him again, visiting all the posting-houses on the road to ruin, crying out, 'One for the road!' He was a solitary drinker, even in company, for his deafness kept him apart. He drank at the bar of the Grand, at Lewis's near the convent where the Sharps and the Jacksons sat around the fire, drinking brandy with Charlie Reynolds the Garda Sergeant, served by Patsy who was thought to wear a corset to keep his figure trim; on to Danns and the Clyda Hotel en route to Delgany and the Horse and Hounds. He drove back at speed through Grey-stones, via Trafalgar Road, Victoria Road, Kimberley Road, Eden Road, Whitshed Road, Portland Road and Erskine Avenue, so that you would hardly know you were in Ireland at all. On one famous occasion he drove across the eight-eenth green in his Morris; and he the vice-president of the golf club!

Now I was to be the minder or golfing companion, a

vegetarian imbiber of soft drinks and holder of the course record (it was a lovely summer's morning), hired to play golf once a day over Braddan public links and to see – to testify to the testy trustees – that he had stayed on the wagon for one whole calendar year.

Thrice a week he walked to the sanatorium for his infrared treatment, for doses of salts and invigorating pep-talks from Dr Howitzer.

We flew in on a grey sunless day.

The details of our arrival, the unpacking of the golf bags, the signing in, all is obliterated from my mind, as the endless wearysome nightshift in the extrusion moulding plant is obliterated, as the details of punishments in three schools are obliterated, swept away.

J. D. Parsons, the Plantigrade Shuffler, *nuestro amigo*, (you should have seen him lining up a putt!), deaf as a post without his hearing-aid out on the course, indomitable battler, the pipe-drill, the tics, the daring recovery shots from deep bunkers, the sunny smile, the gleam of honest perspiration, the extraordinary Waa-waaa-waa of long-drawn upperclass consonants (being deaf for so long, since the age of sixteen, it must have been an aural recall of the posh accents of English fellows at TCD, gone all wonky in the airwaves, distorted by the passage of time, become a parody of what it had attempted to respect – he spoke as Bulldog Drummond and his gang must have spoken, the club drawl).

'The cure takes ten weeks. Perhaps by then I'll have developed a taste for tomato-juice,' he sniggered.

The Plantigrade Shuffler rarely looked you in the eye and then only by accident, busily lip-reading, nodding his head; scuttling into the bar, into the Gents, into the changing-room, a deaf man's extra-loud vocal chorus booming inanities ('Playing to single figures!'), his hearing-aid worn under the arm (the battery buzzing, very loud when he drank soup, if plugged in), the plug in one ear, a sort of harness.

'Hello, Joe, you're looking well.' (Joe Mulderry, the poker

player, looking like death warmed up). 'Hello, Freddy. (Freddy Quinn, his inseparable side-kick). Looking well.'

'Hello, Des.'

He had a furtive abstracted smile, looking down at his shoes, over his paunch, standing at the end of the bar in his accustomed place, rarely sitting, his feet crossed when he began to feel comfortable (after the sixth Dutch Lager), a pedagogic way of making points with the stem of his pipe. The refill, the tamping down with finger, the match lit, the quick insucks, the very flushed face very serious now, sound of sucking in air, bubbling of pipe, waving of match to extinguish, puffing out clouds of smoke, rolling over on the convex rubber soles of his expensive brogues. 'Has Beppa been in?'

Then the short abstracted puffs followed by a storm of coughing, bent double at end of bar, red features gone purple, hand to paunch, pipesteam waved about, fiddling with hearing-aid, to crackling of static, storms of coughing.

A delivery so rich and rare, so *rubicund* it sounded posh, put on, faked, never heard on earth before, was in fact intended dead seriously and so accepted by those who had become accustomed to his eccentric ways at the golf club.

An evening out was an occasion for a loud braying of indiscretions heard across the bar or the length of a dining-room; and every evening was an evening out for the Shuffler, imbibing quarts of Dutch lager, topped up with gin, wine and cognac.

'The Shuffler's a scream,' they all agreed at the club where he was vice-president.

The Shuffler dining out made a real pig's nose of it. The hearing-aid batteries were constantly giving trouble, bubbling acoustics with every mouthful, the battery on the table before him, loud compliments paid to the ladies, Bep and Bimp in stitches, wasn't he a scream! He was an unconscious clown, master of the loud devastating *non sequitur*; and all thanks to deafness. A rum cove was the Shuffler.

'Bep been in?' The Shuffler asked between one hacking cough and another, waving his pipestem about to clear away the smokescreen.

'Not yet, Mr Parsons,' spoke out old Mrs Martin over the bar counter. Astonishing blood-red lipstick daubed across her mouth gave her the alarming look of a whore from *Les Fleurs de Mal.*

Perhaps this unregenerate boozer had his old man, dead but still operative, to thank for the state he found himself in? Old dead Parsons was still clamped to his back by the inflexible terms of the will, as Sinbad the Sailor had the Old Man of the Sea clamped to his back. He had been a martinet in his lifetime and continued to rule from beyond the grave. Having undermined his eldest son's belief in himself, when a qualified architect had become the manager of a boot factory, he had seen to it that his wishes would be honoured posthumously.

The Shuffler was a *softened up* drinker rather than a hard-ened drinker, rendered all round and wobbly by prodigious intakes of Dutch lager and the resultant flatulence.

The caddies kept an eye out for him, recognising the wheels slamming over the cattle-grid at the entrance gate, the car door banged shut almost before the engine died and the Shuffler already surrounded by caddies calling out to be hired. The going rate in those days was half a crown a round with tips optional, a wing.

Who strolled in then but May Fitzgibbon and Dorry Oulton followed by Joe Mulderry and Freddy Quinn, the two pallid poker players of smoke-filled rooms.

Hello Des!
Hello May! Hello Dorry!
Hello Des!
Hello Joe! Hello Freddy!
All agreed that all were looking remarkably well.

The general consensus of opinion in the bar was that he (the Shuffler) was a hoot.

A hoot.

Endless visits to the Gents to empty his bladder; storms of coughing announced his return to the bar where he preferred to stand at the serving hatch. His amiable gossip revolved around golf, the condition of the course, the health of the members, all old friends like Joe Mulderry, Freddy Quinn, John Sibley, John Thullier, Norman Dickinson, Dr Ian Moore, Harry Duggan, Harry Jervois, Major Frank Stone, Captain Simon Pettigrew. The Right Revd Riversdale Colthurst had a plain scraggy spouse who wore a tea-cosy on her head. The Honorary Club Secretary had been gazetted from England and the Rutland Halberdiers; Lieutenant-Colonel Howard Cornwallis Lewis (retired) was a pompous ass. He liked to be addressed as 'Colonel'. It was my pleasure to slaughter him in singles, leave him to go spluttering off down the hill. I nicknamed him Humphrey Chimpden Earwicker.

The Colonel liked to begin the day with a prodigious military evacuation in the club bog. He shat like a Lewis gun. Loud groaning stools were his speciality, with devastating sound-effects, an early morning military barrage with rising stenches finished off in the grand manner with multiple flushings and vigorous application of stiff bumf, the toilet roll sent fairly spinning, like the unrolling of banners.

Then, with much bluff H'RRrrummphing and clearing of the windpipe he stepped out to wash his hands, scrub his nails, comb back sparse bracken-coloured hair, straighten his club tie, put himself to rights. Whereupon he lit up his briar pipe and emerged pristine, set off upstairs to his cubby-hole off the boardroom, his cramped office quarters, to formal acknowledgements of 'Good morning, Colonel!' from staff and whatever amiable member might be about at that hour, looking for an early game; glancing upward at the broad back ascending the stairs in a cloud of good-quality tobacco fumes. He and I had never seen eye to eye.

This testy military type was all the more formally an officer because of never having seen action. When the Right Reverend Riversdale Colthurst (Army Chaplain) had laid a com-

plaint against me for 'driving into him' over the hill at the
11th, the Colonel was pleased to formally acknowledge it.
'Higgins, we have just received a complaint from one of the
members. Should you care to offer some explanation, ahem,
we await your reply. The matter will be brought up at the
next General Meeting.'

Acid correspondence passed between us. He surprised me
with football stockings off, warming my frozen feet at the
coal-fire in the bar; that kind of conduct would not be
tolerated.

'Good morning, *Colonel!*' was balm to his gilead. He was
to die in harness, of a heart attack at Bray GC, collapsing
on the 14th green, muttering his epitaph ('I'm finished!').
This by way of captious aside. We are on the isle of Manx
cats, not Bray.

The daily ritual of a round ('to reduce obesity') was to
continue from the first day, no matter how inclement the
weather. We played for the usual stakes – a half-crown for a
win, a tanner for birdies, dykes and oozlers, half stakes on
the bye, loser pays for the first round of drinks, non-
alcoholic beverages preferred.

Sometimes we returned to the Peverel Hotel for our
refreshments; we were remembered, the barman greeted us.

The Plantigrade Shuffler's round agnostic cheeks glowed a
duller purple as he laboured up the slopes of Braddan
public links, where hills and gradients abounded, following
the high arcs of his drives, struck with determined grunting.
Addressing the ball well teed up, the curvature of his spine
became more pronounced, paunch matched by hump, that
gave him a simian look. Everything about him was curvi-
linear, from round cheeks to paunch, and like the Dodo he
too seemed to totter forward on convex soles. The backs of
his hands were hairy and as he struck the ball he grunted,
following its course with some body English.

He was all roundy, the spine rounded upwards towards

the neck, the neck bulged upwards towards the skull, the skull curved into the inflamed face. The very strokes he struck were perfect arcs, hit with a half-swing from rounded shoulders with a grunt, and looped too was the parabola of the shot, the Warwick dispatched briskly on its way with much top-spin.

Above the sea on the exposed Braddan Hills we followed our drives, one sixty or eighty yards ahead of the other. The days were wretchedly cold. One morning I struck a seabird on the fairway with a low drive, my hands frozen, and had to dispatch it with a sand-blaster.

After lunch I was free to continue my roaming about the port. On the milder days the sky over Douglas turned the flesh-pink of yew bark cut with a knife, a roseate island light. I stepped into the pulpits and read from all the bibles. In St Kyran's Roman Catholic Church (Mass & Daily Communion 8.00 a.m. Daily) the door sighed shut behind me and the street noises abated. A band of diffused coloured light filtered down through the stained-glass windows above the fourth and fifth Stations of the Cross. The wind was humming in the apertures of the long windows above the altar, the noises from outside reduced to a low innuendo, a distant buzzing. It was the first week after Epiphany.

On 10th January 1952 we went to the Christmas panto at the Empress Theatre and I heard the panto girl sing 'Pale Hands I Loved Beyond the Shalimar' (where are you now?), and was much taken with her. I wrote her a fan letter and she agreed to an assignation at two-thirty next day at the Manx Museum.

We began walking out. The nights were so freezingly cold that not even a Manx cat would venture out of doors. We walked the roads sparkling with quartz around the Braddan Hills under an amazing canopy of stars, and she told me that was the Liverpool boat sailing for Liverpool and those lights were not an ocean liner coming in but Lamona

Asylum, where the Plantigrade Shuffler (having gone off his head) was to be consigned on January 21st.

He asked me to spit in his face and I obliged, for why gainsay him if he imagined himself to be Christ, and he an unbeliever?

Frescoes of angels were painted on either side of the confessional. The angel on the left hand had a sly eye and a prudish 'o' for a mouth, with elbows held stiffly by the side and the palms of the hands extended outward, just below the shoulders, in a frozen cataleptic arrested gesture. In graphic capital letters below on a scroll blowing free in the winds of Heaven was inscribed MISERICORDIA.

The angel on the opposite side held a formidable key diagonally across its chest, the angelic brows drawn together in a severe manner, while on a companion scroll was printed ABSOLUTIO. On the half-door of the confessional a card was pinned to the monk-brown curtain:

Rev. Theo. Craine P.P.

On the evening of the 20th Janury the great Naturopath gave a talk to which his patients and members of the public were invited: 'Out of This World to Soft Lights and Music'. It was snowing. The Plantigrade Shuffler and I dined at the Perivale with my panto girl and a friend. The Shuffler was drinking again. He said that the sanatorium was surrounded by a bad cloud, and he was moving back to the hotel. It was to be the end of our silent evenings sitting around the fire. At four-thirty in the morning I was woken by Tom Crowe laying his hand on my shoulder, to whisper that a policeman downstairs wished to speak to me.

I found the Plantigrade Shuffler in an exalted state of madness. He had set fire to the bedroom curtains and might have burnt down the hotel. They were talking of certifying him. He had become Christ expelling the buyers and sellers from the Temple. The sergeant and police doctor converged on us. I refused to sign any papers. They told us that we were going for a short drive, it would be for the best. In the squad car my now deranged employer was squeezed between two huge constables in the back seat, looking like mad preacher Casey offering his wrists for the handcuffs in *The Grapes of Wrath*.

We swept up the curved driveway of Lamona Asylum and piled out. Two inmates carrying a bucket stacked high with dirty washing set it down in order to gape at us. A door in an ivy-covered wall sprang open and half a dozen wild-looking internees in white coats approached us. Me they unerringly picked as the mad one. 'You've got the wrong man,' I said. The Shuffler was undergoing transformations, now he was a middle-aged matron about to bear a child; he was shaking his head with a sweet maternal smile, telling them his time was not quite up. They placated and coaxed him and drew him in with them and closed the door and that was that. I went back to the boarding house and told the Crowes. Mr Crowe kindly booked me onto the first flight to Dublin. I said my goodbyes. I said I would contact the trustees. There was a sister somewhere. It was all most unfortunate I said. We must all hope to be saved they said. We shook hands. A cab came and took me to Douglas Airport, for a flight to Dublin.

On the day he mailed off his mad thesis to Dublin (one copy sent registered to Professor Walton at TCD, one to Professor Erwin Schrödinger at the Institute of Advanced Studies, the first never acknowledging it, the second most alarmed by it) he was fairly flying, a spring-heeled Jack full of helium. Walking to and from the Post Office he seemed to be high-stepping it through a quag or trying to make himself ultra heavy, so as not to fly off the Earth itself, rising vertically until hidden by clouds; stamping down on the pavement as if to increase his weight, assume the leaded boots of a deep-sea diver.

The Plantigrade Shuffler had formerly walked with the

rolling gait of a sailor, but now it was the wound-up clock-work *locomotor ataxi* of the habitual boozer, the hard drinker's roll, en route to the pub named The Hair of the Hound, or the Consul on his way to El Farolito, Casanova incarcerated with the rats.

Neither of us was quite normal; given the state I was in I couldn't see how disturbed he was, behind his habitual twit-ching and eccentric behaviour; if he was going off his head I couldn't see it. I had read the thesis but it hadn't conveyed much sense. He had proved or attempted to prove that pain is palpable; more than that, an objective part of us like an appendix or a pip in an apple, that could be seen and presumably removed, like a cancer. I didn't see what he was getting at; for an unbeliever, a sceptic such as he, it seemed to me a very roundabout way of admitting Original Sin, about whose existence I had little doubt.

Besides, I was myself deep into studies of madness. Thomas Mann's *Der Zauberberg* in the Lowe-Porter trans-lation, Wyndham Lewis's *Blasting & Bombardiering* and a large tome illustrated with schizophrenic paintings made by disturbed minds in institutions for the insane, entitled *Wisdom, Madness and Folly.* Huge coloured spheres were bounding towards a distant horizon or bouncing towards the viewer and about to burst from the page.

In my own days of destitution and misery which were soon to come upon me, brought on by under-nourishment and the pull and stress of a purposeless existence which had become more and more distressful to me, I was to experi-ence something similiar; a sense of doom allied to irrepress-ible gaiety, akin to Herr Mann's pleura-shock, first mauve and then purple, as the hooks go in. A sort of extreme miserable bliss, or blissful misery *in extremis.*

And then?

Dado had resumed his endless pacing from sink to window to command an angled view of Kinlen Road and then the long silent stare out, the abstracted pacing to and fro; the circumspect belch followed by subdued fart told of the eventless passage of Time.

Tyres on gravel, the front wheel of the heavy Raleigh pushing open the yard door, signalled the precipitious arrival of the Dodo back from a day at the office in Dublin, the train to Greystones, the bicycle ride home. A short silence meant he was removing his bicycle clips at the back step, the sound of the flange banged back and the door rattled to its foundations, told us that the Dodo was home again. Everybody opens a door in a characteristic and revealing way, revealing as thumb-prints; the Dodo *fired* open the door and propelled himself into the kitchen, anxious to get in a few holes of golf before supper, or dark, depending on the time of year, before 'Moonlight in Vermont', before the stars came out to play. A rattle of lids on the electric stove told that he was checking out the supper, the silence meant he was changing for golf, following by pissing and flushing and banging of bathroom door; then the slipper in place, then silence, out. A quick sighting of the Dodo carrying his limp canvas holdall and assortment of clubs; head down, puffing out his cheeks, with short fussy steps crossing the path he had worn between the trellised enclosures and out into the back field near the rugby club, and away to the back nine. He was not a member, he was trespassing, resolute in his pleasures as in his work.

No monkey-wrench ever tightened bathroom faucets in any Higgins home, that's for sure.

He had not remarked upon my leaving nor on my return. Life resumed its even tenure as before. He moved like a stout middle-aged woman in a hurry in a hobble skirt, progress impeded by the enveloping heavy cloth. I thought of the *tenue* of the other, which had been extremely odd. He seemed to be filled with helium which was lifting him up and he slapped down his feet as solidly as possible in order to stay attached to the gravity from which his madness was trying to free him. A chemist's window blazed with the display of an outsize bottle of azure blue.

To cut a long story short, I was back safely again in my little pink padded cell, hearing the taps dripping all night long, before you could say *dementia praecox*.

Of the outward flight I have little or no recollection, although it was the first time I had flown anywhere; or for that matter on what airline we travelled – Air Man? Manx Airways? for insignia a black cat *sans* tail sitting up pert and smirking on outstretched tail of crow in full flight; nor can I recall the small island airport where we landed, neat as Menorca.

Of the return flight I recall only the plane tilting over Bull Island and a horizontal line of grey cloud like grey moiré lifting as we came in over Dublin and how it rose up (silently, no orchestra in the pit) like the safety curtain at the Gaiety rising on Paulette Goddard and Burgess Meredith in *Winterset*.

And needless to say I flew in no wiser than I had flown out, and certainly no richer. A week or so later I was summoned by one of the trustees to luncheon at a gentlemen's club on Stephen's Green. An excellent wine was broached. I spoke of a child drowned in a fountain on the esplanade, falling through thin ice and hidden as the water froze solid again, and how they came and found the little dead one, like looking through a window. At the coffee and brandy stage we were the best of friends, the kind-featured trustee in the starched collar and I, and diplomatic feelers were extended. 'As to remuneration for any inconvenience suffered, I think we should . . .'

I held up one hand. I told him they didn't owe me a penny. I was sorry for the man put away, and hoped he would be out and about soon. We shook hands on the steps.

Some time in the following year I had a letter from the Plantigrade Shuffler. He thanked me for what I had done for him. He had put in his time, stayed dry, come into his inheritance, and £66,000 was a tidy sum in those days. He seemed to be in the best of spirits, spoke of another fourball in the Spring, when the greens were cut and rolled. No cheque was enclosed. Life was real, life was earnest, and God was good.

PART II

London

28

Ealing

Nothing is easy in a strange place, at first.

It took me some time to become acclimatised to factory ways and life at Fordhook Road with the frightened French couple who were dreading the end of the world.

Nor was finding Ealing Common as easy as at first surmised. From a perusal of the Tube map I found it named there but be damned if I could find it. I had done the Stations of the Cross many times as a penitential exercise; now I was doing the outer circles of Hell. And Elizabeth Bowen's neurotic mum had it perfectly right: London had a smell of its own.

When I did eventually make it overground at Ealing Common, coming up out of the bowels of the earth, I found a pleasant enough area disposed on either side of the Uxbridge Road, leading east to Acton Town and west to Ealing Broadway, which I had visited several times on the Tube, before taking the next east-bound connection Londonward. A butchery and bakery and cake shop and newsagents with awning were tidily arranged around the mouth of the Tube, out of which came dead air smelling of coke. Fordhook Road was to be my homebase for the foreseeable future. A neighbour with brush and pan was scooping up fresh horse manure, while glancing up at jet skylanes streaming in towards Heathrow, as if this was manna from Heaven – the hot turds carefully collected and carried through the house to his roses at the back. Was this an omen?

My quarters – one room with bed and use of bathroom-cum-toilet – were neat as a pin. I shared digs with Kevin O'Sullivan, a whilom golfing crony of Delgany, who worked at Firestone manufacturing huge tyres for the African market.

In those days the street-criers were still to be heard, ringing their bells and calling their wares; selling and buying ironmongery and odds and ends off horse-drawn drays. Voices from an English rustic past of Cobbett and Jefferies; a past which I had heard echoes of on the Isle of Man. Manx street-criers ringing handbells and uttering strange calls, incomprehensible Manx cries.

London town, when I eventually reached it, had a strange smell all its own. A smell like nothing else on earth – a stale spent smell with its own peculiar murky daylight, unchanged I dare say since the young Konrad Korzeniowski saw *a rusty sunlight that cast no shadows* some forty odd years before, when he had settled himself in digs near the Thames to write his first sea saga, *Almayer's Folly*. Nothing had changed essentially in the interval.

Perhaps it was the dusty miasmic after-stink of the Blitz – that horrific hammering – that still lingered on the air of the early 1950s when I first set foot there, before the end of the smog?

I had sold my golf clubs to a man in Hammond Lane Foundry, paid for a single ticket on the packet steamer sailing from Dun Laoghaire to Wales, boarded the London train and stayed on it until it steamed into Euston, went down steps with great misgiving, bought a ticket to Ealing Common, boarded the Tube and spent several hours shuttling to and fro, mostly underground, but always ending up at Ealing Broadway.

True to my obsession I spent long hours underground, as if bribing Charon to ferry me across the Styx, but could not see the further shore. I had been briefed by brother Bun who had been working for years at the British Film Library at Brentford; and now here I was shut up in a succession of onrushing Tubes.

At last, exhausted, I took the right connection, found Ealing Common when the automatic doors slid wide, stepped out onto the platform a new man. Crossing the Uxbridge Road with a light step I found Fordhook Road as the map had suggested, and the digs brother Bun had put a deposit on in the house so hoovered and polished by the middle-aged French couple who were anticipating the end of the world, a rain of atomic bombs.

Next morning I presented myself at the Labour Exchange and accepted my fate as a factory hand in Ponds Cosmetic Factory in Perivale at the lowly remuneration of seven pounds a week in the old currency, out of which thirty-five shillings would be deducted for rent. I would walk to work.

I prepared myself for a diet of Quaker Oats and milk, tinned beans, Take & Lyle honey spread on sliced loaf, washed down with Nescafé. The work in the stores was not arduous but a 6.00 a.m. shift meant rising at 4.45 a.m. In the factory I wore a brown boiler suit and laboured there for nine months, developing a taste for Watney's Red Barrel ale and Senior Service cigarettes, saving twenty pounds.

It was scarcely an auspicious beginning in the Greater London labour mart, in the footsteps of so many of my countrymen. With Jeffries (a baker laid off) and Tom Davies and Mr Brogan the chargehand in his white coat, and Vic Webb (ex-Army) with his limp, and the dull torment of working on the conveyor belt; beyond a certain speed which I considered inhuman I flatly refused to go, and let the stuff pile up, let the ganger curse, let Minny have kittens.

White froth from the cider factory was blown into Ponds' loading yard and fell like apple blossom or summer snow. At a break from the conveyor belt a group of girls in purple overalls had found a piece of smoked glass and stared through it at an eclipse of the sun and Milly Ashbrook remarked that at the next eclipse none there would be alive. It was July 30th, 1952, in my beginnings. The Bristol lorry driver gave me a present of rhubarb from his garden. He had a pleasant nautical Bristol accent, a seafaring burr, one arm tattooed with a cross and 'Father, Mother, Christ, Forget Me Not' in florid script amid the hair on his forearm.

Belisha beacons were spilling an overflow of ruby light onto the pillars of the Midland Bank on the Mall when I walked again across the Common in the near lightlessness before daybreak and the long-distance lorries were starting up on Hanger Lane.

My next foray involved digging up a back garden in Swiss Cottage, and poor shaly cindery soil it was too; that part-time job did not last long, at remuneration of a half-crown an hour. Then I worked longer hours for a hard seven months for better pay at Punfield & Barstow extrusion mouldings plant out by the Great North Road, reading *La Nausée* and lunching off two thin chops and tinned peas in a transport café. The chargehands here were Bob de Palmo and the whistling German, Martin Muhl, who boasted of the time he had worked flat out on a twelve-hour nightshift with his shirt off.

I sweated it out with Monk the Jew and Blizzard the Jamaican, as black as your boot, who paid extra rent for being black in a white area. Basket the Pakistani and Doody the moody Corkman were on my shift. I had digs in an upper room on Abbey Road, above Wholefart and Angel, a pair of huge decayed floozies who chainsmoked in their bathrobes and ran endless baths, occupying the bathroom – which was also the toilet – for long periods. I alternated day and night shifts, working eleven and twelve hours. Some diehards were prepared to work an hour overtime, regulating polythene in semi-automatic presses while being stunned by a deafening night-long cacophony on maximum amplification, deluging the exhausted workers who didn't appear to mind the pounding percussive beat. It was like being flogged.

Through one of the Musgrave sisters I found piece-work that I could do at home; painting Geordies the size of your thumb, in kilts, as a movie promotional stunt that would drive the sanest person mad. For a time I held down a part-time job as swimming-pool attendant at Marylebone Public Baths; but I saved nothing.

'Use your loaf, mate,' was the embattled war-cry of the weary factory hands and shift workers. Meaning: Wise up, get smart, fiddle.

In 1956 I was either working as a factory hand in Ponds (Cosmetics) in Perivale with Jeffries and Davies and old Bert Pollard or as a trainee extrusion moulder with Basket and Blizzard in Punfield & Barstow (Mouldings) at Burnt Oak on alternating day and night shifts. I recall the nausea of the long night shift and staying awake when working the semi-automatic presses and the incessant barrage of Muzak from the amplifiers – 'The Yellow Rose of Texas' and 'Be My Life's Companion' firm favourites, until they were coming out of our ears.

As with the Muzak and the howling headlines of the *Daily Mirror* so it was with my sandwiches, no matter how carefully prepared, no matter what I put into them, they all tasted the same, an unappetising mush.

Khrushchev and Bulganin – 'Mr K & Mr B' in the overly familiar parlance of the tabloids – had arrived on a state visit in the Soviet crusier *Orzhonikidze* which had anchored in Portsmouth harbour. Commander 'Buster' Crabb the intrepid frogman had swum under it in his flippers and never surfaced alive again. The body was later recovered with not a mark on it. The Soviet diplomats kept their lips diplomatically sealed, the Cold War tactics of not showing your hand.

Farewell the Davall Clock Factory, adieu Cider Factory, the Enna Infants Bath Factory, trio viewed so oft from the loading-bay, a view of the last fields of England. Farewell thin anxious Minny organising labour on the factory floor, Mr Lambert in his blue suit striding to and from the office, farewell old Bert at the shredding machine, Ted Heavens in the stores, farewell early shift and night shift, Nescafé and Quaker Oats, farewell the *Daily Mirror* and Yana ('Britain's Singing Bombshell') and the girl with heavy menses who fainted at the conveyor belt and her sleepy sister with hand impaled on the carding-machine in the Lipstick Room, farewell lovely pay-days and the present of handkerchiefs and the Christmas bonus in the pay-packet.

I was one of the blokes pulverised by a tediousness that could not be contained but somehow had to be endured. It was all a 'bind' (Cockney slang for the intolerable chore) in brother Bun's adopted huff-snuff Limey lingo.

The English factory-hand, your average piece-worker, is likely the most miserable of all working men on the surface of the globe. The centuries-old stoicism of the footsoldier in English lines that never broke, no matter how savage the assault (Malaparte remarked upon this), lives on in a vulgarised form in the bloke or bod you see before you, drowning in his *Daily Mirror*, forever accepting hand-outs, cutting corners, saving his face, bellyaching at his sorry lot, putting in overtime, lowering a few pints at his local, 'supporting' this soccer team or that, a broken-down knacker's-yard animal , a crock with all the stuffing knocked out of it. Brother Bun had found his spiritual home not far from Ealing Broadway in the company of contentious Gorblimeys, the miserable sods of Ailing.

P&B manufactured objects as diverse and various as collar studs to aeroplane parts. One worked, quite literally, by the clock. Fifteen semi-automatic presses thundered away twenty-four hours a day, never silent and stopping only to accommodate a new time-cycle installed by the clever engin-

eers; and the fifteen operators kept their eyes glued on the
clock, a large oval one-handed chronometer that ticked off
the seconds, 39,600 of them in a nightshift that seemed
endless to the operator.

One kept to fixed pressures and time cycles, producing,
say, four articles per minute, per shift schedule as ordained
by the graph hung outside de Palmo's office. It was common
practice to force up the pressure and extrude two seconds
prematurely. In order to achieve a four-a-minute cycle, say,
you were allowed two seconds for opening, two seconds for
closing – opening again on the tenth second, extruding on
the twelfth, closing on the fifteenth and repeating this cycle
four times every minute. But by opening on the eighth,
extruding and closing as instructed, it was possible to close
on the thirteenth instead of on the fifteenth, opening
again on the twenty-first to close on the twenty-sixth instead
of on the thirtieth, gaining two forbidden seconds on every
quarter of a cycle. So we slaved away, opening, extruding
and closing twenty-eight thousand times instead of the regu-
lation twenty-four thousand. This was piece-work put into
practice and a little private gain hard won against the odds;
the carrot of private emolument dangled tantalisingly just
ahead of the whip of the capitalist employer, P&B
(Mouldings) of Burnt Oak.

To see Monk (the Jew) or Blizzard (the Jamaican) wipe
clean the platters of polythene that had been subjected to
heat and severe pressure was to understand the 'hidden
agenda' of the system, the ethos of the Dark Satanic Mills;
the little bit on the side was the factor that made the whole
thing work. And I recalled (in the endless night shift one
had ample time for such trolling back) how old Mrs Henry
(God rest her soul, for she must be long gone to her reward)
wiped a plate clean with a sort of dogged earnestness, with
slow loving strokes (for she herself was also trolling back
into her own past, before my time) as if it were a baby's
bottom. The care and attention she lavished on our dirty
plates was the same loving care that she had lavished on the

Dote's dirty face (tears that grimy fists had knuckled into
his eyes) and thrice dirty bottom, dutifully, lovingly wiping
both clean, as she would my own tear-stained face and be-
shatten bottom, although strictly speaking it was not her job
to clean either end of us, her place belonged below, in the
kitchen. She did it, out of the goodness of her working
heart, to spare us embarrassment with Nurse O'Reilly, that
martinet, or Mumu, that grand lady.

At the end of a shift and without even a shower to clean us,
we departed from the premises of Punfield & Barstow as if
soundly whipped, to doze all the way home in the smelly
tube.

In Wall's icecream factory, putting in overtime, I worked in
cold storage for an extra ten bob a week, fifteen pounds
per week in twenty-three degrees below freezing, putting in
forty-eight hours. And furthermore, in a heatwave in July;
though the last thing any of the blokes or bods craved was
an icecream, least of all a Wall's wafer, after the vomit smell
of the factory floor. Black men lay out on garden benches,
seemingly decapitated.

These were some pockets of the labour mart in the Greater
London area, the equivalent of Fritz Lang's grim *Metropolis*
and not the romantic lies of Carné's *Le Jour se Lève*. In those
years not long after the end of the war, the cessation of
hostilities; being some account of my time locked into the
system – mocked by Beckett as 'the great big booming buzzing confusion'.

Those days of factory labour are now mercifully obliterated by Time, the great fixative and cure-all. Muzak was
piped in day and night through eleven-hour shifts and
rained down on the heads of passive labouring subjects; it
gave me a lifelong aversion to so-called pop music, which I
associated with servitude.

29

Tea With Mr Spender

'Porchester Terrace,' I told the taximan soberly.
One could hear the loud bottle-party from the street. The host was nowhere to be seen, the lighting dim in one room, completely dark in another, both crowded as jails. Presently out of the darkened room sprang lean flamenco dancers in tight black dralon trousers, cummerbunds about their narrow waists, awash with sweat, gruesomely active, their flies stained with emissions from dancing with the girls in the dark.

In they strutted, gesticulating and rolling their eyes, showing the base-metal fillings in their teeth. A Mr Guy Tremlett and a Mr Rory Bagshot introduced themselves. Did I know Riley and Jebby? asked Pigshot or Bigshot, perspiring like a pig. No, really? Not know old Jebby? Never heard of Binky? Their interest waned, was dissipated. They showed no interest in the girls who were drinking cheap red wine out of cups. They had eyes only for the enflamed flamenco dancers with the indecent stains; a right pair of sodomites. No drinks were being offered; one brought one's own bottle.

'I'll snap it off!'

'Damn your yellow eyes!'

An Andalucian song began to whine on the hidden turntable and from the kitchen down the hall came host Peter Upward bearing a plate of spaghetti bolognese, followed by a trim young slip of a thing carrying two mugs of wine. They sat back to back like book-ends, Upward applying himself to the food. From the manner in which he ignored her it was evident that she was to be his that night.

'It was to be either flamenco or booze,' Upward explained, wiping his lips with a tissue. 'So we decided on flamenco. Didn't we, kitten?'

Kitten rubbed her back against his. A tall brunette in tartan slacks stood in a corner with two dull fellows.

'Jean love!'

'Murty!' a strangled voice said.

A middle-aged man went by with a stunned girl in tow. She wore Italian sandals, a tight gossamer-green dress. The dancing girls in the darkened room were screeching, pissed as cunts. They were being agreeably tortured by the young flamenco dancers, ravening and raging, and all dead ringers for Tom Maschler.

'Who, if I cried,' intoned a cor anglais voice, 'would hear me among the angelic orders? None, I fear.'

'Structure,' articulated a thin voice behind the sofa just vacated by the host who was clutching his kitten on the darkened dancefloor within.

'May I?' I asked the mossy green dress, greatly daring.

Couples glued together circled the floor more or less in time to the gluey music issuing from the darkened room where the flamenco dancers were having a ball, their stamping feet sounding like hoofs. I danced close with the mottled man's discarded girl, grasping her resolutely about the hips and girdle, moving slowly, now trapped this way, now that, breathing her scent, feeling her supple spine through the conducting agent of thigh and leg, floorboards.

'You'd never guess whom I had tea with last Tuesday,' she murmured, breathing Martini fumes into my face.

'I would not,' I said.

'James Joyce,' she said. 'Don't hold me there please.'

'Don't quite get that.'

'No?'

'Absolutely no.'

'Oh but it's *true!*' she said, giving me a sweet lopsided smile, and all the honesty of her greenish eyes. I could smell her lipstick.

We circled slowly. I could smell the lipstick mixed with the Martini above or below a delicate sweat, her personal aroma. She was rotating, thinking, absented.

'Not likely,' I said. 'No. Hardly possible. He's been dead some time. Since January 1941, I believe. Buried in Zurich.'

'You don't say.'

We danced about. The room was hot and airless, buzzing with partytalk.

'Oh I'm sorry,' she said, holding her head back, watching my lips as if lip-reading, for what would I say next to disappoint her? 'I mean James Stephens. Last Tuesday I had tea with James Stephens.'

'I'd like to believe you,' I told her.

'You don't – why ever not?'

'He's dead too, unfortunately,' I said.

'Never heard that.'

We were hardly moving, cornered in a clot of sweaty dancers. Then it cleared a little and I steered her backwards, feeling that supple but unsober spine. The same Spanish song whined from the inner room. We danced around, the mottled man observing us.

'Oh but I *am* a fool,' the green girl whispered in my ear. 'It was Stephen *Spender!*'

'Much more likely,' I said, 'considering.'

'Considering? Oh! Isn't *he* alive?'

'Absolutely,' I said.

I could see the green girl taking tea with Mr Spender in a tearoom near the British Museum. She showed him a notebook of handwritten verse. Spender bent forward. The music stopped. A fellow who had announced that he was in publishing asked the green girl for a dance. Rolling her eyes like a doll she was swept away into the shouting throng.

'Structure,' the same voice insisted behind the sofa.

'I must say . . .'

'May I get you a drink?'

'Do forage around.'

I stood next to the mottled man. Very soon I was privy to unwanted confidences of an intimate nature. Most girls who went to bed with him, he said, conceived, and all who did brought forth daughters. But he couldn't make the green girl (apparently her name was Jean) come.

'Come to bed?' I asked obtusely.

'Have an orgasm.'

'Ah-ha.'

'Perhaps it's my fault?' he suggested.

All those who conceived by him bore daughters. Middle-aged and thin on top, with teeth in ruins, they still wanted him, wanted it, and he old enough to be their father. I heard his intestines rumble and groan and a blast of decay issued from his troubled interior along with sundry unwanted confidences and the stink of cheap vino. His breath was foul.

'Can I take her home with me?'

'Tee hee,' tittered the troubled mottled man.

A tall tease with long black hair down her back and a startling white face like Juliette Greco sailed by, very disdainful, very soignée, in the grip of a fellow with double vents. They danced at arm's length, stiff-kneed, with teeth braced in open hostility.

'Ivy Compton-Burnett,' an intense voice sang out, 'and Jack Yeats are my all-time favourites!'

A heavy hand fell like a claw on my shoulder.

'Know Shropshire?'

'No thanks.'

The tall girl in tartan slacks was going home. The host was nowhere to be seen. Unable to restrain himself after the closeness of the dancing he had taken the kitten away with him to an upstairs bedroom. And at that moment the flamenco dancers, the Maschler-clones awash in semen, burst from the darkened inner room, pointing long quivering fingers at each other's drenched flies and shouting, '*Borrachos! Borrachos!*'

I had no coat to collect; I had nothing to collect, it was time to go home.

'Moscow Road,' I told the taximan.

30

The Attic

The last Tube had certainly gone, sucked away into the foul-smelling tunnels, and the stations chained and padlocked for the night. Outside it would be cold; remote stars shone over Truss City.

Narrow stairs smelling of dust led down; I could not tear myself away from that warm attic.

'Stay if you wish,' you had said. 'There's a spare bed.' So I stayed, though not in the spare bed.

My own room stank like a larder, for I cooked and washed there, slept there too; it was squeezed between the high end-walls and cramped as a coffin. No sunlight could ever penetrate into Prince Edward Mansions. My landlady was French – another French landlady! – and believed that all the Irish were dirty in their habits. The place was a warren of admonitory notices and prohibitions of one sort or another: don't do this, don't do that. Madame Sagaison (may she rot in Hell) looked for pubic hair in the bath, stains in the lavatory bowl, puke in the hall. A drugged girl was sent weeping away. No questions were asked. In the near vicinity, two lobotomised patients, one a young woman, threw themselves from windows to their deaths.

I dropped my key down the elevator shaft. Madame Sagaison opened the door resentfully, dressed in pink slippers and gown; was this the time to come home? The morning milk came up in the lift. Movements late at night were frowned upon. The rent was more than I could afford but I liked the area of Notting Hill Gate and Kensington Gardens.

In the daytime the thick carpet creaked; she was standing outside my door, breathing heavily, expecting the worst. The Irish were lazy too, good-for-nothings; an abject race. She was French. But I paid my rent on the nail. So I was allowed to stay. I stayed. It was the first night in Truss City with you, a city transformed. In the night it began to snow.

I walked a station platform under the city, numbed with happiness, felt the dead air of the trains blowing on my face, unmindful of the squalor of King's Cross. Above ground it was still dark but below in the murky warmth the early shift-workers were already heading off for the factories. An obstinate crew, not young, set in their ways; their clothes the colour of mud.

A life of factory work, interrupted by war, perhaps a stint overseas, had worn them down. Then they had their country to serve or die for but now they had only themselves and they were lost, whether they knew it or not. They resembled, if it was anything living, old horses. Broken-winded work horses, their usefulness at an end, nags fit only for the Great Knacker's Yard.

I was with them in the deepest station under Truss City, under the Zoo, Queen Mary's Gardens and the Toxophilite Society. They were bound for Northfields and Osterley, Fulham gas-works and the dreary stations to the West. Factory hands, oil-darkened, clutched *Daily Mirrors* and factory-fatigued eyes stared at the pin-up, the girl-for-the-day, a sultry brunette with little on, sulking by the sea, well calculated to send the circulation up. Hers the swelling haunches of a brood mare; a long shank of dark hair, thighs invoking stalls and hard riding, tumbles in the hay. An expansive bosom was tightly clamped into the twin cups of a minute bra. There was high summer in her haughty gaze. Young, full, with parted lips, she stood provocative and near-nude on a pebble beach, her toes splashed by a cold sea, and pouting bore their hot scrutiny point by point. For she was their lost summer – the one they never had. In all that avid and packed repleteness she was lending herself, giving herself over to the gross pleasures of multiple exposure, reproduced twenty-thousand times, a hundred-thousand times, three million times, held fast in grimy fingers, breathed upon, stared at, devoured, enjoyed by proxy down there, down on the murky platforms under the city, the readers dizzy, nauseous, reeling from bed into this place where no air stirred but dead air, blown through the darkened tunnels by onrushing trains. The hot levelled gaze said, 'Just you dare, mate.' The cajoling pose (one deep breath and all would fall off) said 'Try!' If the opened centre-spread was their morning feedbag, she was their hay. 'Yana, Britain's Singing Bomb Shell!' gushed the caption.

The light that flooded the carriage did not seem to belong to life proper. She was theirs for the morning, with that bold dire stare, held fast, breathed over, desired, dreamed of, prized by famished eyes, stripped, enjoyed. The air was not clean, light changed on a raised sign, the name WIMBLE-DON was lit up and hydraulic doors sprang open down the entire length of the train, a beautiful rapt face flew by. I stepped into the grimy carriage and sat down opposite a corset advertisement. Tread the rubberised surface, grasp the moist pole! The doors clamped shut all together, half-opened again with a monstrous mechanical sigh, then clamped finally shut. The train shuddered down all its length and the empty platform began to flow past and the advertisements became blurred and I was flowing along towards Bromley and Upminster, Uxbridge, Hounslow West and its howling dogs, lovely odd places no doubt, out there somewhere. The galloping train rushed through the tunnels, bored through space, *Würde, würde!* pushing dead air before it, bearing me along the District Line in fine style.

I was travelling, it now occurred to me, studying the Tube map, in altogether the wrong direction; but this did not

seem to matter much, it was a good joke. Misery and hope-
lessness was a good joke; even Rayners Lane, with or without
the possessive, was a good joke. I was alive at last, sudden
contact humming in me. Study the map, consult alternatives,
go back, try again. Go on. A murky sort of light beyond the
racing glass indicated that day was about to break, rise up
again over Truss City.

The cause of it all slept away whatever remained of the night
in her high attic. The covers of the spare bed were not
disturbed. You lived high up and clean like a bird; there
one could breathe. For me you represented freedom. The
W-framed attic with its deep window embrasure was the
secret play-house that a child might build in a tree.

'Can I come again?'

'Of course, if you wish.'

When I changed trains underground the *Daily Mirror* girl
by the sea looked like a rubber doll. I held onto another
sweaty pole, sat on another worn seat, studied the same
Tube map. Where are ye bound for, sad shufflers? Waterloo
and City lines, dirty white for Bank, the city, brown for
Bakerloo, black for the North! I found myself now travelling
backwards in elevated spirits on the yellow Circle Line, heading straight as a die for Hounslow and its maddened dogs.
A carnival mood had taken hold. On I went.

Above me a day hard as iron was breaking, as I stepped
out, breathed snow. It was snowing on Moscow Road. Leaving behind me the acrid stench of the cage and the touch
of hard shoulders, I felt my shoes crunch in thin snow. The
outlines of buildings loomed up with windows lit here and
there. Two Indian girls in saris were laughing and attempting to catch snowflakes in their open mouths.

I returned to Prince Edward Mansions, rising up in the
elevator to Flat No. 8 like Jupiter Tonens. The milk delivery
was outside the door. My room stank of monkey, the alarm
was just about to go off. I changed into my working clothes,

warmed a saucepan of milk over the gas-ring, spooned Nescafé into a mug, prepared for another working day at Ponds.

It was at a South African party at 18A Belsize Lane attic to
which I had not been invited that I become friends with my
future wife, Jill Damaris Anders. I had come on the sugges-
tion of Michael Morrow, an inveterate party-goer; it was a
party for friends, with slivovitz from the Yugoslav Embassy
laid on. In attendance were: the Pinkers, the Harringtons,
oily Tom Maschler (briefly), Pat Godkens and the two inverts
from the flat below, Chris and Luther. There was dancing
in a very confined space. Michael Morrow and I sat back to
back on the spare bed and drank slivovitz and smoked
Balkan Sobranie. We stayed on after everyone had left; eventually we spent the night there, head to toe in the spare bed
like Mr and Mrs Bloom. I did not get a wink of sleep.

I waited five weeks before phoning. Again I visited on my
own, found the door open as before, the phone in the hall,
the number on the dial; when five weeks passed I had
plucked up enough courage to phone the Yugoslav Embassy.
A friend wanted to know something about the French
Cameroons. It was merely a tactical ploy, moving crabwise
like a dog. I was invited around for a meal. It was then I
must have stayed the night. You were my unknown mistress.
In you I was to find both mistress and wife; rarely are both
united in one person.

Your life, as narrated by you, was to me in the highest
degree fascinating.

The pederasts in the flat below liked to talk to you while in
the tub, scrub your back in the communal narrow bathroom
shared with the Pinkers, and photograph you as screen
siren of the 1940s pouting over one naked shoulder at the
camera. Luther from the island of Mauritius spoke French,
was black as a pot; his philosophy was simple: 'Life is a
rugged path which we try to make smude.' The islanders
dreamed of buried treasure, dug great holes in the beaches.

Chris, who moved the false teeth of his lower jaw like a pike, taught art in a school at Crouch End.

They were a loving couple long together, and good company for you, in whom they both confided.

There had been a third, Lonny, a gentle boy who had died young. His mother had come from Natal for the funeral, and you had collected flowers on the Heath for a wreath and a man had exposed himself.

Everything was photographed – the gentle departed one smiling on cue at the piano, the two pederasts cross-eyed with lechery, the Harringtons posing artfully; it had all taken place in the confined spaces of your attic with the long window embrasure, before my time.

You were Balance. Libras can be both tyrannical and conciliatory, blowing hot and cold; don't try to reason with them, logic is not their forte, nor patience. On her small turntable she played Jacqueline Françoise, and composed lapidary verse.

> Inhabit and bring
> To the pale shell your
> Body as an offering
> And a promise of life.

In a rubber-goods shop down gloomy Goodge Street, into which I ventured with extreme reluctance one grey afternoon, I was sold large brown horse-pills the size of bulls'-eyes which a sallow-complexioned dispenser of condoms assured me would do the trick; at least nobody had returned to complain.

There had been dancing in the confined space between two beds and Eonie Harrington fell into my lap. There I danced with you, call it dancing, held you within arm's reach and saw close up the clown's face. Sure I must perish by your charms.

I had been introduced to her by Michael Morrow from a bed in the Mile End Hospital ('This is my South African

friend'); she had brought him sketching pads. I had come
with Mad Meg, bringing Player's cigarettes. Mad Meg, sens-
ing trouble, had hurried me out of the hospital and into
the Coach and Hound.

31

Billy

B oys in the garden were blowing up frogs. Figs rotted and fell from the fig tree, all the fronds of the palm trees rustled in the breeze. The scent of pine, roses, dry earth, the watered garden at sundown, pepper trees, bougainvillaea and syringa all summer long fill the tumid twilight air and the pigs are screeching in fear, held down by African butchers; she and Fiona Doran ran with hands over their ears but still heard the frantic screeching. A bad smell of death wafted up from the tannery when the breeze blew from the wrong quarter.

Miss Weir her piano teacher assured her that she had 'near-genius'. They played games of forfeits. The Everett sisters drove by in their phantom Buick. Hoarsely, with feeling, Miss Weir sang the Burial Song from *Aida*.

Boarding school was a time of prolonged physical discomfort. The girls of Kaffrarian High wore unbecoming blue uniforms 'always damp and smelling of laundry'. Billy played the lead in Anouilh's *Antigone* in an amateur production in the King Town Hall in aid of the Red Cross and was photographed by the local newspaper, staring pensively from a papier mâché castle window at the mess backstage.

The fellow who played opposite her – could it be Reg Gasson? – had struck a classical pose, pressing the back of one hand to his brow in a gesture of anguish. He wore grey

worsted tights and the press photograph in black and white
showed a large stain at the crotch; evidently nerves had got
the better of him.

Billy worked in Bat Whitnell's law office in East London
and dreamed of London, England, and the West End stage.
The Reverend Herron thundered out his Hellfire sermons
but a ghost stood between Billy and brother Lloyd; Elwyn
had crashed his Miles Master when he was eighteen and his
sister twelve.

Now Nells was in love with her.

His hair was trimmed short like a convict's. He sat behind
the wheel of the truck that was piled high with furniture and
cooking utensils en route to Kidd's Beach for the summer
vacation. The sun shone through the skin of his large protuberant ears, lighting up the blood vessels. Tongue-tied, he
stared through the insect-smeared windscreen, mashing the
gears, too shy to speak to her or look her way, seated beside
him, he humming to hide his embarrassment, the over-
heated engine panting and stalling. He pitched the bell-tent
a hundred yards from the sea. They heard the deep grunting
of baboons in the thick shelter that grew down to the water's
edge. Shadows on the canvas at night, the oil lantern swinging, incey-wincey spider climbing up the spout.

Then: Sunset over a vast hot landscape and the beginning
of hot nights with trains shunting, the squeal of hot metal
getting into motion again, hiss of escaping steam, the
mournful bellowing of cattle (now it was their turn) on their
last night on earth and the hollow Baptist bell banging away
into the small hours.

She and Stephanie Weir with skirts hiked up about their
waists climbed the picket fence into forbidden ground, saw
light shining in the ground floor of the Stewart's house and
Syd the diving champion naked from the waist down and
hands active at hidden crotch, engaged in 'some secret male
thing', so they crept away, mystified. She was the youngest,
and only daughter in a family of three, one of whom died
in an accident. Her parents had wanted another boy; the

old man called her Billy. Done your homework, Billy? Been to the dubs, Billy?

Her parents were not hitting it off, they rarely spoke to each other, old Jonathan Carl spent much time in the office. The home atmosphere was distinctly chilly. Spirit mediums were consulted. A glass serving-dish broke neatly into four parts, a chair moved itself a fraction, ectoplasm curled from the wall, a dog barked at the framed photo of the young pilot with crewcut and cheery grin, framed on the sideboard of the livingroom and observing every meal served with much sighing. Her mother never laughed, her father rarely smiled. A partner lost company funds and a pile of debts accumulated; Jonathan swore to work even longer hours, every tickey would be returned to the investors. Gauche suitors invaded the house. Her mother went sighing from room to room.

Thousands and thousands of needles of rain struck her face and shoulders, scattering over the public baths where she swam lengths alone; then home in the rain to a deserted house and a meagre supper in the fridge. As she prepared for bed she heard again the evening commotion of pigs and a terrible smell wafted itself up from the tannery. Her brother Elwyn had to kill himself larking about in a Miles Master that went out of control and exploded on a hill. Gone were the days when her mother, erect by the open patio door, sang:

> I gave my heart to one man,
> Loving as only woman can . . .

As soon as Billy came of age she sailed for London on a Union Castle liner, embarking at East London with her best friend Fiona Doran, daughter of Dr Doran. The last she was to see of her father for some years was the old man standing on the dockside holding up bunting made from a number of handkerchiefs tied together, growing smaller and smaller on the quayside, calling, 'Goodbye, Billy!' She and her friend Fiona wept their hearts out on the rails.

32

The Ice-cream Factory

The ice-cream factory was vast: a brown windowless bulk somewhere beyond Willesden Junction. Trucks assembled in the loading-yard at night in the heat-wave. Because it was nightwork and there was overtime, I had ten bob extra again for working in cold storage. It was difficult to stay awake, even in the freezing bays.

A tall shell-shocked worker threw a fit in the canteen. One night on the loading-bay a small coloured man went berserk, shouted, 'Fuck your sister!' at a huge dull Irishman who backed away; he was given his walking papers on the spot. The gates opened, a Black Maria pulled up, factory guards led him out, a small insubordinate figure walked away, a free man. Downcoming tins jammed in the exit points and had to be knocked free, bursting open on the cement floor and the stuff pouring out. The factory itself smelt of vomit.

I worked in the freezing areas, drawing good wages, but exhausted all night, half-asleep on my feet and all sandwiches tasted alike. In the garden, during the night break, exhausted black men in white overalls were laid out on the benches, as if headless and armless. I was saving up money for our first holiday on Inishere. The regulations said I had to be clean-shaven; the freezing cold stung my face.

When the two heavy doors were thrown open high up by the ganger an Arctic scene offered itself to my eyes: snow and fog, rime and mist and the bays iced up.

Palsied with the cold I stopped the run, started another line, sent it out, blowing into the iced-up intercom. The ganger cursed me. It was soft as shit. 'Try an' stay awake, matey.'

On weekends Mick Swords of Tipperary caroused with friends in the West End, walking back to Shepherds Bush after the last tube had gone. In Kensington Gardens he saw a fellow mounting a whore who drank from a bottle. Irish whores, Swords swore, were the worst, the most inept. 'Dormant fucken rats'.

It was a sort of underground place reared up into the sky, spewing ice-cream and smelling of lost hopes and vomit. You came with me once to the gates. You were aghast at the squalor. 'Do chaps work there?'

'This chap does.'

You were staying with your friend Pat Godkens on Campden Hill. Our marriage banns were posted. A keen young priest was giving you Catholic indoctrination at the Church of St Thomas More, not far from our old quarters at 18A Belsize Lane. We were to be married there; since a wedding in a Registry Office seemed as impersonal an act as, say, purchasing a dog licence.

We walked in Holland Park by your old office in the Yugoslav Embassy, by white statuary laid out on the grass like corpses of Holland House. The husband of Pat Godkens was a beast, you confided to me. He drank double gins, overfed and overweight, overbearing, a mother's boy. Silence was called when the Prime Minister spoke on the radio. Eden spoke on Suez.

33

Galustian & Co.

A
n unknown mistress possesses a unique charm, Bayle avers.

But while the charm of novelty yields progressively to the knowledge of character, bliss comes only with intimacy. First it's victory; afterwards comes pure felicity, provided one is dealing with an intelligent woman (a very Froggy rider).

'The nicest feeling,' you admitted in my narrow bed in the murky room (daylight slanted in, meagrely apportioned, fresh air not at all), 'is waking up in bed at the wrong end of town. Finding yourself in strange territory, and going home in a taxi.' Where we found ourselves now was home, had to be home, at 18A Belsize Lane (her eyrie, at the topmost attic on one of the topmost hills of North London) or No. 8 Prince Edward Mansions (my coffin at Notting Hill Gate); home is where you start from.

To get to work you took two buses to Kensington High Street and walked to the Yugoslav Embassy through the poplar blossoms blowing like snow from Holland Park. Wherever you walked extraordinary climatic conditions prevailed.

Two fat men met, wheezing, on the stairs and embraced under the portrait of Tito. You brought back booty, slivovic

and Balkan Sobranie from Embassy parties which occurred
quite frequently.

Your life before me teemed with admirers. Some of them
still hung in there, phoning HAM 348 at awkward hours,
breathing heavily. You neither encouraged nor discouraged
them. Vuck Eisen lived around the corner, strikingly handsome, homesick for Rijeka. Admirers abounded, phoned or
hovered near, just out of sight.

By night in that first summer we swam in the Women's
Pool on Hampstead Heath and I covered you in flowers.
Members of eccentric religious sects came floundering down
the hill with arms outstretched, calling out incomprehensible incantations. A small 'combo' composed of alto sax,
guitar and harmonica played Satchmo numbers (had he just
died?) all night long under an oak tree. We obtained the
signature of Josh White after a concert at Burnt Oak. 'Hey!
Gimme a raincheck!' signed *Josh White*. He promised to play
at our wedding but never showed up. Josh never showed up
to sing 'John Henry'.

In winter you walked in fur-lined bootees and a short
tartan tweed skirt of Royal Stuart on the damp or frozen
earth as if it pleased you. You said you liked the cold days
and the last leaves dropping from the trees. And now you
wore a white angora poloneck with tartan slacks.

'She has a really soiled face, that Jeanne Moreau.'

Many of your judgements were incomprehensible to me.
I just couldn't see that. Jeanne Moreau had a lovely face.

'I must have fruit!'

You went shopping by West Hampstead station where the
Punch and Judy show was performed near the pub where
Ruth Ellis shot her lover and the price of vegetables lower.
You kept a ten-shilling note in the vee of your glove, put
aside weekly for fruit, which seemed extravagant to me, the
Mick paying out three pounds for renting out one room
sans daylight or air, told that I had the palate of a dog, that I
must experiment, open up. Ever try avocados? persimmons?
pawpaws? yumyums? Never heard of them. The Cockney

greengrocer smote his mittens together and boasted that all his market produce came fresh that morning from Covent Garden. 'Ain't got no dud 'uns 'ere, Miss.'

I frequently felt at a loss; your past was becoming more real than my own. I, the sombre cooker of dull spuds and carrots, my staple diet spaghetti bolognese in a darkened room that stank of cooking, unwashed clothes. I lived poorly then. Once I had invited you to dine there; once only.

You had a clown's sad face.

You were not prudish ('*Je ne regrette rien*'). In a dream you sat on Orson Welles's great lubbery lap and looked close at his blubbery Rosebud lips, his sneering mouth – well then, a mouth capable of sneers. (Wasn't rosebud a sneer?) You thought him mean and told him so. 'You're so mean,' you told Orson, 'it's coming out of your ears. Can't you feel it?'

Orson jerked his head back, opened his mouth wide ('like a cave'), beckoned to someone. 'Get her!' Throwing back his great head he gave a rich expansive laugh. He was not fooling you. 'He watches you craftily to see how you take it. His eyes are inquisitive.'

Orson Welles was no fool.

Even your dreams were rich and fanciful; perhaps one day I too would appear in them with Orson Welles? You marched down Rosslyn Hill past the George IV, our local, heading for Chalk Farm with a Spanish basket a third full of fruit and vegetables.

Did I know Gascoyne? Did I know Derain?

Were these more exotic fruits, gascoyne and derain?

You were driven down to Sussex to meet George Barker and who sat next to you in the friend's car but Gascoyne who did not utter a word. Appearing at Barker's door he took a naggin of Scotch out of one pocket and handed it to Barker without a word, then another naggin from another pocket and handed it over, walked in, sat down and not a word.

Not a word out of him all day, just drinking Scotch and

looking from face to face. On the way back to London he
ventured two remarks: 'That's supposed to be a good field
for mushrooms . . .' And: 'There's an underground river
there.' He had given up writing poetry and painted pictures
that were like Persian miniatures. He had threatened to
blow up Buckingham Palace. Gascoyne was perhaps a little
unhinged.

Your former boss had been a priapic Persian.

A handsome brute, most amorous, by the name of Haig
Galustian.

'Nothing miniature about him.'

He had designs on her; the day began with a chase around
the office. He was deadly serious and carried an erection
like a spear. He was most persistent, hot and hasty, never
had a South African girl. One or two orgasms and an English
girl was finished. 'You cannot begin with me,' she told him.
He was slung like a stallion. The races continued. He was
operating in something shady, munitions or arms deals. One
set of files were top secret; he had the key. One day he
phoned, instructing her to burn the secret files at once, the
duplicate key was hidden in such-and-such a drawer. If
the police came, she was to admit nothing, he was out
of the country, the files never existed.

It was a hot day and she had been sunbathing nude in the
garden. She burned the secret files, raking up the charred
remains and buried them, waiting for the police to arrive.
An hour later Galustian phoned to say it was all a mistake.
Too late, the files were destroyed.

He was hot and hasty.

She shared a flat with two other South African girls. The
thing to do was to have a black lover. Nirodi Nazunda had
a skin so black it was almost blue, sat stark naked on a rug
and was greatly admired by the girls, when in walked an
even prettier brunette, Diane Liebenberg.

Billy was going out with a cad from the FO. She had to

lie naked on the bed and say, 'I want to be focked.' He was hard to please, cruel, overbearing, took taxis everywhere.

When the two queers moved from the flat below a tall shy admirer moved in, with terrible halitosis. He ate nothing but fish, painted nothing but fish, and the flat began to stink of nothing but fish.

Meanwhile I searched through Islington for a lost earring, dropped when we came out of Collins Music Hall where a stripper was pushed naked on a bicycle across the stage. Pauline ('Take 'em Off') Penny wore nothing but a fixed smile and the gallery hooted. You laughed at the serious nudist on the bike, but I never recovered your lost earring. You had a habit of losing things.

Leaning perilously out of the attic window, naked as the day you were born, you called down to the milkman four storeys below, to leave Gold Top Cream. 'Milkmin!'

I lay between the blue sheets and marvelled. The sheets were fresh, the room aircd, fresh air blew in, there were flowers in a vase. I had bought a second-hand wedding ring in Kentish Town; we were to be married in late October. We had breakfast with fruit. Anthony Stanger of the FO with his kinky tastes was a thing of the past, with the blueblack bucknaked West Indian, the priapic Persian who had given you a going-away present of a black French corset, very fetching on, and you had wept buckets.

In the National Gallery on Trafalgar Square you stood under the giantesses of Paolo Veronese, the most flittering light of the old Venetian school, under the huge torpid sprawl of brown-skinned lethargic propagators whose oakenhued limbs were as the wide branches of great oaks, whose breedy boles were their well-fleshed haunches, whose spread hair was as the colour of beech-leaves stirred by a serene breeze in autumn, whose opthalmic eyes (the sleepy eyes of born breeders) were bursting from their sockets, as if stunned or drugged, drugged with life, with sensation, staring out from

the boscage above the door where a sleepy gallery attendant
was trying not to doze off.

So had I worked as a store-hand in Ponds (Cosmetics) at
Perivale near the Great West Road, then at Punfield & Barstow (Mouldings) as an apprentice extrusion moulder on
day and night shifts near Willesden Junction, while you
worked for Haig Galustian, and in the Yugoslav Embassy,
then as the personal secretary of Randolph Churchill who
paced to and fro with a hangover, unshaven and unkempt,
dictating on his feet. Then we were both taken on as trainee
puppet operators by John Wright in Hampstead. He had
rented a room in the corner house of Professor William
Empson, set up a marionette stage and we practised how to
operate the puppets before a wide mirror in cramped dusty
quarters, as we would later in Mlini in the stifling Adriatic
heat of August.

Your fond dream of a career on the West End stage had
come to nothing. An interview had been set up with John
Gielgud at the Old Vic. You had a drink in a bar to steady
your nerves and told the barman where you were going. He
said 'Read hit to us 'ere, luv. We'll be yer h'audience.' So
you delivered your audition piece in your best Antigone
voice to the morning boozers and it was a total fiasco. The
boozers just looked down at their pints, cleared their throats,
shuffled their feet, and you knew it was no good. You
marched out of the bar, threw the script into a refuse bin,
and shortly after that went to work for the priapic Persian,
began running.

I moved into 18A Belsize Lane while we were being
trained as puppet operators. The arrangement was that the
company would go ahead in a newly acquired custom-built
Bedford truck; we would visit my parents in Dalkey and re-
join the company near Dubrovnik towards the end of
summer, at Mlini.

In the meantime you told me the story of your life.

The to be continued tale of the wife to be. We were
married in the Church of St. Thomas More on November

26th 1955. Best man: Hubert Mary Bermingham, B. Arch. Music (an organ voluntary by Telemann): John Beckett. The words were extremely bawdy; we had just the airs.

34

Your Life Before Me

Jill Damaris Anders was born on 21st October 1930 at 2 Raglan Street in King William's Town in the Eastern Province of South Africa, within sight of the Amatola Mountains which stood up to the west as a reminder of native cruelty and barbarity, short rations, prisoners inhumanly dispatched. Born of a Welsh mother and a German father under the tricky astrological sign of Balance (Libra), when lawyer Jonathan Carl Anders was already an old man.

He was a notary or family lawyer who made out deeds of possession in a miniature script as he sucked little black pastilles to keep his breath sweet for clients. He wrote in the neat precise hand of another age – fussy, industrious Samuel Pepys. Debit and credit, profit and loss. He wasted nothing, ate the core and pips of apples.

He wore a stiff wing collar, a choker, and button boots well polished; and had a distinct look not of Pepys but of General Jan Smuts, that thorn in the British side. I saw him ever in a vapoury daguerrotype fumed and framed in oaken leaves with cannons going off in the background and natives being impaled. He would have been a patriot in whatever country he found himself. German settlers, Lutheran missionaries, were all around; there was even a village called Berlin not too far off. As vain as he was deaf, he would not wear a hearing-aid or ear-trumpet, being obliged to shout at his clients over the pipe tobacco he had spread to dry on his desk. He was a sweet-natured old man, a gentle soul. All his life he had worked hard. In his middle and even late eighties he was putting in eight and ten hours at the office, as he had when aged fifty; still shouting at his clients, still with mounds of tobacco out drying on his desk, still deaf as a post. He was the best Pop in the whole world and she was his beloved Billy.

Her moody mother had no pet name for her and showed precious few signs of affection, let alone love. Billy with her amiable clown's face, who tended to drop things when nervous, was merely 'my girl' – addressed with a cutting coldness.

We sat on a public bench in the sun and watched the kites fly. Below us in the Parliament Hill Fields the ground fell away to the ponds surrounded by willows, poplars and copper beech.

'Pop had me too late.'

'Why too late? You're here, aren't you?'

'He'd turned sixty when I was born,' you said. 'That's too late. Anyway he wanted another boy.'

A small Oriental person was flying a silken kite, a bloodred tarblack dragon with glistening scales, a good twenty feet long with a mouthful of dragon teeth and fierce glazy eyes. It lifted in the sudden breeze and went wobbling and jerking up over the stand of trees, swelling mightily as it ascended, filled with air, while its owner, running backwards and clutching the cord, shrank away to nothing, a mere mortal.

'It's too late.'

'Too late for what?'

'To be a father,' you said, smiling now at the frantic antics of the dragon-keeper, 'at sixty.'

'Pish, pish.'

'Yes, yes.'

'Not in Ireland. At least not in the old days.'

'Well for God's sake look at Ireland!'

'True.'

Now the dragon was far up and still rising on the thermals, its tiny owner calmly unreeling a mile of line that curved and bellied away from him, up and up to where the mighty dragon was butting its head bloodily against a low cloud.

Presently we would go down to Highgate village and into the Flask where Hogarth had once caroused, sitting snug with a covey of wags. We passed Gaels with scorched faces at fierce hurling, strong country boys (looking demented in crash helmets) roaring out the Holy Name as they whirled and pucked in a lather of excitement, sending the dun-coloured ball down the field to where a pile of discarded clothes served for goal-posts.

'Now Tom avic, into him!'

'Now Tom Malone!'

Tom Malone with white hair and a pale green ganzy was smooth as oil, hard as teak, wriggly as an eel, pucking goals from all over the place, no holding him.

'Up Down!' you called, but no one heard.

They didn't hear you; they were back in Kerry, in Kilkenny, in woody Kildare, pucking and blaspheming. The sun was sinking behind all the horizons of the heath and Truss City had vanished into a dim grey haze below; now it was just a glow in the sky off towards Neasden and Dollis Hill. Tomorrow for sure would be a scorcher.

Now the hurlers were struggling and swearing mightily near one of the makeshift goals, upraised hurley sticks of ash smacked fiercely together.

'Oh Jaysus you eejit!' a voice called in agony.

'Blood will be spilt,' you said.

We walked down past the ponds.

35

The Pond

I lay on the moored raft and watched the white blossoms drifting off the poplar trees that grew around Hampstead Pond. Through slitted eyes, peacock-twittering, the stagnant brown water resembled a motionless river. The causeway was a bridge. Serious men fished there with gaffs and waders as if after fighting salmon in a running stream.

When a swimmer dived off the raft, it tipped and brown water washed over it. For a time I was alone there. An odour difficult to describe arose from the bed of the disturbed pond, a blast from an upset stomach. Girls in tight costumes swam in the dirty water, breast-stroking, holding their heads high, Professor Empson among them with something foul (snot? emission?) caught in the forks of his mandarin beard. He did not know me; I closed my eyes. The sun was hot in Hampstead high summer. The raft began to tilt. I opened my eyes.

Professor Empson was breast-stroking back, stately as a paddle-steamer, and a plump girl in a yellow costume was hauling herself aboard. She had left a wake of scent on the water, now it was on the raft. The sun shone on the oiled sunbathers, poplar blossoms drifted by in the breeze, carried on the surface as though the pond-water was moving. The plump girl had stretched herself out on the damp boards.

She lay there calm as a leaf, caught in a fluid sensual dream; her diaphragm heaved mightily with every breath.

A rowing-boat was putting out from the bathing place, the little lido among the trees. At the end of the duckboards of the wooden jetty the sunbather ostentatiously immersed in *Malone meurt* (purchased in Paris) sat still with feet submerged, staring down at extremities that appeared to be severed below the knees.

The raft tilts again. At the end of the wooden jetty the cadaverous reader of Beckett stares down aghast at his reflection without feet below the knees. The sun shines. It shines on sticky sunbathers oiled and creamed with Nivea; a rowing-boat is pulling away. The oarsman pulls easily, not to disturb the swimmers or the moorhens hidden in the overhang. As he comes on I see that he strangely resembles Ussher who resembles the dead Cavé, the friend of Dégas. The boat leaves a line of bubbles behind.

High up in the azure an unseen jet fighter bangs through the sound-barrier and (as though there were some casual connection) more blossoms are shaken from the poplars that line the pond. Turning in mid-pond and casually shipping his oars, Ussher-Cavé now begins retrieving something with a grappling-hook.

I lie there letting time drift. Impressions offer themselves, briefly focus and slip away again; the raft rocks, brown water washes over it. The plump girl, heavy as a stove, has dived off. A line of bubbles shows where she has gone under: her hands surface, then her head. Her scent lingers, sweetly cloying, not pleasant. Professor Empson breast-strokes in his stately way through the filth. A tall auburn-haired beauty in a red dress is crossing the causeway with a towel under her arm. She waves to me.

I leave the raft, letting the water receive me; not only filthy but tepid, both bidet and toilet, the used bathwater of thousands, hundreds of thousands over the years. Trapped water; the blossoms are scum. As I touch the jetty you appear above me, having undressed in the ladies' section, hung up your red dress, covered your purse. You stand adjusting your rubber bathing-cap; your face changes subtly with the hair hidden.

She leans forward, poised to dive, taking a deep breath. The boatman is closely examining a dripping object. She launches herself from the jetty above me, passing like a swan over my head.

Now in the Oxo-tinted pond I am holding you up, lifting you above the scum, the mire, and you are laughing. Laughter comes so naturally out of you, childlike and hopeful. Do clowns laugh? No matter. We are in the shadows, in the chilly water; as I sink you rise, held up by the waist. Aloft in the air you are laughing. My head is below the surface but I can feel the laughter in my hands, your laughter, as if it were the best joke in the world, the world gone from us and we are slipping away. *Do as I bid you and you will find out my form. There are no pure substances in nature; each is contained in each.* We are slipping away. All around us the scum, the spent blossoms floating on the dark Oxo-brown water. The raft is empty; we are the last. The boatman watches us. He has a weatherbeaten face, long countryman's cheeks, and smokes a pipe, looking thoughtful. Noble it is to decay growing wise, as metaphysics wears out the heart. We were happy in a drugged manner; supposing Balance and Pisces can ever be happy together. It was a start.

In the dingy purlieus of Camden Town I'd bought a second-hand trunk the size of a wardrobe, weathered oxidized green as if recovered from water. The shopman, dingy as his premises, hove it onto the pavement to demonstrate that it could take hard knocks. I had some trouble getting it aboard a bus – Crusoe lugs his painted chest across the Ox Mountains – passengers had to force their way past it. We were preparing for the Adriatic voyage.

Your dream: an open matchbox contained a miniature Field Marshall Montgomery, a little figure that rolled its eyes when you tilted the box. The real Montgomery stood on a knoll nearby, with rolled maps under his arm, looking over your head in a far-sighted military sort of way. When you put down the breakfast tray your dressing-gown fell off. 'Make me warm,' you said, climbing into bed. Your life before me was full of admirers.

36

The Ghost of Elwyn Anders

My poor parents had not yet moved, or been forced to move, from Dalkey to Dun Laoghaire, in their slow but remorseless progression downward. They were still living in Dalkey, on the fringe of respectability in Breffni Mansions, prior to their last move to squalid underground quarters at Haigh Terrace.

Dado had aged. That morning we surprised him mowing the grass by the Georgian granite steps as we came in the gateway, to be welcomed like royalty.

They occupied the upper floor while a family who never appeared had rented the basement flat. The double flight of granite steps led to the hall door, then more stairs to their living quarters, too many steps for my overweight mother.

Mumu too had aged. With long white hair combed down over her shoulders she was sitting up in bed in a woollen cardigan with all the stitching gone along one arm. My recently acquired spouse received that pointed stare as of yore, and for you a sweet smile, and you heard for the first time Mumu's high sing-song voice asking rhetorically: '*Is this Jeel?*'

Mumu's bedroom was a large bare room devoid of carpet or family suite on the bare boards; all that remained was one uncomfortable high-smelling leather arm-chair, strategically positioned facing the high bed, the last of the suite sold at discount by Jack Ellis the much maligned Jew. In a corner a great mound of old newspapers reared up, high as the hill of Tara, mostly back numbers of the *Irish Times*.

Three long windows overlooked Dublin Bay. When I threw open one of them the sea with its smells entered the room. The wind boomed all around the house; yachts were tacking towards Howth, the line of the granite harbour wall stretched away to the north-east. Now the invigorating smell of new-mown grass was in the bedroom. From where I stood it would be possible to follow the course of the mail boat arriving and departing. We had flown in.

Dado, acting the butler, now carried in a tray with tea and gateaux. They fussed over the preparations; was it strong enough, there was no cream but would milk do?

'Of course,' you said.

'Is it all right?' Mumu inquired anxiously.

'Perfect,' you said, your legs crossed in tartan slacks, a black beret, high-heeled black boots, a grey highneck pullover, a wedding ring. The angle of the beret had been nicely judged and stopped just in time.

Dado was taking all this in, this was how the international set dressed; he was more accustomed to stocky broadbeamed types with the complacent rumps of brood mares. Horsey women.

'Anders,' Dado said, looking at his tea-leaves, head tilted judiciously to one side. 'Now what kind of name was that?' He was seated like a garden gnome on an upturned orange crate as if on a throne. You had given him a present of a gold tiepin with turquoise inset and he was wearing it already. 'Is it German or where does it come from?'

Dado knew where it came from right well, for I had written many letters from London and he was thoroughly *au fait* with his new daughter-in-law's background.

'Sugar?' offered Mumu, dispeller of mystery.

'My father is German and my mother Welsh,' you said, crossing your long legs.

'Now are you satisfied!' cried Mumu, smiling at her daughter-in-law who sat with legs crossed and beret removed, quite at home, eating gateaux from a saucer.

'We put on no fine airs and graces here, my dear.'

Here Mumu threw Dado one of her most withering looks. He was staring at you and wobbling his head and seemed to be quite taken with you, as with all sirens and tall good-lookers; at least I hadn't landed myself with a flibbertigibbet.

They had made up twin beds for us in a room without furniture or carpet. We pulled them together and threw open the windows to let the strong sea-air and all the aromas of the sea and garden flow in. There were cut flowers in a bowl.

'Oh this air!' you said, naked at the window. 'It's not true. It's just like Hermanus, only stronger. I grew up in this kind of weather.'

Billy was quite a specialist in air.

Odours of seaweed and brine all night long, of newmown grass, odour of drifting space. All night long the house swam through space as dogs barked in the quarry behind the town. The Dalkey night was hectic with moon-maddened dogs barking their heads off at the full moon sailing resplendently over the quarry. We were home.

Next morning even before I had opened my eyes I recognised the distinctive sound of my progenitor's arbitrary stop-and-start method of mowing grass without a catcher attached, conserving his strength and trying to make enough noise to waken us. Sunday church bells were ringing all around and from the kitchen the aromas of breakfast were wafting.

When you appeared dressed at the window Dado called up that breakfast was ready when we were, but to take our time, and already he called you 'Jilly'.

We drank draught Guinness in a rundown Dalkey bar. Out in the bay in a rented rowing-boat we watched the church spires sink and the Wicklow hills put on more bulk. White clouds drifted on the breeze as I dropped the lures over the side for mackerel. The silver sank like shot into the green depths below us, but were the mackerel running?

'I had a peculiar dream last night,' you said. 'A dream that Elwyn had come back.'

You told me your dream.

It happened at Jan Smuts Airport. 'He was flying in on such a lovely day.' They were there waiting, all the Anders, and one can imagine in what a state. You saw the glimmer high up like a silvery fish in the blue sky over the burning Rand. The Anders family watched it come in as if it were an ordinary flight arriving at Jan Smuts.

She didn't know what to expect when it touched down – would it burst into flames and a winged horror come bounding out, a black Elwyn racing towards them, screaming, '*It's me! It's me! I'm back!*'

It circled, made its approach run, touched down, taxied in quite normally. The steps were pushed up, the door opened and the passengers began alighting.

'I recognised him by the way he walked. He wore a tall hat but carried no hand-luggage, no briefcase even, nothing. Waving, if you please, an outsize stetson! It was Elwyn alright, my long-lost brother whom we hadn't seen in fifteen years, had come home. He was all grainy and colourless like a photo that's faded, walking among the others in a kind of mist. It was most odd and disturbing. On this strangely bright unreal day to see my dead brother come towards us, not hurrying, carrying the stetson and smiling, coming up to us waiting there at the barrier. My mother had begun weeping already.

'He came right up to us. I was so happy to see him, grinning from ear to ear and holding this outsize ridiculous stetson.

'My mother was becoming smaller and smaller, weeping with happiness, her eyes shining. Elwyn spoke all our names. Mom and Pop, Lloyd and Sis. I was still his little Sis. Did we embrace, shake hands? I forget. Mom just kept on weeping and shrinking, Pop was growing younger and younger the more he looked at Elwyn who was saying very little, just grinning away all the time as if this was the best joke in the world. He'd brought no luggage because he wasn't staying, apparently.

'In photos his nose turned up, but it didn't really. He was very calm, took my arm and then *I* was crying because he was back.

'We enquired where he had been all these years? He clapped the stetson right back onto his head, onto the airman's crewcut, tilting it over one eye and winked, those bright devil-may-care eyes amused and observing us. "Oh, I've been around," he said. He was a real grinning devil.'

You had the collar of your donkey-jacket up about your neck and the beret down over your ears. It was cold out on the bay. A beam of sunlight lit up Howth Head. Below us, deep green water and stuff streaming down. I felt the strong drag of the tide on the lures down on the bed of the bay, pulled at the oars, facing you, reduced to just a nose and amber hair emerging from the donkey-jacket. Water and air were cold, the tide on the turn; such opaque peace!

'What happened?' you asked Elwyn.

He rolled his eyes.

'I got too cocky and over-confident, you know. I lost control and went into a high-speed stall at an altitude too low to pull out of. After three hundred hours flying time you think you can do anything with the crate but you can't. You can't fly the kite upside down. You have to learn to talk upside down in a Miles Master. Your Adam's apple comes up into your throat and you can't get the words out.'

He was laughing and rolling his eyes in a droll way, making a joke of everything, even his death. His loving mother had carefully kept the SAAF heirlooms, the medals mounted on black velvet, the Flying Logbook, his wings and dress uniform, and a school exercise-book preserved from the time when he was aged ten.

He had crashed his Miles Master on a farm called *Donker-hoek* (dark corner) not far from Bloemfontein in the Orange Free State, which was not a free state.

She didn't know the name of the krantz in the Amatolas where British soldiers were thrown during the frontier war, known as the Kaffir Wars in the history books. In the country of the clicking Xhosas, Kreli (1820–1902) was Paramount Chief of the tribe during the first part of the nineteenth century. Her loving Pop never spoke of the war or the English POWs thrown from the krantz, except to tell her that it was there he had learnt to eat the whole of an apple, core and all, so he must have been hungry.

'I was only twelve then,' you said (now mysterious as an oracle seated in the stern of the boat, with the hills behind you; you disguised, suffering, speaking in tongues). 'When he went missing. In the dream he would have been, let me see, thirty-one . . . supposing the dead age, which is hardly likely. They are always at whatever age they die at; isn't that right? They always remain the same. But I hardly knew this joker. I'd loved him much and he me, I suppose, I being the youngest and all that, the baby. Mom loved no one else but him, as she made clear enough to me. Certainly she didn't love *me.*'

Dead brother Elwyn had once attempted to teach maths to his Sis, but it was a total failure. You can take 1 away from 2 but where has it gone, where is it? He was patient, he said: 'It still exists somewhere in some form or other. Nothing ever disappears.'

Nothing he said or did could surprise her; she expected that of him, surprise packages, delights. He thought he had control of the Miles Master but he hadn't. Hold onto nothing; nothing lasts.

I rowed to new fishing grounds off the Forty Foot. To one side, among the grey boulders, a corpulent nudist was going in on the sly, crouching; with a male head but female appendages, just lowering itself surreptitiously, flinchingly dipping its androgynous extremities into the now-swelling-rip-tide, bobbing up and down before the quick total immersion and being jeered at by some wheeling gulls.

A year passed, a cloud going over. My mother found that she could not take the steps and they moved again, going underground at Haigh Terrace, for a cheaper rent. They were going down.

37

From Fiume to Old Ragusa

We had come from Ostend by train, watching pilgrims embarking for Lourdes. A heavy woman was carried aboard from an ambulance. Her face turned purple with embarrassment when the wind lifted her skirt and exposed unsightly maroon bloomers to the gaping crowd of idlers at the ship's rail.

We passed from winter and rain in Belgium (stations with names from the Great War, hard rain on the restaurant-car window in Köln) into high summer after the Alps. The white butterflies *Kohlweisslinge* dipped and dodged over a shallow clear river where Austrian cattle waded; we changed trains at Köln and again at Ljubljana and reached Rijeka in the early hours of the morning. The tourist office was open. It was not yet seven and they were selling steamship tickets near the harbour. A brown skeletal porter in a loincloth was most persistent and took our baggage away. Shabby soldiers in baggy uniforms were being drilled by a furious little officer. Jill wept with exhaustion and frustration and the strangeness of it all. I bought tickets and we went on board, eating tomato sandwiches on deck when the ship sailed, and you went below into the cabin, shared with two huge German Fraus.

After interminable hours of heat and sea the sun sank and the moon appeared. The Dinaric Alps looked like a mountain of ashes. I dozed in a canvas chair on the open deck, listening to the pleasant sound of the prow cutting through the water. The other passengers sat silent as ghosts all about me. The air was clammy, I smelled pine forests. In the middle of the night a storm came up and raged for an hour. Then all became still again.

We entered Dubrovnik, old Ragusa, around six next morning. We were going on to Cavtat and Mlini, climbing hundreds of steps in the great Adriatic heat of high summer, to where the Puppet Master waited in duck shorts; to Epidaurus in the old dispensation.

On a small pier in the middle of nowhere between Rijeka and Dubrovnik the steamer was offloading melons and machinery. A young woman stood and watched. She was brown as the dry earth she stood on with one good leg and the other a wooden stump to the hip and a kind of sarong about her waist but nothing else, barefoot she observed me while breastfeeding a small brown infant covered in flies.

It was close and humid and when she moved the strong shape of her showed through sweat-soaked cloth. When she spoke to the infant she showed gums the colour of yew bark.

She put the child down among the water melons, took one up, tested it with her fingers, cut it quickly in two with a kind of panga and approached me on the rail. She might have been rolling and fornicating on the dusty ground, so sweat-soaked and dusty was she. Streams of sweat poured down her face and torso as she offered me the fruit, lactating freely (waters tumbling down from Lahore), saying something in her own language which I could not follow but had a nearer whiff of her reaching up with ancillary tufts drenched and she was chewing some sort of nut that stained her teeth and lips.

Then she went back to the child, picked him up and set him to one of her bursting pomegranates, set him to suck. She watched me eating the water melon. When the steamer cast off with a thick black plume of smoke rolling back from the stack and a merry ringing of bells from the captain or helmsman, she stood on the pier and watched us depart, the child still sucking away for dear life, covered in flies, dreaming the day away. It was somewhere down the coast there, miles from anywhere known. Our puppet tour would take us to Sarajevo where Wright was to be fêted by the Yugoslav puppeteers and fondly embraced by a bearded, homosexual puppet man. We were offered slivovic and Hadji Bey Turkish Delight.

PART III

South Africa

'Mourning airs of forgotten childhood, mingled with premon-
itions of one's last end.'

Images of Africa (1971)

38

The Shore of Africa

The approaches to a new continent are ever prescient. When we took the plunge over the Equator, flying-fish sank to starboard, porpoises surfaced aft and every evening the sun went down in formations of cloud, furnace-like, dramatic as Doré's illustrations to Dante, in old Mrs Warren's library that became ours. Such lovely leewardings must lead somewhere. The first sight of Africa low on the horizon on the port side, a dim white skeleton coast; a mirage that goes.

We toured Europe with the John Wright Marionette Company from August to November of 1956, beginning in the great heat of the Adriatic near Dubrovnik (oh Mlini, ah Cavtat!), touring Yugoslavia and Germany, before the North Sea cold of Holland; refitting and rehearsing in Amsterdam for the coming extended tour of South Africa and both Rhodesias.

Early in December 1956 we sailed on *Die Waterman* for Kaapstad. My diary reports: '20th Dec. 1956, Cape Town. Prancing airs of the Cape of Good Hope. Table Mountain looms over us, balancing on its summit a single white cloud. It's a hot day in high summer here. The passengers crowd the rail. A blinding glare comes off the sea in Table Bay. Here everything is on a grander scale (even the swallows are bigger).'

257

Blossom, Le Roux, Zebra, Power, George are our stops along the way. The ostrich farms; a lady in a picture hat stands before an easel on Mossel Bay.

On December 24th two engines pull a long line of carriages through the Blaauberg Mountains in a long train travelling on the Garden Route from Cape Town to East London in the Eastern Province. Wheatlands go right up into the foothills of the mountains which are lime blue; the horizon seems very far away, bright and luminous. Jolting over the points on the bridge above the Zwartkops River, passing New Brighton location outside Port Elizabeth at dusk, lines and lines of hovels give way to arid land where the dark relocated race remain invisible in the native hut called Heart-of-the-Beast. An African internment camp sprawls featureless in the growing darkness; nothing can be added and nothing can be taken away from the African shanty town. Most mournful aspect. Where huts end the barren land begins again. Clatworthy, Funeral Furnishings All Parts.

But wait, life is here! In the twilight, clinging high up on the wire fence like bats, naked piccaninnies stretch out their skinny hands towards the lighted carriages that glide slowly by, the dining-car passing last. They are the colour of dust, chanting 'Hippy!. . . . hippy! Hippy!'

Happy Christmas in Sud Iffrika!

On December 25th I wake up on the upper berth of a first-class carriage in a long train travelling on the Garden Route through the Drakensbergs to meet Billy's parents at King.

Prancing airs of the Cape of Good Hope. The train is stationary out in the veld and I feel the warm air coming through the carriage window and all along the track the crickets are going like wildfire.

Then the long train begins to move again with much creaking and groaning and pissing off of oil and steam and jostling and colliding of bumpers. Onward from Hex River,

Mossel Bay, Plettenberg Bay, to Port Elizabeth, to East London, to King William's Town by the Amatola Mountains.

To good old King, to good old King, where I am to meet Billy's aged progenitor (who was in the Boer War) and anxious progenitrix, which fills me with foreboding.

We arrived by night in an immensely long dark train pushed by two steam engines belching flames and smoke, that went snaking around corners, one end emerging into open country, the veld, with the other end still out of sight, negotiating rocky curves. On leaving Cape Town days before we may have passed through De Aar, Graaf Reinet and Adelaide before East London, and now we were drawing into King William's Town, Billy with her head out the window and telling me, 'There they are!' and already in floods of tears.

Her parents were waiting sedately among Africans in striped blankets under an illuminated clock in a darkened station where great wooden crates marked KWT in stencil were being trundled up and down alongside the now stationary train – was it the end of the line? It was a scene from another age; the night departure of the troops for the Sudan in *The Four Feathers*.

Since all handsome young heroes arriving from overseas were variants and eidolons of the dead airman, Gwen Anders became coquettish at once; a peck on the cheek was in order, I was after all her new son-in-law. The old man was making a great to-do of fondly embracing his long-lost Billy. He drove us slowly and carefully to their high bungalow on the edge of town; next morning I would see the open country, the veld stretching away into the distance where a line of hills rose up, all trembling in the sunlight of the Cape.

They speak odd languages here, echoes of other languages; your Afrikaner (Boer, pronounce boor or bore) with his kitchen-Dutch, not duden-Deutsch, but a sort of strangled

Low German (the strongest word is '*braaivleis*', before '*veld*', and '*coon*'), the lowly 'Kaffir' (their fated body-servants forever) utters his clicks; the English-speaking settlers speak in their pinched way, afraid to open their mouths: 'Mai wiff. Pseude-Iffrika.'

Ireland would fit comfortably into the Transkei if they rolled it up, maybe smaller than the great Drakensberg Range, the Great Karroo or the Orange River basin, where we swam naked and saw the weaver birds nesting, where the sun shone all day long, the water free of bilharzia and crocodiles.

Meals tended to be a little formal, with much play of starched napkin (touched to the lips, fiddled with, adjusted under the chin for soups), and one did not dress too casually, certainly not go barefooted, like a piccaninny.

'If you accept the hospitality of a country,' said lawyer Anders over the breakfast table, fixing me with his steadfast honest-to-God old watery blue eyes with the vapoury anxious stare of a hare or bream, 'then you *cannot* write against it. It wouldn't do.'

We digested this morsel of commonsense.

He was German down to his buttoned boots, believing that one representative male white voting citizen simply did not go out on a limb or go against Judge and Jury; and most certainly did not disobey the law of the land – particularly if the land was South Africa and the laws Dr Hendrik Verwoerd's.

He let it be inferred that any rational bias of his against integration was an impartial bias, for white after all was white and black distinctly black. I could detect Bible bigotry in this – the drunken helotry of the Old Testament – but did not wish to argue the point.

'It would be a grave discourtesy.'

He did the needful, pouring out the tea.

Gwen smiled at me. She was quite content to treat 'them' as subhumans, her black domestics were semi-wild semi-trained black pets kept in kennels – the smokeblackened cement hut at the rear. They understood orders if the orders were simple enough; this she contrived by addressing them in a slow distinct manner and by dropping the definite article. That was as far as African progress should be allowed to go.

The old paterfamilias, heaving a sigh, having folded his napkin and put it into its plastic ring, rose now to indicate that breakfast was over. We had partaken; he had spoken, we were free to disperse.

He disapproved of the amount of wine and beer we had stocked in the ice-box but we were overseas folk after all and had our own customs, beer after breakfast being one of them. He and Lloyd, the son with the gun, voted for the United Party led by the absurd Sir de Villiers Graaf up on his white charger; the token opposition with the token liberal jackass in charge.

It was a party that could always be relied upon to defer to Nationalist will when it was a matter of closing ranks and all Blankes worth their salt voted wholeheartedly for white solidarity or voted in fear of outright black majority. Dyed-in-the-wool liberals – pseudo-liberals in the secrecy of the voting booth – such as Jonathan Carl who displayed the anti-intellectualism of the sincere Positivist to whom all explanation is suspect, were for the status quo at all costs.

Old man Anders was ninety if he was a day, having served in the South African War, but still remained in full possession of most of his faculties. Suited and cravatted as if the denizen of a previous age, he sat stiffly in his rocking-chair on the patio, facing his surviving son, with the temperature already risen into the high nineties, and both invisible to each other behind generous open spreads of the *Cape Times* which they rustled at one another in lieu of polite conversation, the deadly daily commonplaces.

Brother Lloyd had married Elaine Tutt, one of the East London Baptists, having bought a revolver to scare off a rival suitor.

The rocking-chair tipped, the big pages rustled stiff as palm fronds, a faint breeze wafted through. Barefooted and in khaki shorts the tolerated visitor from overseas, an awkward son-in-law under an African sunhat, sneered at Sir De Villiers Graaf and read Gibbon in the shade of the fig tree out of the atrocious heat of mid-morning, sipping ice-chilled Lion beer, hearing African voices passing by on the dusty road below. Up the way were the blue Amatolas and the krantz down which British soldiers white as sheets, as ghosts, were pushed to their deaths by order of cruel Kreli of the proud Xhosa nation. Down the way was the King tannery with stinks as atrocious as the heat.

But, lo, an African postman glistening with honest sweat came ambling up the path, taking from his postbag a neat package which he held up and called Bwana Higgings. It was a rare find. Basil Fogarty, a Scot with a bookstore in Port Elizabeth, had traced and procured the unprocurable – an American first edition of Djuna Barnes' 1938 novel *Ryder* (Horace Liveright of New York). He had laid his hands on a novel I had been after for years (Hi, Basil, if you're still alive!). The postman, who knew his place, handed it to his Baas, who handed it to his guest; the old German jaw most resolutely set.

'You must respect our ways.'

So I began again, jobless.

For two years we had toured South Africa and both Rhodesias, from Windhoek in Namibia to Worcester in the Cape; from Humansdorp to Plettenberg Bay to Louis Trichardt in the Transvaal; from Blantyre back down to Eshowe and Port Shepstone, saving £200, old currency, to salt away in the British Kaffrarion Savings Bank in King. In all we played in over two hundred towns and dorps.

39

Touring with the Puppets

John Wright's Marionettes
National Theatre Organisation 1957 tour

22–27 Jan. 1957	Cape Town	Town Hall
	Wynberg	Town Hall
	Woodstock	Town Hall
1 Feb.	Bellville	Communal Hall
	Rondebosch	Town Hall
	Paarl	Town Hall
	Somerset West	Town Hall
	Stellenbosch	Botha Hall
	Wellington	Town Hall
	Worcester	Hugo Naude Centre
	Robertson	Town Hall
	Swellendam	Town Hall
	Riversdale	Town Hall
	Mossel Bay	Town Hall
	George	Town Hall
	Oudtshoorn	Drill Hall
	Graaf Reinet	Town Hall
	Cradock	Town Hall
	Somerset East	Town Hall
	Kirkwood	Church Hall
1–2 Mar.	Uitenhage	Town Hall

	Port Elizabeth	City Hall
	Grahamstown	City Hall
	King William's Town	Town Hall
	East London	Selborne College
	Durban	Wesley Hall
	Pietermaritzburg	Rowe Theatre
	Estcourt	Town Hall
	Harrismith	Town Hall
	Bethlehem	Town Hall
	Kroonstad	Town Hall
	Vereeniging	Town Hall
1 Apr.	Van der Byl Park	Rec. Club Hall
	Johannesburg	Technical College
	Pretoria	Grootkerk Hall
	Brakpan	Town Hall
	Springs	Town Hall
2–3 May	Benoni	Town Hall
	Krugersdorp	T.H.
	Roodepoort	T.H.
	Randfontein	T.H.
	Germiston	T.H.
	Boksburg	T.H.
	Heidelberg	T.H.
	Standerton	T.H.
	Ermelo	T.H.
	Bethal	T.H.
	Middelburg	T.H.
	Potchefstroom	T.H.
	Klerksdorp	T.H.
	Kimberley	T.H.
	Bloemfontein	T.H.
1 June	Smithfield	P. A. Venter, Hairdresser
	Burgersdorp	*Albert Times*

	Queenstown	Venetian Blind Centre
	Molteno	Town Clerk
	Steynburg	Pretorius & de Kock
	Tarkastad	Tarka Distributors
	Indwe	Ko-Op Handelsvereniging
	Elliot	R. H. Thompson
	Matatiele	Central Pharmacy
	Harding	O. T. Bowles, General Dealer
	Margate	Ports Limited
	Port Shepstone	A. Ross & Co.
	Scottburgh	*Scottburgh News* Agency
	Ixopo	Mr Ross, Ixopo Hairdressing Salon
	Ladysmith	*Ladysmith Gazette*
	Greytown	George's General Store
3 Aug.	Pietersburg	de Bruyns Shoe Store
	Tzaneen	Lenel Shoe Store
	Potgietersrust	Impala Winkels
	Groblersdal	Corrie's Hairdressing Saloon
	Bronkhorstspruit	Town Clerk
	Brits	Transvalia Meubels
	Koster	Harmonie Cafe
	Rustenburg	Uitspan Cafe
	Lichtenburg	J. J. Smit, Hairdresser
	Kuruman	Model Bakery

17 Aug.	Van Zylsrust	Primary School Hall
	Askam	Hostel Hall
20 Aug.	Gochas	Hostel Hall
	Stampriet	School Hall
	Aranos	Primary School Hall
	Leonardville	Pretorius Cash Store
	Gobabis	Headmaster, High School
27 Aug.	Windhoek	Messrs Nitzsche-Reiter
	Okahandja	Mnr. E. Gelhar
	Omaruru	Mr Gloeditsch
1 Sept.	Uskos	Mr F. A. Jensen, Turnhalle
	Kalkveld	Mr Christies, Dealer
	Outjo	Headmaster, High School
7 Sept.	Grootfontein	Mr Zechokke, Nord Hotel
	Tsumeb	Club Hall
	Otavi	Mr Mutavszik
	Otjiwarongo	Mrs L. Kunze
	Swakopmund	Mr Clajus, Faber Hall
15 Sept.	Mariental	Mrs U. Massman, Charneys Hotel
	Keetmanshoop	Dr Burger
	Karasburg	Volkswinkel
	Ariamsvlei	Principal, Primary School

	Upington	Café Royal
	Keimoes	Pietersen se Modewinkel
	Kenhardt	Voortrekker Cafe
27 Sept.	Williston	Amandelboom Cafe
	Calvinia	J. W. van Staden, Auctioneers
	Van Rhynsdorp	Town Clerk
	Clanwilliam	J. J. Louw, Municipal Offices
1 Oct.	Citrusdal	P. de Villiers, General Dealer
	Moorreesburg	Handelsvereniging
	Riebeeck West	Mr Kruger, Municipal Offices
	Tulbagh	Mr J. H. Theron, Tailor
	Ceres	P. F. de Kock, General Dealer
	Wolseley	Mr Groenewald, Central Café
	Laingsburg	Die Scriba, N. G. Kerk
	Ladysmith	C. H. Wessel & Son
20 Oct.	Beaufort West	General Hairdressers
	Loxton	Town Clerk
	Carnarvon	Central Café
	Victoria West	Karroo Printers
	Britstown	Mrs Sarel Daneel
	De Aar	Brits en Roos
	Hanover	du Plessis & Keun
	Richmond CP	Ruchof Koffiehuis
	Middelburg CP	*Die Middellander*

	Colesberg	v.d. Merwe & Bezuidenhout
1 Nov.	Bethulie	Attie du Plessis, Hairdresser
	Aliwal North	Kruger's Hairdressing Saloon
	Zastron	N. J. de Wet, General Dealer
	Wepener	Frasers Limited
	Maseru	Secretary, Memorial Club Hall
	Ladybrand	Central Café
	Ficksburg	H. B. Kruger, Hairdresser
	Senekal	Springbok Outfitters
	Winburg	*Winburg Post*
	Ventersburg	The Town Clerk
	Welkom	Manie van Rooyen, Radio Shop
	Odendaalsrus	Sonop Limited
	Bothaville	Venter & du Preez
	Heilbron	A. Howell, Vermaaklikhede
	Sasolburg	Secretary, Amateur Dramatic Society
21 Nov.	Volkrust	Metro Café
	Newcastle	Newcastle Hairdressing Saloon
	Glencoe	Stey's Electrical Service
	Vryheid	Empire Theatre

	Wakkerstrom	Uitspan Café
	Carolina	Miss Welman, Butows Chemist
28 Nov.	Barberton	C. H. Coertzen
	Nelspruit	Central Café
	Lydenburg	Die Scriba
1 Dec.	Belfast	C. J. J. van Vuuren
	Witbank	Coalfields Trading Store
	Delmas	Delmas Radio Shop

The South African tour ended at Delmas, about which I remember nothing. Our 1957 itinerary took in over 150 towns; en route here and there we encountered the full force of Afrikaner bigotry, the laager mentality in whose language the strong words were *Voortrekker* (helot), *braai* (bigot), *veld* (patriot), *kaffir* (a racist jibe). The only English word on their lips was deployed as an expostulation – as one might say 'Fiddlesticks!' – 'Shame!' as in 'Och shime min!' All words were spoken in their language with relish, assurance and familiarity, as of something you could not take away from them; the hard ring to it echoed their innermost convictions: *This lind is ours min.* Well certainly it was a lovely land of gorgeous vistas, if only the blight of apartheid could be removed from it, the scales dropped from bigoted white eyes.

The 1958 tour of Southern and Northern Rhodesia began on February 23rd at Umtali in torrents of rain. We were all injected against cholera, smallpox and yellow fever. Crossing Beit Bridge we travelled as far north as Kariba Dam. Scotch 26s. a bottle and all the African loaders weak with bilharzia. We played:

Bulawayo
Fort Victoria
Gwelo
Gwanda
Chipinge
Umtali
Salisbury
Kariba Dam
Livingstone
Victoria
Lusaka
Broken Hill
Mufulira
Kitwe
Zomba
Gweru
Que Que

to name but these. I recall: baboons grunting in the baobab trees at Wankie, the tintinnabulation of the diamond-doves in the suffocating heat, the air-conditioned bar in the Baobab Hotel, the early departure for Victoria Falls, flamingoes in a lagoon at evening, elephants cropping the tree-tops on the way to Kariba Dam, and the lioness running before us in the headlights of the Bedford truck. The Arab dhows tacking across the fast-flowing Zambesi at Tet, the bad-tempered monkey on its perch, at the end of its chain.

In the Rhodesias they speak yearningly of the Yew Kai or 'good old Yew Kai'; landlocked Afrikaners never speak of Holland as home. The tour ends somewhere south of Salisbury. Exhausted, tired of the company, we are going back to Johannesburg, to begin again. Goodbye John and Jane, Margaret and Tim. Adios vile Brink, our Afrikaner driver with bloodshot eyes and stomach ulcers. Brink by name and brink by nature, the bane of kaffirs and munts. *Hasta la vista,* cackface.

40

The Child of Storm

Our first son Carl Nicolas was born on the fourteenth anniversary of the Hiroshima bomb, 6 August 1959, named after careful old Jonathan Carl and reckless Nicolas Chamford (1741–94), the friend of Mirabeau, in Johannesburg at ten minutes past ten of a winter night, the seasons being reversed there.

Next morning I brought mother and son home to the spotless apartment, the new cot looking out over the distant mine dumps of Bez Valley. Mother Superior would not dream of parting with the swaddler until the father had disbursed a cheque; for this after all was lawless Jo'burg. Amigo Trevor Callus, intemperate poker-player on the green baize of Adamczewski's Bellos Guardo, drove us home at a stately forty miles an hour in his racing DKW. In the top-floor apartment neat as a pin, the fridge was stacked with Mateus Rosé, fine Rioja and champagne from the Pa Petousis off-licence to fitly celebrate the storm-child's home-coming.

I saw a white angel-child in Jill's arms on the deserted station platform at Blaney. The low white walls reflected a positively intractable heat and even the African porters had taken cover. I bade my travelling companion adieu – a surly soldier – collected my baggage and alighted.

I hadn't seen my son, aged eleven months, for a month during which I wound up our affairs at Johannesburg and said goodbye to friends. Carl Nicholas no longer recognised his father. The white angel sat on my knee and suffered himself to be embraced in the roasting car with the smell of heated leather. Beads of perspiration stood out on his forehead, but he did not recognise this over-familiar fellow with goatee who seemed to know his mother, now making a balls of gear-changing and telling her husband some bad news. Her old Pop was far from well; I would have to sail alone and they would follow when they could. I buried my nose into the sweet-smelling hair before me.

Under the fig-tree's shade in the great heat of King I read Gibbon and watched my son crawl at speed down the sloping lawn, heard the high-pitched screeching of African women passing on the road. Child-bearing is the lowest form of creativity, said Plato sourly; but Plato was wrong. In the cool of the bungalow we drank gin and tonic. The trunks were packed. The black nanny adored the crawling child, grand-father had recovered and a date for sailing was fixed. My son began to recognise the man in the shade.

Our ship, the *Warwick Castle*, was already berthed at East London docks. It had sailed in convoy to the Middle and Far East, ferrying Hurricanes and Spitfires with medical sup-plies and condoms for the Allied war effort.

In a garden-flat in Ranelagh I would begin to support a wife and small son on a modest stipend paid monthly by the publisher Calder who had accepted the first book of stories, most of them written during the two-year puppet tour.

Soon we had moved to Nerja in Andalucia where I finished my first novel. It was a new beginning, another life; for we live again through our children and, as the first was to be joined by two more bouncing boyos, I was to enjoy three extra lives and be thrice-blessed. The first, the child of storm, a hot-tempered Leo as befits the fire sign, was carried in state (there was no elevator) to his high home on the fifth floor back, above the double line or honours guard of jacarandas shaking their little blue bells all along Isipingo Street above cosmopolitan Hillbrow.

PART IV

Dun Laoghaire

41

The Gentleman Rider

Flaky distemper fell from the low ceiling and lay as a greyish slush on the damp linoleum that had perished and buckled here and there, by the door that would not close, under the draining-board, around the dented and seldom disinfected bucket that had no handle, before the stove with its coating of thick grease, as Sharpe the taximan moved in the room above. He was their landlord, and the rent was low.

In the cold basement flat below, the old somnambulist, sodden with tea and porridge, stared out over the soiled half-curtain with its design of cornstalks and sheaves of wheat. In the narrow patch of earth outside finches flitted among cabbage stumps and valerian withered on the granite wall near the postern-gate; and then a tabby cat appeared on the path and birds flew out of the apple tree and the cistern upstairs began to choke and splutter.

My father heaved a sigh, turning away from the window to walk slowly in creaking cricket boots over the faded surface that sweated all winter and entered the room off the kitchen where he slept. A barred window admitted some light, the pavement was level with the top of his head, he could follow pedestrians from their knees down going by. At one time it might have been the larder. He made up his bed. It had no sheets; a narrow bed that sagged, covered in soiled and threadbare rugs, a poor man's rest. He threw on his overcoat and muffler, prepared to sally out.

My mother was waking in the shadowy front room in stale air. A low table on which were scattered miscellaneous objects stood by the fireplace where she had burned papers. A single uncomfortable leather armchair was piled with newspapers. The damp stain had come back on the wall. The ship's clock from Irish Lights – a hand-out from her sister Evelyn, Joss's widow – stood on the sideboard; the sorry sideboard itself had come second-hand from Andy Hand of Cumberland Street. It was Autumn 1961 and the clock hands were three-quarters of an hour slow.

Through the persistent drizzle of impressions and half-impressions filtering their slow way sluggishly through his (Dado's) morning brain, one effacing the other, interspersed with yawns, farts, rifts, sighs, the sound of the hour came from the bell-tower of the church on Royal Marine Road. In Monkstown, Glasthule, Sallynoggin, Killiney, Dalkey, Kill o' the Grange and Cornelscourt it was nine o'clock where he stood among fifty thousand others preparing to face the day in Dun Laoghaire, the old Irish royal dun, now a place of church spires and dog turds. In No. 5 Haigh Terrace underground it was still 8.15.

Dado crossed the dark hall to Mumu's room. He needed money to fetch milk and bread for her breakfast. She brought out a purse from under the mound of pillows and from it extracted a half-crown which she handed across in such a way that her hand did not touch his, saying: 'Mind you bring me back the change. Not like last time.'

Their roles were reversed. Now it was she who managed the money, the dole, such as it was, and issued the orders, such as they were, for him to obey. Poverty had chained them to each other and this ritual. Whereas before it was she who had been the solicitous one and he the strict one, now it was she who was strict and he solicitous. She had had to 'put her foot down' as to who should visit and who should not ('I don't want that one in the place. Don't talk to me

about that fellow!'), Aunt Mollie but not Aunt Gerty. The
flat was 'too shabby'; it was a disgrace, she hadn't the heart
to clean it, and would be just as pleased if no one came. So
no one came.

Corcoran, the retired publican who was interested in
antiques, called and was turned away. Mumu had never
needed friends and now towards the end of her life she had
none except Mrs Bowden, a widow who worked in the Irish
Sweepstake offices at Ballsbridge.

'Are you finished with these?' my father asked, pointing
at the pile of newspapers on the armchair. My mother hid
the purse under her pillow. Yes, she was finished with them,
there was nothing in them. She watched him collecting
them, folding one upon the other, pressing them down, He
read nothing but newspapers and he read them thoroughly,
omitting nothing, competitions in the London tabloids,
sports items, lists of runners at racetracks.

A languor and weariness seeped up through the worn
carpet, coming out of the floorboards. This had happened
before; this would happen again, with modifications. The
very air was tired. My mother turned her face to the wall.
Footsteps made a hollow sound passing by on the pavement
outside. A man and a woman shape passed. People were on
their way to work. My father left the room.

What kind of a day would it turn out to be? Good or bad,
wet or fine, ordinary or exceptional, a great sum won at
long odds, a few hours of forgetfulness in the bars? Snuffling
up his nose, my father retired to his room, piled the day-
old newspapers on another great pile already mounted
there, hid the half-crown in an empty Player's packet, took
a florin from its hiding place, put it in his pocket, pulled
on a pair of woollen gloves. There was hoarfrost on the
window. News items of general interest were impaled on
great nails, what he termed buck nails. The window gave
on to a terrace that led to the Mariners' Church and the
grey harbour, the mail boat docked at No. 2 berth. My father
had been down that morning shortly after seven o'clock to

watch the passengers disembark. Three or four times a year
he would see someone he knew; it made the day for him.
The habit of going there had become a ritual for him, this
small indomitable man with bowed back and vague eyes and
wavery talk. Sharpe had been summoned to drive us the few
hundred yards to Haigh Terrace on our return from South
Africa with grand-child. But on that raw morning no one
known to him had disembarked. Sharpe had a few fares. My
father returned, lit the gas oven, left the oven door open,
the only heating available. The kitchen warmed to a humid
body-heat as he prepared porridge; it was like attempting to
warm an igloo. He ate his porridge, plugged in the electric
kettle (a handy present from his daughter-in-law), went back
to his room to change into his only good pair of shoes.
Other figures passed the window, huddled against the cold
wind blowing off the harbour. He changed out of his cricket
boots. Now the passers-by were walking above his head, as
he bowed down to tie the laces. Above his head the school
groups from CWC, the crossword puzzle that almost won
the big prize, the charm-contest that had ('Dalkey Man Wins
Jackpot!'); spot-the-ball competitions. He had received his
cheque on the stage of the Savoy Cinema. The DJ had asked:
'How do you pick the pretty ones?' He had answered: 'I
married a pretty one'; that went down well.

'That bloody fool,' Mumu said, bitter as corrosive acid.

Once well-off, he had lived improvidently; now he had
nothing but the old-age pension and the rent that my
brothers paid between them. He collected the pension in
Glasthule where he was not well known, or not known at
all, whereas in Dun Laoghaire he was known. For getting
through the winter, those interminable winters that he
hated, a sack of low-grade coal or turf came with the pension. He burnt it extravagantly and then went without heating, opening the gas-oven door, turning the gas half on,
sleeping half-asphyxiated, sending out great droning snores.

Whatever he won he spent immediately; that was his
nature; given a little he became a spendthrift. Money burnt

holes in his pockets. He liked the open-air life, out in all weathers like a cab-horse.

The brilliant unsurpassable past and its retinue of cronies, good fellows, yachtsmen and ladies in white, flowed by, borne along by the Shannon and waved to him from the white deck, calling out, 'Batty!' My mother was among them, waving a parasol.

In return for light gardening duties in a Glenageary home he had the price of a suit off the peg from one of the seven married sisters, all well off; he being one of three sons, the odd one, the mollycoddled boy.

In my father's family there were seven girls and three boys. Margaret who married a Newman, Anna who married a Delaney, Bridie who married a Connolly Fagan, Nora who married the famous athlete Jack Healy, Tessie who married a Stevenson, Mollie who married a Smyth, Gertie who married a Moore; and the lads Tom, John and Batty, my father, who married Miss Lilly Boyd, whose father was the Peace Commissioner at Longford. Her brothers were Aubrey and Herbert, her sister Evelyn who married Josef Moorkens of Hertenfels in Belgium, the go-between. And was there not an Aunt Ada who married a man called Lynch who had a grey son called Herbie who played with the Dote and I in those endless summers in Springfield in the long ago? There certainly was.

Kind sister Molly bought him new shoes, the ones he was wearing. His friend Corcoran stumped up twelve pounds for a winter overcoat; he was fitted out. He accepted charity in the spirit it was offered, did not complain of his lot, wore the collars of one shirt, the cuffs of another, the body of a third (the tail of the latter cut up to make the former parts), wore another as an undershirt, for he was thin and felt the cold. For the same reason he washed irregularly; the narrow bathroom with its peeling walls and cold water was not very inviting. He never took a bath. In the toilet the cistern was out of order, the chain wound about a wire scrubbing brush; you flushed with a handy chamber pot. It would do.

For most of his life my father had dressed casually, tight cord jackets with single or double vents (true mark of a racing man or a bounder), thin-stripe good-quality shirts, ties that stood out from the chest when secured by a tiepin, three inches of cuff on display, gold cuff-links (when he had them), a handkerchief up one sleeve, a display handkerchief in the breast pocket, highly polished tan brogues with pointed toes and perforated uppers, a centre parting in the quiff, a dandy's socks, a whiff of eau-de-cologne. He never wore a hat.

A short, amiable, nimble gent who was sometimes – to his great delight – mistaken in public for this or that professional jockey, Smirke or Quirke, which he accepted as a compliment. After all, he had ridden in his day, been a gentleman rider. Lifted his elbow at the Horse and Hound.

Often he spoke of the great jockeys of his time: Joe Canty, Martin Quirke, Morney Wing, Dinnie Ward, Martin Maloney and Charlie Smirke ('a Jewboy but a great jock'). For him they represented the golden age of racing, at a time when he himself had money, money to burn. His time was the best and only time. And those were the jockeys he had watched going over the jumps and galloping on the flat. He had seen Steve Donoghue win the Irish Derby at the Curragh in 1916. Donoghue and Smirke had each ridden three Epsom winners. Dado and Mumu saw the Irish Grand National at Faeryhouse every Easter Monday, once in the snow. My mother in a cloche hat and a fur coat, my father peering through binoculars.

In August they drove in the Hillman or the Overland for the Galway Plate, drank whiskey in the Great Southern Hotel and walked in Eyre Square, drove home late to Springfield, none too sober, to the roaring fires.

At Jamestown uncle Jack Healy had bred and trained race horses. At Springfield he sucked raw eggs, the diet of athletes. He had won the Liverpool Grand National in 1938 with a horse called Workman, T. Hyde up. Mumu's other brother Jimmy rode thrice in the Liverpool Grand National, coming second once, third the following year. But was there a brother Jimmy? Was not that rather Jimmy Brogan? Search the records for the amateur champion jockey Jimmy Boyd.

Dado himself, once an amateur rider, had always dressed like a swank. Nowadays, with the going a little harder, he still dressed like one. A dark suit, patent-leather pumps, the relics of his dancing days. When the patent leathers wore out he wore my old discarded cricket boots, two sizes too large, which he stuffed with wads of the *Irish Times* as undersoles. The paper shredded as he walked, bits of newspaper erupted from his heels, making him into a winged Mercury. Walking about the flat, farting, he shed stale old news, the stamp scandal, the fellow who absconded with the funds.

Another more resourceful breeder more methodical in his ways took over the running of Springfield and other racehorses were exercised over the seventy odd acres; Ringwood Son and Cabin Fire flew over the jumps where One Down had faltered and Grogan had come down.

My father spent much of his time in the men's bathing place at Hawk Cliff in Dalkey, a fair walk for an oldish man. He gossiped with the swimmers in the summer, kept an eye on Corcoran's clothes in the winter. Corcoran, retired publican and reformed alcoholic with ideas about physical fitness, swam in the icy winter sea, did exercises in the buff on the cement ramp. He had a bald pate which he daubed with brown boot polish, bought my father an occasional packet of Player's, instructed him how to bid at auctions, further to his interest in the antique trade, for he was too shy to bid himself, or did not want to be known ('Too damn cute', Dado said), a silent man with a shaky hand ('The jigs', Dado said), a speech impediment.

'That fellow would drive you mad,' Dado said. 'He's cracked himself. Who else but a madman would want to jump into the sea? Do you know what temperature it is? Forty-two degrees. Corcoran's mad.'

The undercover bidding at auctions was not done on a percentage basis, my father (no businessman) neither asked nor was offered remuneration other than packets of Player's, for after a lay-off of about fifteen years Dado had begun to smoke again.

'Corcoran's stingy,' Dado said. 'Tight with his money. And he has pots of it. Keep it and you'll always have it.' I suspect that Dado had hoped to inherit some of it, if only by outliving Corcoran, though Dado was at least ten years Corcoran's senior but always spoke as though he himself would live to be old as Methuselah. His credulity, when it came to base human responses, was matched only by his ignorance; his faith in people had the naive quality of primitive superstitions. What he firmly believed had a charming inaccuracy about it, an arrested stage of knowledge or ignorance like the mythical basis of the heavenly bodies as seen through pre-Copernican eyes. He was gullible to the furthest extent imaginable.

'The bug,' Dado croaked, coughing to demonstrate it. 'I've got the bug.'

It (pneumonia) was 'going' in Dun Laoghaire; in due course he would catch a 'dose' of it, be laid up. About the workings of his own constitution (marvellously healthy when you consider how little he ate) he knew about as much as he knew about the language of the Copts.

Still, ever optimistic, he bought tickets in the Irish Sweepstakes, as he had done all his life; half shares once, now quarter shares. He lived in hopes.

'By the living Jaysus this year my luck will change, I have the feeling,' he said, staring fiercely at me with his weak blue eyes that were always watering now in the cold. The *Arcus senilis* had spread, vague hopes swam there, vague dreams of prosperity at the eleventh hour, all addled together.

'Begod it can't get any worse,' said he, laughing.

'Mind your language,' Mumu said sharply. 'I'm sure Jeel isn't used to such language where she comes from.'

'Grow up woman,' Dado said with a devastatingly vulgar sniff at the door.

'Very trying,' Mumu said, shaking her head. 'That fellow is very trying.'

Trying was one of her dismissive terms.

She was jealous of his attentions to my wife, had mistaken his inbred courtesy for incipient senility; so in the ashes of their old love there was still a little fire. At all events she resented the gallantry displayed for my wife's benefit.

Mumu came by bus to see her grandson, changed at Appian Way, with a rice pudding in a plastic bag, with love, with fondness, making that journey across town to see us all, to give us her fondest love.

We had called on them once or twice a month, hardly more than that, from Ranelagh with two changes by bus via Merrion Road to Dalkey, generally on Sundays. And at two or three o'clock in the afternoon we would find them still in bed in separate, dark rooms with the shutters drawn, the light already beginning to wane and a fog-horn sounding mournfully out in the bay.

Dado, dressed and spruced up, brought out the tea and plates, mentioned a new light-ship or floating lighthouse that was to be moored on the horizon on a sand bank; of its usefulness he was highly sceptical, as he was of all services in the public sector or any improvements from any Fianna Fáil government (the new car ferry would ruin the three yacht clubs), for had he not been to Blackrock School with Éamon de Valera and beaten him in the 880 yards.

'A killer,' Dado said, 'that fellow's a killer.'

'Talk about what you know,' Mumu said sharply.

'My dear woman,' my father said, 'my dear woman.'

Truth to tell, I had grown very tired of these barbed exchanges and wished they would end. A fog-horn moaning out in the bay, the low-kilowatt bulb already on in the afternoon, the feet of pedestrians passing above eye-level above the half-curtain, the great damp stain on the wall, my mother bringing out a Monument Creamery Cake from the cupboard where scraps of food were hidden away, my father in creaking cricket boots fetching a lemon for our tea. So was ending a long and latterly acrimonious association, at the beginning of which I tottered across the nursery to be received into the open arms and scent of Mumu who assured me warmly that I was a little dote.

From her lair my poor mother stared at me, as though I were far away. The room stank of women's old stale things, cheap perfumes, old clothes. A stoop-shouldered man coughed in the vegetable garden that was restricted as a prison exercise yard. He wore a cloth cap, a muffler about his throat, a sallow face like the tubercular Collins who had died in Seamount Sanatorium. Perhaps he was a war-veteran, gassed or shell-shocked? He had a closed and miserable air about him, and no civil word for anyone. My mother said that he watched her at her toilet behind the half-curtain, but that was impossible, for the half-curtain reached up to the lintel. An apple tree with dark rain-saturated boughs kept out the light. The garden was planted in cabbage, the apple tree yielded bitter cookers, the tall granite spire of the Mariners' Church rose above the granite of the garden wall which had a postern door let into it, used by the surly fellow in the cloth cap. He was a roomer in the flat above Sharpe. The church had been built in the early 1700s by convicts hauling the stone from Dalkey quarry.

The auctioneer's notice for the sale of Springfield, discoloured with age, was impaled on one of Dado's buck nails. The four sons had scattered to the four winds.

The grounds of the Marine Hotel were infested with cats. They stared through the railings at the stout old lady with white hair walking painfully by. Mumu had put on considerable weight, her ankles were swollen, she advanced with a pronounced roll, uneasy on the slopes above Moran Park.

There was the bowling green popular with English summer visitors, there was the pond with its ducks and geese.

My mother's health was poor, she did not look after herself, she liked a drop, injections for pernicious anaemia kept her alive. 'Without those lads,' the doctor had warned her, 'without those, Mrs Higgins, you wouldn't walk the length of this room.' Sometimes the injections were painful, though she never complained; she drank JJ green label to put a little fire inside her, spent hours in Woolworth's in the winter, for the warmth. I had seen her in the bookie's with her face pressed close to the list of runners, the lens of her spectacles criss-crossed with innumerable fine lines, an intricate spider-work of fine white lines delicate in texture as the lines in Pavel Tchelitchew's *Inachevé*, but no good for her failing eyesight. It must have been like walking through a snow-storm; she was living in a twilight world at the end of her life. How could the good God be good if He overlooked or ignored the fate of the Jews, for wasn't He a Jew Himself? How could He let that happen, then? And if there was no justice to be expected in Heaven, what hope had we? Ask His Mother, I suggested.

Mumu felt the cold.

For a while she blinded herself wearing her sister's castoff reading glasses, her eyes grown huge and froglike and confused. Study the list of runners in the Turf Accountant's, fancy the chances of certain favoured jockeys (Piggot, Scobie Breasley, Joe Mercer), slap a bob on the Tote, win a bit, lose a bit, drink when you can, avoid people, endure life. Grief brought to numbers cannot be so fierce.

The fog-horn in the autumn, the leaves rotting off the trees, Cork Road, Tivoli Road, Ulverton Avenue, Corrig Road, Oliver Plunkett Road, the Orphanage, and one day like another, winter turning into spring and spring into summer, and that into autumn and then the winter again, delayed daylight shining weakly on the Muglins, on deserted

Bullock Harbour, filtering at last into Haigh Terrace and into her stale-smelling lair.

One dark would be just as another dark. A patch of white out at sea meant gulls over sewage, 'stormwater' drifting out or in on the tide.

Dado retired at eight to rise at two in the morning and make himself a pot of tea, drinking it alone in that morgue of a kitchen, sleeping the thin sleep that the old sleep, awake at seven in the morning in the dark, and then down to the railway tracks, the barrier, like a crow in a cold field ploughed up, watching his travelling fellow-countrymen, the Irish back from England on their holidays, the tired faces coming through with poor baggage.

On the pond below the Mariners' Church leaves and scum had gathered, bloated white bread, geese, reflections of bare branches, iron railings and the trembling image of a granite wall. A breeze passed over it, the images changed, shifted, the bowling green lay deserted, clouds were reflected in standing water, life was passing, opportunities wasted; a tracery of leaves and feathers, the hair of the dead drowning there.

Dado passed down the hall and let himself out with a yale key. Opposite was the Marine Hotel with its granite bulk and scuffled gravel, the cat-infested grounds. He went on, huddled into his raincoat, resentful of the interminable winter that 'took it out' of him, weakened him and made him anxious for his health. Mumu had a touch of bronchitis.

She had had herself photographed on a public bench at Salthill, squinting into the sun; in a capacious handbag the letters I had posted in Johannesburg. She has watched the old *Dun Aengus* beating out towards Aran, the last landfall before America.

They had stood on the pavement outside the Monument Creamery and called to us, standing on the platform of a No. 8 Dalkey bus inbound for the Pillar, holding up our

grandson, to please come soon again. My father tapped the
window when we had taken our seats, Dado nodding, smiling, to please come soon again, and Mumu waved and
nodded, come soon again.

At Booterstown we had seen the twenty-foot model of the
TIME ale bottle, an illuminated beacon for thirsty travellers
by the sloblands and the sign of Kinch.

From draining-board to kitchen table five anxious creaking
paces, glare out through the half-curtains (a yellowish flaw
near the shocked blue of the iris); from there to the open
bedroom door five and a half slow, anxious creaking paces,
snore through the nose, break wind circumspectly, draw
away, pull away, be patient.

My gull-eyed father put down a sliced pan loaf and a pint
of milk on the sideboard by the clock that was still three-
quarters of an hour slow at the last reading and began
slapping his pockets in a crafty way and frowning, saying
(lying again!),

'You won't believe this, Lil, but that bloody bitch has given
me the wrong change again.'

He was a tanner short. Two tickies.

'No, I don't believe it.'

Dado, a true Stoic, accepted good or bad fortune as it came,
like a gardener who instead of watering his plants, waits for
rain, confident that it will come sooner or later (as it certainly would in Ireland). He devoured the tabloids, a lifelong
and insatiable consumption of bad news; his was an insidi-
ously lazy mind. O Angel of Time, you who have counted
the sighs and the tears of mankind, forget them and hide
them away!

Dado's expressions were these: A 'rip' (an exasperating
person) or (more forcefully) 'a right rip'; impudent bitch.
'Dough' (the American inheritance, or money in general).
'The wind always blows cold over graveyards.'

Mumu's expressions were: A 'lug' (a thick fellow, stupid), 'slushy' (romances), 'ructions' (rows), 'biddable', 'barging', 'farfetched'. 'Thick as thieves'. If someone was 'all over you' with flattery it only meant they were smarmy and insincere.

Brother Bun's expressions: 'A bit dicey, what's the gen?' 'Hunky-dory, not half, jolly good show, haven't a clue.'

42

The Hospital by the Sea

That morning the bell had rung early, someone kept their finger on it. I put on a dressing-gown and went down the chilly passage to hammer open the stiff rainsoaked door of our garden flat. There was nobody there, though the gate into Charleston Road stood wide open. I shut the door and returned to bed and must have dozed off for this strange dream came to me.

A World War II Sunderland flying-boat was blundering slowly through clouds at no great altitude and being fired at by persons on the ground armed with antiquated rifles. There came a shout from the door: '*Here she comes again!*' I ran out and took up one of the heavy rifles, a Lee-Enfield that I recalled from Local Defence Force days at CWC when we had fired them at the range.

I could see the shadowy bulk of the Sunderland flying through clouds, it had a white fish-like belly. If I hit it I knew it would explode, as a whale hit with a harpoon that carried a charge in its head. But as I fired, the recoil strong as the kick of a mule, the dream ended. I didn't know whether I had struck it or not; allowing for the trajectory and altitude I had fired ahead of the flying-boat, passing high up through clouds white as snow. If I had fired well ahead of the white belly, it was me the bullet struck.

Some warning there, a premonition, I felt uneasy, bad

news was on the way. An hour or so later the doorbell rang
again. I opened the door this time to a motorcyclist in black
leather and a crash helmet, taking a telegram from his
bulging satchel. He said, 'Higgins'. I said yes I was and he
handed it across; it was brief.

'MA GONE TO HOSPITAL × COME OVER × DA × DUN
LAOGHAIRE'

The hospital was by the sea.

It stood near the harbour and the three yacht clubs,
near the railway station. Saint Michael's was a bleak-looking
edifice in grey stone. The Dalkey bus dropped me near the
gate. Clouds hung low and I could see my breath in the air.
Before midday it was already twilight. In the damp the snow
had turned to slush and the slush to water soon after it
touched the ground, forming irregular puddles in the hospital car-park. Nothing kept its shape. The name of the hospital was reflected upside down in puddles of water. I saw
the lame man going by and called to him but he did not
hear me, chose not to hear me.

It was late autumn, in as far as there can be an autumn
after no summer; for me it was already winter. Everything
was grey, lead-coloured, not a stir of air, the low clouds
releasing a drizzle of snow.

A resident medico beckoned me into a small well-heated
room near the grim reception hall. He told me in effect
that my mother was dying; her lungs were gone. We could
but hope was his way of saying there was no hope at all, but
I could call him at any time. 'Any time,' he repeated
firmly. I thanked him and we shook hands. I went up to her.
She was in St Cecilia's ward, the ward for the female dying,
near the service lift. I walked past the curtains and saw that
she was certainly dying; her caved-in features and leaden
colouring did not belong to the living. Her lower jaw had
sunk. They had removed the bridge and the flesh of her
face had begun to collapse as the bones came through.

If she lived through it, she would most likely be paralysed;

opinion varied as to the severity of that paralysis but none
was sanguine. It was better, perhaps, that she should die
knowing nothing and feeling nothing. The nuns were looking after her. They were dressed in white habits and moved
silently about the ward. In that hushed room the light was
going. They moved past the windows, wimpled and pale-
faced sentinels of twilight, ghosts of this gloomy, fatal world.
They did not represent the world, to be sure; they were the
sexless gate-porters into the next. My mother was in good
hands.

She, a great student of obituary notices, had feared death;
first with religion and then without it, she embraced it again
towards the end of her life; it's a strange Catholic fear, the
fear of death, very Irish, in a religion that harped on agony,
last things. A little light, a last feeble glow of intelligence
about to be snuffed out, a little hard-won breath, and then
it would be the end.

It was hard-won all right, pulling her down. She was dying
with each heartbeat; her sorrows and pleasures shut up there
for seventy and more years would die with her, she brought
her past with her. Something of me too would die with her;
I was watching part of my own death. It did not seem to
belong to me, yet it was mine. Will my own death be like
that, for another?

Brother Bun materialised out of the shadows and stood
by her bed. The Dote had come briefly but had returned by
boat to London; he would have to return again to be there
at the burial. The Kerry nun had let it be known that the
nearest and dearest should be around, time was short, and
where was the husband? 'Ah, let the unfortunate man rest,'
murmured the compassionate brother Bun. Her favourite
was absent, circling the hospital, wrestling with his silent
demons; his love was too great to attend.

For now the long-brooded-upon, the long-feared had
caught up with her at last and soon there would be no more
light, no more thought, no more injections or pain, no
more breath; she was going out, knowing nothing of this,

advancing step by step in darkness, going out in deep coma.
She would know nothing of what had finished her – the
cerebral haemorrhage, the night stroke. I took her hand.

She was hardening already, tending towards the inertia of
matter. I could not think of her dead, gone, any more than
I could think of myself dead; but nonetheless it was only
too apparent that she was going. Long ago in the garden at
Springfield she had sat on the rug and read Hans Andersen
to the Dote and myself as red pulpy berries fell like drops
of blood from the yew tree full of missel thrushes. She had
been a beauty in her day, and a local poet had composed a
sonnet in her honour, the beauty sitting on a public bench
on the Mall. Rhymester Jim McGinley had inscribed his little
book of doggerel to her, Lillian Boyd. Printed on poor
quality paper, it had once been an object of wonder to me.
Jim McGinley's verse was printed in the *Evening Mail*, which
seemed to me a female newspaper, reserved and rather dull.
It ran the 'Mandrake the Magician' strip which the Dote
and I followed with the closest attention. The magician's
cold shaved features would never change or age, he was
always Mandrake, his coal-black shiny hair was slick and the
precise middle parting was like Dado's. Cloaked, he was my
father in tails. He had a gigantic Negro with thick lips who
went about dressed in leopardskins as body-servant. Dado
subscribed to four morning papers and two evening; the
Evening Herald was masculine with the head of a Crusader
stamped on red as banner on the front page. The Dote and
I followed the adventures of Bud Fisher's 'Mutt and Jeff'
and Inspector Wade and Donovan. Inspector Wade was
another eagle-nosed type, also with centre parting, and a
quiff like bow waves which we attempted to imitate. The
Herald was hot bread just out of the oven; whereas the *Mail*
was a glass of cold milk.

All of that happened in the long ago; and so remote in
time it seemed to belong to someone else's past, not mine,
when the three of us sat under the oldest tree in the garden
and the yew berries fell about us, disturbed by the thrushes

feeding. The smell of freshly cut grass, the smell of the lime on the tennis court, the odour of grass decomposing behind the stand of bamboos, this belonged to my childhood, and my sweet-faced mother reading patiently to us there in a voice that breaks my heart. The straight white guide lines were for mixed doubles at tennis and Billy Odlum, stout as Billy Bunter, playing in braces and falling heavily; and they were the lines I must follow out in the world, the guided world that the nuns and the Jesuit Fathers spoke so often about, the world I had never found. The bamboos whispered of the advantages and pleasures that awaited me there; the stand of silver birches behind the summerhouse said the same.

She had reared us gently. Taught us to like books and paintings and suchlike, art, all the things that my father rather despised in his heart; he had the horses and the farm – those other bright fanciful things were beyond him. My parents were kind; putting our interests before their own, they had pinched and saved to give us a preparatory school and then college education which they could ill afford; an education that dropped off me like water off a duck's back. I took only what I wanted from it, the residue and hard drupe of my exasperation with it, and myself in the toils of it; boarding school for the sons of the privileged is a sort of penitentiary. From it I learnt the strange art of making myself invisible and travelling free on public transport through Dublin and London, as if I were already an old-age pensioner, in my middle twenties. The Jesuitical fiction, those pious lies, telling of the world's essential order and goodness, may have dropped off me like water but had made me an invisible man.

I looked now into the caved-in closed eyes and wished for her that she should not survive, not continue to suffer, but rather depart in sleep; the bad colouring and stertorous breathing, the white hair soaked in sweat and arranged in an unfamiliar way, made her a little strange to me, and I had not seen her in a nightdress in many years. I wished this for her who so dreaded death.

The previous year had been a year of deaths; too many too near to her. She had lived with my father in that damp place below street level, poorly enough towards the end, and had got at him, taken out her resentment on him, the last man able to defend himself, for he had no guile, no hidden resources, whereas she had her boiling resentment – if her life had gone wrong it was all his fault. Everything he did (and he did little) and everything he said (and he said much) annoyed her, yes and beyond all endurance. She was dying, as women sometimes die, of their man's equanimity.

The days refused to change, the living living and the dying dying. Funeral cortèges passed slowly through Glasthule, the shiny complacent hearses laden down with flowers, of the death-fleets owned by Creegan and Fanagan (both CWC), moving in the narrow way by the pedestrians doffing their hats to the unknown one who had passed out of life, was free as air, or who knows, plunged in Hellfire for all Eternity. Was it Eudora Welty who remarked on the ominous feeling that 'attaches itself' to a procession, as hinted at in the story of the Pied Piper of Hamelin? Droves of the dead went 'in all directions', my mother said, prone to exaggerate when her stronger feelings were aroused. She meant the ceaseless activity of the living into life and the dead into the ground, where she herself was now heading. Dun Laoghaire itself, formerly Kingstown, the ferry-crossing to England, had something of the River Styx about it, the boat-train packed with commuters drawing out for Westland Row, tired Irish faces gaping from the carriage windows in winter, the level-crossing passed, rain on the tracks, the gate closing like the end of one of those prodigious watery yawns that bring out a tear and a groan, and my father huddled into his thin coat going home.

Your dear father, she said, disassociating herself from him; your *dear* father, meaning that abject fool.

He still loved her in his way, but that was also too late; the life they had shared together had gone sour on them, they had drifted apart over the years, as I from them, as my three brothers from them and me. We had never been what is called a united family.

At five that morning the tide had begun to go out for her.

It was the turning point, entering the third day of deep coma. My father had been visiting her day and night, haunting the hospital. He had seen her at eight that morning and was convinced that she would not survive the day. It was her last day. Sunday in Ireland.

The streets were deserted, the sky grey and overcast by mid-morning, threatening snow. As I was shaving, the bell sounded. My father had come to say that she was sinking fast, not expected to last the day.

'Oh she's very bad,' he said, shaking his head. 'Very bad. I'm afraid she's going on us. Get over to her quick. I'll try and get the other fellow.'

The other fellow was the Dodo, who had flown in from Scotland but was not visiting the hospital; he was kept informed of progress. He had cultivated a princely hauteur that was most unbrotherly. I told Dado to stay where he was and try to rest. He was worn out with worry and grief; if anything happened I would phone. He needed rest. I built up the fire and he sat before it in his overcoat. Then I left. It had begun to snow. At Ranelagh Circle I recognised a heavy figure emerging from the newsagent's with English Sunday papers tucked under one arm. The Dodo! He pretended not to see me and turned quickly away, going by the wall with short, rapid, fussy steps, a furled umbrella in one gloved hand. He would not go to the hospital, only near it, to feel he was somewhere near her, but he could not bring himself to watch her dying, and he couldn't talk to me. Some intuition had warned him that she was dying that morning. I let him go. There's love for you. I too turned

away. A crosstown double-decker would take me via Appian
Way to the Dalkey or Dun Laoghaire bus stop.

I reached the hospital before eleven. The house surgeon
told me what he had to tell me. I went upstairs to sit by her
bed until she died.

When I reached the curtained bed I did not know what
might await me – a death's head, my poor mother transformed by dying into some kind of horror. A dull heavy
breathing came from behind the curtain and told me that
she was still alive, just about. I stood by the bed. A nurse
came with a chair. I sat down.

For two days death had been harrying her, drawing closer
and closer, and now it was very near. It was doing terrible
things to her; she was holding on with all her remaining
strength, mumbling with pinched-in and discoloured lips,

For me? Is it for me this time? Me?

Unmistakably it was for her; death was already stirring in
her. She had been relatively passive for two days, two days
of more or less quiet dying; now giving way to this internal
turmoil that would end it. Her spirit was now engaged;
before it had only been her body fighting with the blow, the
hard night stroke, now it was her spirit – the weary breathing
of a stubborn pilgrim ascending a penitential hill, a stony
way. A bird lost at a window.

For me? Is it this time for me?

The bridge of her nose was bruised on either side where
the useless spectacles had pinched, or it was the mark of
when she had fallen in George's Street, one windy night
when we had been out drinking hot toddies with the lame
man in Mooney's bar.

Now she was ascending a steep hill, going on at all costs,
puffing at it. It took all her strength and more but she was
obstinate, going at it, her nose pointed, my poor mother
wearily persisting, her eyes sunk, her mouth collapsed, looking bitter and deprived, attempting the last impossible hill.

Who may say what humiliations can be borne, what the
body can endure, what the mind can stand? I sat by her,

held her hand, called to her (and it was here that brother Bun entered the ward and approached diffidently), felt her pulse where the feeblest lymph fluttered and ebbed away only to come fluttering back again, as if uncertain of its welcome, the blood that had given me life. I put into her unconscious hand her own rosary beads of mother-of-pearl, listening to her hard breathing, intermittent snoring, and wished this indignity ended, her troubles over. Her cheeks sagged and filled, loose on the bone, and a little white froth or scum had accumulated at the corner of her mouth. This sac wavered, agitated by the air brought up painfully from her lungs. It soon dried out and another began to form. Each breath dragged up with such painful and persistent effort disturbed the bedclothes where she lay on her side, offering to us her final agony.

Then another followed, hard as the preceding one, harsh as the one that followed, and the little scum wavered on the dry breath issuing from collapsed lungs, torn up from deep inside her. All this interspersed with sighs such as a child might give, uncertain of what was happening. Then silence as though she were listening, harkening to something. She had begun her death. I held her stiffening hand where *rigor mortis* had already started. Her hair was damp with the terrible effort of giving up her life, as all about her the ghosts moved, whispering. A moth was burning in God's holy fire.

It had become quiet in the ward, a feeling of the Sabbath prevailed, the minute hand moved around the dial of the ward clock and the hour hand dragged itself after; time went by sadly and slowly. The nurse on duty made an entry in the Day Book and went past, disturbing the close air, her starched uniform rustling. The ward was warm and full of nuns moving about at their business silently. On the table by her bed stood a bowl of water with a white towel over it, cotton wool, a glass tumbler, a black leather Prayer Book, a priest's crucifix. She must have received Extreme Unction.

The thin gusts of snow blown against the long windows

soon melted and ran down the panes of glass, but it was close and humid in the ward. My mother was the only one dying. The gob of spittle hovered in the corner of her dry mouth and an old arthritic nun with a mushroom complexion inside her white coif came and laid a white and speckled hand on my mother's forehead and her fingers lifted her eyelid. *Leave me alone*, the hazel eye said; *I am soon leaving you.* That famous fixed stare. Her eyes were fixed on something moving within herself, something reflected there. World-weary flesh, unbend; eyes, look your last. I was offered rosary beads.

I took them in my hand but declined to kneel, for I wanted to watch her while she was still alive, so that if she opened her eyes it would be me that she would first see, as she had been the first person I had seen in my life, without even the light of intelligence to inform me it was Mumu looking down at me over the end of the cot and begging to be recognised.

But Mumu's eyes would not open again, ever in this life. The dutiful sisters were kneeling around her now saying a decade of the rosary. They went at it sing-song, a patter long learnt by heart, drifting with it, telling of the termination of another life soon to be ended, that bulk of sins (Mumu and sin did not go together) at which their prayers were pointing, prodding, urging *Sanctify! Sanctify!* as a thurible swung to and fro by a server with his mind far away – more lullaby than dirge, pleading and lamenting in high sweet voices.

Oh now, thought I, if she who so dreaded all this mumbo-jumbo were to open her eyes! They wanted to hurry her away, make all decent, change the sheets, put up the screen. *No more sensual fret*, they chanted, lost in their dream; *relieve her of her hard cross, oh Lord!* But her eyes did not fly open. The difficult breathing went on. Now it would pause, as if she were listening, harkening, then continuing as before. A heavy sigh fetched up, then another breath taken, then the subdued rattling in the throat, a snore, then another breath pushing out her cheeks, and the pitiful effort to live began anew.

Ledge by ledge she was climbing, turret by turret, looking in all the windows. *Relieve her of her sad cross,* the chorus of nuns chanted, staring at her. *Lead her to the light,* they murmured. *Take from her her hard burden! Let her have respite from her hard labour, oh Lord!* To one side of me brother Bun shifted uncomfortably, his adenoidal breath snoring discreetly.

But she was still down at the foot of the hill. Grown cynical in the face of innumerable setbacks, a deeply disappointed woman, I daresay, she would carry her cynicism and disappointments with her like banners or campaign medals for valour, into whatever region she was bound for, eyes tight shut (and here the laboured breathing faltered, as if she was following my thoughts; it carried on a little way, faltered again, slower and then, quite abruptly, stopped).

'She's going,' the old nun announced, falling forward on her knees and dashing holy water into my mother's face. They began the prayer for the dying.

It was most urgent now; the nuns raised their voices (the thurible swung faster, sending up clouds of incense), hunting my mother's wilful spirit hither and thither, trying to tell her that it was not like that, that it was not like that at all; but it was eluding them, rising up through the smoke of the incense. The snow was melting down all the long windows of the warm ward, the nuns' breaths going together as if to help her on her way. It seemed like something I had witnessed before, though performed in a manner more accomplished; this was a botched rehearsal for something that had never happened, would never happen.

And true enough the harsh and troubled breathing did begin again, hesitantly at first, uncertain of its welcome (for her spirit in anguish had just flown over the Abyss), and then resumed as determined as before, rasping and wheezing now – the obstinate effort to scale the impossible hill. The candle in her limp hand tilted at a dangerous angle, dripped candle grease on the sheet and holy water rolled down her cheeks like tears.

Nonplussed by this turn of events, the old nun came to observe, felt her pulse. The breathing was weaker but still persisting. Mother Superior made a sign and the nuns left the bedside to go about their chores as silently as they had come. Then she too followed.

I looked at my brother who raised a sigh. Then at my mother, who had only been pretending to die. Her humour had always tended to be on the grim side, rarely if ever aimed against herself. Was this another of her grim jokes? One directed against herself? She was obstinate and set in her aversions, had not anticipated much; now she was dying at her own pace and in her own way. The prayers of the nuns had not touched or even reached her and they would never reach her. She had always scoffed at nuns – their dubious piety and questionable humility, holiness; nuns and male hairdressers, barbers. Like slugs, she had said.

The pleas of those who have turned away from the world in order to pray for it – their lullaby could not touch her or reach her (drops of holy water rolled unheeded from the sunken cavities of Mumu's eyes). The candle had been snuffed out and taken from her; it would not be much longer now, this was the pause before the end.

Presently the old nun came back, watching her suspiciously, as if my mother might leap from bed and run from the ward; she felt her pulse, whispered something to the young nun who looked after my mother. Then she went to another part of the ward where a strong female voice was calling. I held her hand. It lay limply in mine, life was all but extinct there. I liked the young nun's calm countenance and unhurried ways and asked her name. She told me that she was Sister Alphonsus Ligoura, Sister of Mercy. I sensed a different sensibility; nuns with hair shorn and vanity gone were distinctly different. I had found a prayer for the dying by Cardinal Newman on a card by the glass bowl, the wadding and heavy crucifix, and asked Sister Alphonsus Ligoura if she would be kind enough to read this prayer. 'If you wish,' she whispered. She knelt down and I with her, below the mound that was Mumu dying, and she began to read it in her white voice: *And my Guardian Angel whisper peace to me*, the white Sister of Mercy read in a white voice bled of all inflexions. She finished the prayer and looked at me. 'Again please,' I said. And my mother, her face discoloured, her breath going ever slower but resigned to it at last, down at the bottom of the hill, harkened, heard the prayer whispered by the nun.

I was handing her back her copy of Hans Andersen that she had read to us: the Dote and I stricken with measles in the darkened bedroom, or out and about on a rug in summer, and Mumu, young then, dressed in a summer frock with Japanese prints, took the book in hands that were not discoloured, saying brightly, 'Enough for one day I think.'

It had a pale-blue cover and no illustrations, the dust jacket lost. Enough for one day. The tormented breathing stopped, this time for good, and she had gone upwards out of her ailing body (clutching Hans Andersen to her breast), past the unavailing prayers of the Sisters of Mercy, past the falling snow, the accumulated slush. Slowly from the corner of her mouth some pale matter flowed.

Now the nuns were back in a flurry of kneeling and relighting of the candle, the candle lit and thrust into her dead hand and the Prayer for the Dying set out after my mother.

When they had finished they blessed themselves, rose up and moved off, the old Kerry nun and another nun hid the bed with screens, I could hear them whispering behind, church gossip, technical stuff.

Inside the ward it was warm. Only my mother was cold. Outside the snow whirled away, over the pubs where she had liked to drink whiskey, out over the yacht basin and the harbour, out over Ireland's Eye. The old Kerry nun offered us a cup of tea. It seemed to be the custom; I did not want it but took it without milk or sugar and swallowed it scalding

hot. The old nun questioned us about the family. I told her
that I was married, this was brother Bun, brother C. was in
London but would be present for the funeral, and brother
D. (the Dodo) was hovering around in the vicinity. She
offered no comment on this, was small and bent and
reached only to my shoulder, had rough manners (the way
she had lifted Mumu's eyelid) but no doubt a kind heart.

'Was it your first?' she asked me.

'Yes,' I said, the tea scalding my insides.

'Ah, that's hard then. For it's worse when it's your own
poor mammy. But sure God is good and He will be good to
her, poor soul.'

'Yes,' I said.

Behind her the nuns filed silently by; the curtains blew
inward and I saw a darkness of shape as if thrown down on
the bed. I had not been able to weep. Going out, I looked
for the last time at where she lay. Her mouth had fallen
open and she was all dark and angular and stiff. When a
thing lies still, it will be still forever, is a truth that no man
can deny. Death had fixed her in this inimical pose – dark
and punished, she no longer resembled my mother. The
jaw had fallen in, the brown lisle stocking stuck out, I saw
it all before the curtain fell.

'Go on now,' the old nun said at my elbow. 'Don't be
needlessly troubling yourself. You can do nothing for us
here.'

'I suppose not,' I said.

I let the curtain drop, blotting out the face that was not
my mother's known face; that dark and monumentally stiff
figure.

'She had her wish anyway,' I said.

'And what was that?' the old nun inquired, smelling of
mould-mushroom.

'To die in Ireland,' I said.

The old Kerry nun gave me a crafty sideways look and the
hand that she offered me was almost as cold and unreceptive
as Mumu's.

l thanked her and left with brother Bun.

Outside it was cold and overcast. The snow had stopped falling. I felt some relief; pain and decay, fishing just below the surface; decay and pain, it was like leaving the dentist's following an extraction, some decay in the system had been removed. And now that it was removed one was glad to be rid of it. Something of myself had been removed with some pain and now I was free to go on without it.

The water in the harbour was still and the colour of lead, and there were the masts of the yachts bobbing on their moorings and there was the gutted church. I waited for a bus to take me back to Ballsbridge, from where I would take a taxi home.

I found the old man sleeping in his overcoat, the sink blocked with his endless tea-leaves, the electric kettle out of order, my wife and child away, no light, no fire. No matter. I made him tea and brought it to him, told him what had happened, that she was at peace, that everything that could have been done was done, that the nuns were great. He sat wringing his hands and staring at me.

All had been done and everything was over.

He had grown old in a few days, now he was an old man.

He lived in his overcoat, a gift, dreaming of summer like the flies, only emerging from winter-long hibernation to lead a summer existence hardly more purposeful than theirs, setting out each day for Hawk Cliff to join Corcoran, keep an eye on his clothes, watch him dive into the sea. He expressed a wish to see her.

'Later,' I told him. 'They said to come later. They are laying her out now.'

He stared at me in horror.

'Drink your tea, Da.'

Later on we would both go and see her; see how she was. I tried to recall some verses by the recluse Emily Dickinson; how was it they went? A death-blow is a life-blow to some?

A Death blow is a Life blow
　to Some
Who till they died, did not
　alive become—
Who had they lived, had died
　but when
They died, Vitality begun.

My peevish elder brother was nowhere to be seen, on or off the premises.

The Dodo, unknown to us, was flying south; squawking on the wing.

43

Mortuary Chapel

D ado and I, a little the worse for wear, visited the mortuary chapel after dark on the day she died. A young nurse led us to a wooden shed to the rear of St Michael's Hospital. She went ahead of us and unlocked the door and stood aside for us to enter. She had a small watch pinned to her bursting chest. We went in, my father with bowed head as if being punished; gallantry itself with the ladies as a general rule, he had nothing to say to the pretty nurse with her chestful of breasts and her robin's bold eye.

An open coffin stood on trestles to one side of the altar. We stared at what was in it: my dead mother, his dead wife, in her blue shroud. She was alone there in the silent chapel, calm and composed; nothing would ever touch her and she would never come back, dressed in the cerements of the grave. She had been a beauty in her day and now her looks had returned. I, who had a lifelong dread of touching a dead person, kissed her forehead. It was cold as winter stone. The Ice Queen received my homage icily; she was hard as granite yet gentleness glowed from her; with her beauty, her good nature had returned, her mouth was no longer bitter. The strained and worried look that she had worn for so long had gone; I had never known her, as her expression – disdainful, frigid and yet sweet – spoke to me.

No one had ever known her. The petty annoyances of her
life were over and done with – husband and sons who loved
or didn't love, couldn't love, it was all the one to her. I had
the feeling, looking at her there, so sedate and still, yet so
sweet, that one is always being observed, under constant
surveillance. Underlying theme of the overlying earth that
would presently serve as blanket; soon she too would be
anonymous as earth. She who had such a mistrustful nature
had spoken dismissively of 'cock and bull stories' and 'tissues
of lies'.

Now it was someone else who watched and guarded her,
and from under her closed eyes she still watched me. We said
our silent prayers and prepared to go. My father hesitated
between the coffin and the altar and, raising his right hand
as if addressing a living person, said, 'Goodbye now Lilly!'
saluting the stone effigy in the coffin. He went out then
with head bowed, not looking at the nurse. She locked the
door behind us. Crossing the moonlit yard we entered
the hospital again. He stopped in the corridor, and the
place was a warren of corridors, to say: 'I can't believe it.
Fifty years married and look at her there.' His voice echoed
down the corridor where an old nun dressed in white was
coming towards us.

'She was a beauty in her day, you know,' he said.

'She's a beauty now,' I said, watching the nun coming on.

'It would have been our Golden Jubilee this year,' my
father said. 'We'd have both our names in the papers. She
said she'd never live to see it, but I don't think she meant
it.'

The old nun came up and spoke to us. They all agreed
that my mother was a beauty; the Child of Mary blue shroud
suited her. The Sisters of Mercy would be going down
through the night to pray for her. Going out I tipped the
doorman half a crown.

'I'm sorry for your trouble,' he said.

It was freezing again, a cold night with the moon flying fast through white clouds, and the wind whistled down the hill from the direction of Dalkey. Across the narrow way light shone in the shop selling funeral items, wreaths and printed requiem cards, hire-purchase terms, artificial flowers in domes of glass, tributes to the dear departed – the usual forlorn objects that one seldom notices when passing by. Stained glass, blue shadows, arpeggios, funeral organ music, mental somnolence. Mother dear, goodbye!

One may hope: Never again all this agony of life. Certainly it's not supportable on a hedonistic basis; it is only supportable, if at all, when one digs down into oneself. And then? And now? Soon for her, poor dear, would begin the 'barehead life under the grass'.

Mumu would belong to the earth soon and it belong to her, and the past also, and not only her own past but all past, it was there waiting. She had existed as part of the seminal substance of the universe that is always becoming and never is, and had now disappeared into that which produced her, coming out between my grandmother's legs. Many grains of frankincense on the same altar; one falls before, one falls after, it makes no difference.

'Thou art a little soul bearing a corpse,' quoth wise old Epictetus. St Paul called the human body a seed. It was sown a natural seed; it was raised a spiritual body. Some things are hurrying into existence, others hurrying out of it, and of that which is come into existence a part (Mumu) is already extinguished. Everything is only for one day, both that which remembers and that which is remembered (I had stood with Mumu in Doran's snug in Baggot Street in my warm Menswear overcoat and thought I would never die as Mumu, Powers in hand, told me of the sweating corpse that was Joss in the morgue). Persephone protect her; and Xochipili, the Lord of Flowers.

The sad signs of approaching spring that my mother had waited and watched for were all about us; the earth hardening in April, the birds nesting, swallows on the way, soft days when her corns gave her Hell, announcing rain. She had moved about more easily then, burdened with too many clothes, the wintry load. Spring bloomed in Baggot Street.

The auguries of summer at Springfield had been the corncake grating rustily in the upper field where a hare decomposed in the well at the ring-pump and grass sprouted through the perished boards and cuckoos were calling in the Crooked Meadow. Then the mated starlings, the same pair every spring, with an oily sheen to feathers that resembled fishscales, returned to nest in the wall of the rockery between the broken limestone and corrugated-iron roof of the shed.

Kick over a stone and out come familiar grubs.

We were hardly into the steaming pub when whom did we run into but one of Dado's cronies, a man by the name of Larry Ball, with drink taken. He seemed unmoved by news of my mother's death. Hearing of my travels from my father, proud as punch, he informed me that he, bouncing ball, had sailed twice round the world.

'Ah Larry,' Dado said, ball of malt in hand, holding him with his watery blue stare, 'if she was here well Lord knows she would be laughing with us now.'

Stout and wheezing, with soiled protuberant boozer's eyes, Larry Ball was packed into a worsted grey suit. He had a blunt mottled complexion and the cloudy eyes of a cod, and sat with stout legs wide apart, mopping his brow.

Magnified prints of racing yachts lit from above showed them running before the wind; Howth, as ever, lay in sunshine. The soiled protuberant troubled eyes studied me (I could see a dull question formulating in that gudgeon's eye). So this was the artist of the family. The mournful music came from tapes behind the bar: *Sundays and Cybele.* It had been played while she was dying, while I drank gin in Mooney's and spoke to an aunt on the phone, while the snow was still falling, now it still played and she was dead. Nothing had changed in the bar. She had died on Sunday.

But who was Cybele? one of those dying and resuscitating female Mediterranean divinities who carry towers and temples on their heads?

'Ah God now, Batty, the world has changed a hell of lot since our young days,' roared Ball, looking at me with deep misgiving.

We left gasbag Ball sunken in gloom when the pub closed and bought a bottle to take home. A great deal of handshaking went on. My father was by this time in a maudlin state, inundated by the past and no one to share it with, Ball waving a meaty palm and disappearing towards the taxi rank. We went home in our own taxi, I built up the fire, brought out the bottle, put on the kettle, and my father sat before the blaze, glass in hand, his eyes watering. I have his hands, he has mine, depending on how you look at it. My wife was asleep in the front room, our child tucked up in his cot.

On the morning of the funeral I lay in bed covered in coats. Rain had fallen or was still falling. I heard a car pass on the road. The sound came clearly – the slap of wetted tyres on wetted asphalt, a savage mangling of gears at the corner and the pitch of the engine rising. It passed, and the sound died away. I heard another approaching at a dangerous speed, all out, driven by a maniac, slamming into a gear-change at the corner, the driver impatient, taking it too fast. I felt it inside me, the wet tyres shuddering at the sudden braking, the whine of the engine risen, ready to burst through the walls, scatter my thin morning sleep, pierce my eardrums, the fan-belt screeching, '*Oxte! Oxte!!* Awake!' A fearful blast of sound, like pent-up rage released in damaging blows. I was tightened up, waiting for an accident to happen.

Then something immense and airborne almost lifted the roof off the house. I saw its shadow blunder across the wall, onto the cornice, and whip away as the whole house shuddered. It went on into silence. The roots of my hair stood up, for it wasn't any car driven by a lunatic or a jet airliner flying too low through cloud, but her own unhappy spirit that had plunged past, looking for Hell or Purgatory, before disappearing for good and all; and I recalled the dream, the spectral bomber.

My father had woken and was calling for us to rise. Quinn's black funeral limousine was coming at nine sharp. My wife would come with us, a friend would look after our child. We followed the hearse to Glasthule Church; it was lowsprung, packed with flowers, the lights on inside illuminating the coffin, looking almost festive, so that people stopped to stare at it going by. That was the evening before, the Removal; this would be her last journey among the living.

After the Requiem Mass we rode in high style behind a liveried chauffeur to Deans Grange Cemetery, following the flower-laden hearse. Out of the main traffic it picked up speed, threading its way through the lanes. There were other hearses there before us and groups of mourners standing before plots or walking here and there in the barren fields of the dead. We were directed to the wrong grave, under a yew. Four rough fellows, grave-diggers in wellington boots, came stumbling across, waving their hats and calling out, 'Higgins! Higgins!'

The open grave was on its own away from the congestion of headstones and crosses (as if in deference to her claustrophobia) and deep – eight feet of opened earth, livid clay, a plot in semiperpetuity. The brand-new coffin would not be brand-new for long, down there in the dampness of earth. It was cold, a cold exposed place, with groups of dark-clothed figures gathered around open graves or moving away. There was snow on Three Rock Mountain. Few, as she had predicted, were there to mourn her. The Dodo was not present; Swift had not attended Stella's funeral, the woman who may or may not have been his wife; and Wilde had refused to leave prison to see his dying mother. The Dodo, holding fast to his own inexorable nature, had kept away. One may assume that all three had their different reasons.

Fearing a nervous breakdown, the Dodo wrote in his neat and precise hand, he had thought it best to leave immediately after the Requiem Mass, and I did not see him again. O be thou damn'd, execrable dogge!

Thereafter, per brother Bun, he wintered in Tasmania, home of the waddling duck-billed platypus (*Orinthorhynchus paradoxus*) and Tasmanian devil on that remote island off the end of Oz in the Tasman Sea at the extreme rim of the globe; returning to Largs in Scotland each spring for the golf (more shanking and hooking and missed putts and blue language, no doubt). The Dodo returned home before the swallows dared.

Mumu had died on Sunday 16th October 1966 in St Cecilia's Ward of St Michael's Hospital in Dun Laoghaire, formerly Kingstown, and was buried on 20th October in Deans Grange Cemetery outside Dublin. There were many buried there who had gone before her. She was the first of us to go.

44

Sedna

It was said of Henry Cavendish the famous scientist that he had probably uttered fewer words in the course of his life than any man who lived for fourscore years and ten. No doubt he had his own reason for being silent (as Crusoe on his island hidden behind his palisade and terrified of encountering savages), immersed in his work. The Dodo too had been immersed in his studies when qualifying to be a quantity surveyor, in his lifelong silence, his separateness, that long intransigence – even Crusoe had.

Certainly he was most retiring and reticent; you wouldn't meet a quieter fellow outside an enclosed order of monks. He had addressed to me his brother, not more than a hundred words in his entire life; not that I saw much of him after the time in Kinlen Road and my stay in Clonskeagh Fever Hospital where malnutrition and scarlet fever had laid me low.

Our paths had not crossed in ten or more years when he came down from Scotland for his mother's funeral. Like the war that had he had missed, the combat missions he had not flown by night, so with Mumu's funeral; he came as if to attend, but in the event did not, could not face it, but turned aside. He hadn't anticipated the coffin lid being off and when invited (silently) by one of the mutes to pay his

last respects, he had turned away, gone out into the yard,
and paced about, troubled.

He had not changed, merely put on weight, grown into
a corpulent middle-aged man still awkward on his feet, a
Buddha wobbling on an insecure base, moving on convex
soles like a penguin, the creature that flies in its sleep, or a
toddler learning to walk. He was still keeping his distance,
keeping his trap shut, addicted as ever to prolonged Trappist
silences interspersed with heavy sighs and sorry eructations
of wind in his gullet, as though he were somewhere else,
thinking of something else. I had the unsettling impression
that he was far away, sipping his gin and tonic with a shadowy
version of myself, though we stood side by side in Mooney's
bar, listening to *Sundays and Cybele*, silent as ever. I had
nothing to say to him. But oh hadn't he such a lovely smile,
if he cared to use it. Not that he, so sparing of his benevol-
ence within the family, had ever cared to use it on me.

His head wobbled as if loose on an insecure base (Buddha
nodding), a Black Baby bowing on its plinth on receiving a
penny for the Foreign Mission and the saving of heathens.

When had he begun to go all silent? Was he a silent boy
already at Killashee? I had never actually touched him; for
you would no more touch the Dodo or shake his hand
then you would pet a python. He was broody and inaccess-
ible; that unapproachableness was his deepest lair, his high
nest or Secret Place (a child's cubbyhole), his covenant with
himself.

What could I say to him, after the long silence of those
years? 'Once I was set upon by two surly louts in a bar in
Drim. They seemed to think that I was an undercover Brit
agent sent into Connemara, drinking bottled Crusaders in
the heartlands of the Provos. They frisked me, claiming to
be Provos. What do you say to that?'

Silence. The head wobbled, the ghost of a smile quivered
at the corner of the thin lips. He continued to sip gin. Once
had I not asked him for a loan of a thousand pounds (Irish).
I needed the return air-fare to Texas. I wanted a stake to

take me to Austin for one semester at the University. But did I, by any chance, get it? No. Had he even answered my letter? No. Would I mention that here? No. Would I ever in my heart of hearts find forgiveness? No.

Brother dear, I could have said, laying a placating hand on his arm, hear me now. Never had I felt less welcome than in that faraway bar on the western seaboard on that drenched peninsula where all old Irish grievances fester. I was drinking bottled Crusaders with an authentic Englishman, an ex-British Army Tank Corps man by the name of Foss. They took us for a couple of Englishmen and gave us the hard eye. Maybe they *were* armed at that, maybe they had a mind to shoot us. Who can say? The youth of Drim took home good money from the Japanese canning factory and reeled into the bar already high on potcheen.

'Provos,' I told them, 'I spit in your eye.'

Taken aback, the blood-brothers-in-arms (James Joyce's 'sanguinivorous bugaboos') exchanged swift eye-messages before beating a retreat to the far end of the bar where they put their heads together to mumble their mouths in the Gaelic.

Were they proposing to shoot us out of hand? Our boon companion, the fair Contessa Rosita (who had a smattering of the old tongue), now threw discretion to the winds, her dander up. She marched down the length of the bar with her hair on end to formally accost them.

'I know what you're saying about us, you fuckers, and I don't much care for your tone. If you want to make something of it just follow me!'

Over to the door she marched, flung it open on the wild black night without, daring either of the bold boyos to step outside with her. The lads looked shifty and went all silent. Outside! No thanks.

They backed down. Johnny O'Toole said later that they were pirates; but how was one to know? Maybe they were armed and high on potcheen before they came in. What do you think brother-of-mine?

He folded his wings, heaved a heavy sigh, voided a few knotty evil-smelling turds, held his silence, by way of response.

Silence (the deep silence of incertitude). The Dodo continued musing, staring into his gin with a reflective half-smile graven on his thin lips. He would slip away before the funeral cortège got moving.

We had somehow assumed that he was in the second hired funeral car *en route* to Deans Grange Cemetery, when in fact he was already on his way to Dublin Airport. Oh he was a strange fish: none stranger in our waters. Communication with the Dodo was like trying to fathom a new and unpredictable chess opponent; the hidden strategies would reveal themselves in time.

That voice of his – when it came, propelled into reluctant speech – was faint and mournful as the distant fog-horn mooing out in the bay, with neither lung-power nor will-power behind it. He was a strange one.

The Dodo had grown stouter and older, wore a good-quality suit on his back, and walked – or rather rolled – as I had remembered from Springfield days, the path by the beech hedge; awkward child or shackled somnambulist or sleep-walking penguin tottering on the cement ramp at the Dublin Zoo.

A great Anglophile, he followed the cricket tests and rugby internationals with the closest interest, kept meticulous records, rugby programmes from Lansdowne Road, cricket score cards from Phoenix Park, Trinity College and Rathmines, sets of Wisdens. He had a room for his files and records which he kept locked. The shelves reached from floor to ceiling, the files went back ten or more years, the place stank of Jeyes Fluid.

After the moves from Springfield to Greystones, to Dalkey, and then the nadir, the Haigh Terrace garden flat, a damp underground warren, the files were dumped in tea-chests where the contents went mouldy on the damp tiles. One

day I dragged them into the garden, doused them in petrol
and set fire to the lot – saving one diary from the bonfire.

It was bound in bottle-green leather, the dark green of
the old corked Guinness bottles and also the green of the
smelling-salts bottle which Mumu kept to hand; there was a
loop for a slim pencil that was missing. The *School Boy's
Notebook* compiled by Marc Ceppi for the year 1934, contained much useful information and 'many tables helpful
for his work and play', The author of *French Lessons on the
Direct Method* had brought out a list of Sovereigns on
the English throne – a stale breath of the past – a table of
Latin, French and Greek verbs, some 'strong' German verbs,
mensuration formulae, a handy table of logarithms, a list of
possible careers in the Colonial Service and Indian Police,
or anywhere in his Majesty's armed services spread through-
out the world.

Since leaving CWC in 1937 the Dodo had subscribed to
the college annual. It hadn't changed its format or editorial
policy in the intervening years. The same smooth-faced
Imperators and Prefects gazed complacently at some goal
out there in the real world of Law and Finance and Engin-
eering and Science and Shell Oil.

It was typical of the Dodo, given his withdrawn and evasive
nature, that he didn't subscribe directly but sent a postal
order to Mumu towards the end of each summer to buy it
at Smyth's on Stephen's Green. I open a page at random:

August 9, 1934, Thursday.
Woke up at 6.30 & roused Ma and A. & went to look for
mushrooms in the field opposite. Got a good few at first. Got
tin can from lodge people after. I brought some to Mrs Coyle
(in bed).
August 11, Saturday.
Half Quarter Day. Cardinal Newman d. 1890. Hammond 302
not out. Very hot.

The long field was still damp with dew at six-thirty in the
morning of 9th August 1934, sparkling with light. Among

toadstools, thistles, cowpats, spider-webs sagged on the tus-
socky grass, going with a checking motion in the breeze,
throwing off drops of moisture and lightness. White pupae
were hidden in the still centres of grasshopper cocoons.
Mushrooms, counterfeit fairy-rings, and the sun shining over
the river; the resurrection of the body! It was the twelfth
anniversary of the Battle of Liège and two days before the
fortieth anniversary of the death of Cardinal Newman, when
the three of us went out looking for mushrooms, Mumu
aged forty-two, the Dodo sixteen and I seven years old,
walking to and fro amid thistles in Mangan's field bounded
on four sides by walls, with Killadoon wood facing the Charter School. I remember the dewy field and the search for
mushrooms; spears of grass shone, puffballs went sailing
downwind, we trod in liquid cowshit.

We had come in by a five-barred gate near Brady's corner,
the gallant Dodo throwing it open for Mumu to walk
through, saying 'Thank you, Desmond.' Was he not the
perfect gent in his purple cricket XI blazer?

Oh he was. Yes he was.

Our No. 8 went bowling merrily downhill at a good lick by
Dun Laoghaire harbour and out by the Top Hat Ballroom
and the pond and bandstand at Blackrock Park heading for
Rock Road and Booterstown. All the windows were thrown
open on the lower deck and some kids from the Coombe
were singing glees. A strange whitish emulsion of afternoon
light filled the lower deck that had become a fish tank where
sprats darted; the kids had stopped chewing bananas and
were in constant movement, pulling at the seats, looking
out the windows, and their brazen mothers had got them
quiet and now they sang glees in high sweet voices. The
poor of Dublin had little enough to sing about, but they
sang glees. The sour whang of the unwashed came from
them, returning home after a day at the sea, at Bullock
Harbour or White Rock, and nothing could diminish their
high spirits.

So those were the songs of praise sung at your passing: *Sundays and Cybele* and glees. You could not be disappointed any more. Your final presence – leaden, serene and descending – had intimated: *Take heed of what you see, my son; for as you see me now so shall you one day be*.

You had changed, become cold and austere, become Sedna the Earth Mother who lives under the ice. White birds flew to unknown coasts over your head and the Aurora Borealis danced in the sky. But you saw and heard nothing but the roaring in your ears, down among the walrus herds and the seal herds and the big fish; you yourself had become one with the deep fish, you *were* a deep fish; half-fish, half-human, my little soapstone mother. We had buried you on a grey autumn day, slightly head-first (you were always impetuous), dropped a framework of wreaths on top and left it at that, no thumping of clay on the coffin-lid. Not many attended your last obsequies. It was almost nice to be going to earth before the winter. The grave, *das Grab*, in the old Gaelic dispensation it was The Dark School. You were reduced – no, refined – to that; you had learnt to prop up the earth with a stone. Hands long still in the grave . . . oh look at the clouds!

Farsoonerite Fears, Preverbal Chaos, Undertow of Time, the Mulligrubs

'To return to childhood haunts is to retreat into a land which has since become unreal and hermetically disturbing; a paler shade of grey prevails there.'

Ronda Gorge & Other Precipices, (1989)

i

The sullen art of fiction-writing can be a harrowing procedure; an inspired form of pillaging. The writer has never scrupled to beg, borrow or steal from other sources, languages and times when occasion seemed to demand it; as I have had to 'borrow' money from my father, as my three sons borrowed from me in turn – the commodious *vicus* of recirculation that keeps the world turning.

'Borrow' may be a misnomer; say rather, put to better use, refined and improved out of all recognition. Both *Balcony of Europe* (1972) and *Scenes from a Receding Past* (1977) are out of print, and will remain so in my lifetime. I have freely pillaged from both for sections of this present work – bold Robin Crusoe ferrying booty from the two wrecks.

The transported elements of these 'liftings' now serve different purposes – as Crusoe had to cut down a great hardwood tree to make a plank – so too the castaway's necessities when conveyed within the stockade contrived a cave-dwelling from the side of a hill.

They have become my own stories again.

In an ingenious technique of survival Crusoe had to multiply whatever meagre resources lay to hand, *multiply himself* – in direct and open disobedience to his father's wishes, always working against the well-intentioned paternal advice to stay at home – and would be transformed into a fully manned and armed encampment if the dancing savages ever returned in greater numbers to smoke him out. Significantly the first word he teaches his man Friday, in the command structure of language is . . . 'Master'. Me Master, you slave. Carping reviewers, those journeymen ever hasty in their judgements and not too prone to split hairs, have objected to the prevalence of lists in the Higgins *oeuvre*, still emerging and changing, which they took at best to be an indulgence and at worst as a poor imitation of James Joyce's worst excesses (Lestrygonians; organ: Esophagus. Technique: Peristaltic). But hold your hearses, carpers.

Lists or catalogues of proper names can be ambiguous – and sinister – as processions, be they military, religious, funeral or Klu Klux Klansmen burning effigies by night, preparatory to hanging some unfortunate next day. Eudora Welty, the Natchez Trace yarnspinner, instanced the Pied Piper of Hamelin luring the children into a cavern that opened and closed on them. I took the notion of lists from Rabelais, via Urquhart two centuries before James Joyce. Crusoe was obliged to keep lists in his head, ink being in short supply on the island. A chronology, arbitrary as our evolving history, introduces Ur-Provos into Connemara somewhat prematurely; logically they were still merely a misty, reflective gleam in the eyes of their fond parents. The sap risen in the tree-to-be, flies astir in the Irish ointment, gangrene growing in the wound.

Now at the risk of spoiling old work for new readers, it must be admitted that the four apathetic spinsters of *Langrishe, Go Down* (1966) were my brothers and myself in drag, subjected to a sea-change and all the names altered except the dog's. The real (once living) Langrishe sisters were a pair of prim spinsters who occupied Springfield before old Mrs Warren. Rumour – the greatest of all whores – had it that they were partial to a drop and had to be helped up the front steps and possibly tucked into bed by the yardman who acted as postillion, on returning home inebriated from social calls and, who knows, uncertain of their whereabouts, (as at public readings I myself have sometimes been introduced as the renowned author of *Langrishe County Down*). Horses for courses.

As a spell or curse might be cast or hurled in a fairy tale, the four old biddies living in the country have, hey presto, become the four-fold mystery of myself and three longlost brothers. (Joyce thought that a brother was 'as easily forgotten as an umbrella'.) For the purpose of this bogus autobiography, bogus as all honest autobiographics must be, I have changed them back into my own brothers again, nettle-shirts and all. Wasn't it Orwell's contention that autobiography is only to be trusted when it reveals something disgraceful? I have attempted, by stealth, to discover the snake in the garden.

I am writing of a time of Aladdin oil-lamps when all lay in darkness outside the charmed family circle; of the time before television, before bicycles had to be chained up; so much has changed within one lifetime. I was hoping to catch some lost cadences of my mother's voice – an echo reaching back into the previous century, to the voice of my maternal grandmother; into the true darkness before my time.

ii

All subject peoples must deem their natures to be – however obscurely – biologically inferior. All Paddies are patsies at

heart. This assumed base inheritance induces doubts as to
the cast of one's countenance and produces a characteristi-
cally uneasy stance before superiors who now encounter the
shifty eye, the cringing look and evasive response. Doubts
as to one's exact whereabouts and precise *raison d'être* for
occupying (polluting) that particular spot, must linger in
the breast. Why that particular space in that particular time
and why me? And all further progress impeded by certain
distinct doubts as to the rights (disputed rights) to be there
in the first place, even if under the most adverse circumstances and restricting conditions imaginable; a set of galling
tallies and intolerable limitations guaranteed to produce
stasis; the haven (purely Irish) of exquisite inertia.

Accidie was the disease of monks, a lay version (as a long
wet winter produces slugs and weeds) being the mulligrubs
– the celebrated Celtic shiftlessness or civic inertia.

Joyce's term for such negative capability was 'farsooner-
ite', in the sense of copious alternatives, all negative. I'd-
sooner-do-this than that, I'd-sooner-be-there than here, the
Irish way of prevarication.*

Neville Chamberlain's disastrous foreign policy of
appeasement to Hitler was decoded as 'umbrology'; a neat
neologism for the act of nervously fiddling with a rolled
gamp while taking umbrage; prevaricating diplomacy,
dithering.

The imagination of a people long oppressed tends to
produce, down the ever-narrowing lanes of possibility, curious and wayward simulacra, shadowy substances, deceptive
substitutes – the 'hoax that jokes bilked', in Finneganese.
All our hopes and fears are joined together in an inexplicable way, our weaknesses with our strengths. The Celtic

* The Duce had snorted like a stallion when Harold Nicolson
remarked (diplomatically, disarmingly) that rearmament no more produced war than umbrellas produced rain. But beyond the Brenner the
Führer entertained other ideas.

imagination was *bestowed* upon us by centuries of occupation. Bite, aginbite! Sting, inwit, sting!

Natures wrung by obscure abstract hatreds must come by the most devious ways to understanding, if needs be via mayhem (with us almost a family affair), and all in the name of thwarted love.

As a pale shadow cast in weak sunlight, fear has always been my constant companion. Fear, the basis of all nastiness. The lengthening shadows of King Billy (pronounced bully) and his henchmen, the bounders and bouncers, hovered over my cot.

Prototypal Irish hospitality with its compulsive amiability, the cottage as open house, a place for quarrels to be settled as vociferously as possible, the clamorous argument fairly bawled out, is highly suspect. Such twisted pseudo-liberality must indicate something other than mere friendliness; it suggests fear and uncertainty. A hundred thousand welcomes is excessive, in all conscience; *Cead mile failte* is an awkward formulation, more an attempt to put the visitor at his ease. For the giver knows right well that there is almost nothing to offer, the larder bare.

'*Mi casa es su casa*' say the open-hearted Spaniards a little speciously, an old grandeur still duplicated in the stilted formality of their epistolary style. My house is your house; but one was not supposed to take this offer too literally. The over-generous host, fallen on hard times, begs the favour that the guest overlook this temporary poverty. The good heart must stand as collateral against the empty larder. The giving hand would never waver, at least theoretically; convention would have it so.

It is a beautiful form of courtesy. The true civility is to be generous with what you haven't got. King Ferdinand and Queen Isabella spent years on horseback campaigning against the Moriscos; they had no home to go to, it having been taken away from them by Bobadilla. The Spanish royals were poor as church mice. They had started the fashion of offering the freedom of their house, quite forgetting that they had lost it and had no royal largesse to offer; all that remained was Spanish *dignidad*. The Spanish and the Irish, with miserable histories not too dissimilar, are much alike in their fervent phobias about open homes and giving hands that must never waver. The fear and uncertainty that underlie such token hospitality is an Irish Catholic neurosis which can be detected behind the wish to please so evident in the works of 'Frank O'Connor' (a Cork civil servant by the name of Michael O'Donovan), the Monaghan bogman Kavanagh and in the broth of a Borstal Boy himself; here again the craven urge to please, to be amusing at all costs. Behan of course carried the notion of the Stage Irishman to its logical conclusion; legless incoherence and wild abuse terminating in fits of projectile vomiting.

The Stage Irishman, the butt of all butts, represents the nadir of the above stasis in a petrified form; a sort of Irish Aunt Sally, a sorry figure in the stocks, a bad joke.

iii

I was ever a prey to ogres and demons.

In that cold echoing vault of a Georgian mansion, every room creaking and groaning upstairs all winter in storms of wind and rain, they were threatening to come down the chimney, drop into the freezing nursery where my young brother and I lay shivering: to fall upon us as their meat, their allotted prey and gobble us both up. Huffing and puffing and covered in soot they had us at their mercy, Dado having gone off boozing with the Bogey Man who lived in the cellar with the arrowheads and empty wine bottles gone mouldy; Mumu having run off with a soldier.

The roof demons were pastmasters of disguise and transformation and could transform themselves at will into many kinds of horrors, now reduced to the size of toads or eels to force themselves down our throats or by puffing themselves up, fill the room as elephants or elks.

Liebnitz has most ingeniously suggested that the function

of monsters is to help us recognise the beauty of the normal. To learn is to submit to have something done to one. Everything is already known, provided you know where to look for it. Prejudice is a state of mind brought on by experience. Or, if you wish, 'common sense is the deposit of prejudice laid down in the mind before the age of eighteen' (Einstein *dixit*); distance being the perquisite of happiness. One can only love one's neighbour at a safe distance, *pace* one of the Karamazov brothers.

Perhaps every child's animistic view of the unknown world which they unaccompanied must enter fearfully, is the truest view of our world and the cosmos at large which we are likely to be vouchsafed?

Just because that world-view is so circumscribed by a desperate and anxious love and need for mother and assured home; *just because* it is so saturated with fear lest something (a slithery demon! a goggle-eyed ogress!!) or some dark enemy come swiftly to snatch it all away; *just because* so threatened, might not it be all true?

Even if it is, as it must be, fear-ridden as the morning noon and night of Prehistoric Man fairly gibbering with terror and afraid of every step he takes and – most alarming of all – with a name for nothing. Existing perpetually in that preverbal chaos, in the limitless darkness of nameless fear (the Earth unnamed!). Earth as the unknown, the nameless ground he stumbles across; with his timid will and perception stalked by another Unknown that shadows him, continues to multiply itself, never defining him – it (the Other) the arch-enemy, a dark hole, a Nothing where an incalculable Time runs away (look, no hands!) from him or drags him down, pulls him under.

All this must the child suffer.

What year of storm saw a gravid speckled cow dead a day or two, with stiff uplifted legs and stillborn calf half-emerged from under its tail in a mess of blue guts, killed by fright

when struck by lightning near Sadlier's shop that sold harness parts there by the bridge?

A river flows through the village; an old humpbacked
stone bridge bisects it, a five-arch stone bridge of pictur-
esque Irish antiquity.

A ford of stepping-stones led across there before the
bridge was built and there is another by Castletown estate
on the road to Leixlip. In lawns sloping down to the Liffey
the cock pheasants strut with gorgeous tails erect, cocks of
all walks. A rare breed of black rabbit colonised the river
bank and grazed there where the cock pheasant and its
mate patrolled as masters of all they surveyed. The narrow
gravel avenue led to the Batty Langley Lodge, a loony-look-
ing artifice, a consternation of singular shapes as though
her Ladyship had taken leave of her senses or had caused
it (the peculiar-looking gate-lodge) to be erected both as
charming whimsy and overt threat. With Wonderful Barn
and Conolly's Folly these large and ostentatious monuments
stood as souvenirs with clout and undoubted cachet, casting
their rapacious shadows.

Every race to its own wrestling.

No matter how miserable its history, every race on earth
sees itself, fitly and properly, as exemplar of the entire
human species, its prototype and paradigm; the *mere Irish*
being no exception. An English Pope on the Vatican throne
had granted an English King sovereignty over the poor little
magic nation dim of mind called Ireland for short, so oft
short-changed and cheated; and the Second Henry gave it
to Strongbow who having portioned it off, handed Kildare
(follies, ruins, rich grazing and all) over to Adam of Hereford, the Norman knight who had brought Kildare to heel
– ground Celbridge under his spurred boot, dug in the
rowels. Thomas de Hereford built the Corn and Tuck Mill
of Kildrought early in the thirteenth century and his new
tenants, walking as if on eggs, brought corn to be ground
and wool to be woven and got the place going.

In 1202 Adam de Hereford founded St Wolstan's monastery; and so the community and the village began to develop around the church, the castle, the mill.

Many townlands in the Celbridge area owe their present names to prominent Norman lords and knights who had settled there. Oldtown and Newtown, Parsonstown and Griffinrath, Posseckstown and Barberstown with Simmonstown, to name but these. In Ireland, go where you will, you are walking into the past. Stone effigies hunched up in the niches of Catholic graveyards are silent representatives from that past; the long-dead ones staring back at the living with round shocked afflicted stone eyes.

An awkward squad of soldiers in mould-green baggy uniforms fired a volley over the freshly dug grave of some brave patriot at Donycomper where I stood by a cypress tree that wept in the rain. Nurse O'Reilly stood near, her face darkly flushed.

Less than ninety years before I was born the bog people of old Kildare were reduced to living underground in the bog itself, from whence the carters with their turf-carts and small donkeys carried loads off to distant Dublin, and came back asleep in their empty carts. To the mid-nineteenth century the bog people of Kildare were living at a bare subsistence level, poorer than the nomad tribes of northern Norway. The Irish peasantry knew hardship as they knew their bogs, they were intimately acquainted with both, being residents of sod-hovels on the very bog itself. The Stoics and the Romans after them believed in signs and omens, unable to envision a world without cruelty and inequality.

The Anglo-Normans of Kildare planted as Agronomist Soldiers and builders of castles, constituted a hard-headed fighting stock not too given to hair-splitting or abstract thought, were content enough to live out their lives on confiscated lands, behind high estate walls protected by broken shards of bottle-glass, hidden away behind masking ambuscades of 'Protestant beech', an enclave within an enclave. In the secret recesses of their inherited estates they asked each other: 'Are not the requirements of the rich greater than those of the poor?' Not hearing the forlorn echo: 'Aroo adin, Maaaster? Havoo nara crust for us?'

All hidden and secluded places pleased me. Behind old Mrs Henry's voluminous warm petticoats, where reaching back she could secure me and press me to her, for I was only skin and bone. Or behind the mangle under the sheila-maid where the cats made their stinks, or in the orchard or in the shrubbery, the attics or stables, or in the plantation where I could keep the house under close scrutiny and watch the comings and goings in and out – the Bowsy Murray smelling of entrails and carrion cranking up the avenue on his butcher's bike, a sack thrown across his shoulders and an old weather-beaten hat clamped down on his head, arriving punctually with the Saturday roast, a bloody side of beef wrapped in yesterday's *Evening Mail*, Mumu watching him closely from her niche in the bedroom window.

We cannot allow our hopes to rise too much, since history has branded us as malcontents. Flat unaccented blurred speech distinguishes the Joe Soaps of hereabouts from those of, say, the Kingdom of Kerry, whose strong reflexive diph-thongs have powerful Gaelic roots.

All my life have I had vivid and disturbing dreams of Springfield; dreams disturbing as nightmares pulling me down. Perhaps it was the memory of the fragile front door thin as cardboard set into the portentous porch with its stained glass – a door that any determined lawless boot could kick in, which caused the ever-circling ever-returning revenant such uneasiness?

Duties and land taxes and labour levies were anathema to him (Dado) who hid in the long orchard grass when the Taxman called every five years or so from Dublin. Major Brookes of Pickering Forest hid in a bush on his own front avenue, where our land steward Tommy Flynn surprised him when calling with a spayed collie bitch for her Ladyship. He saw the curl of smoke rise from the bush before the carriage sweep and, looking in, saw the Major complacently smoking his pipe.

'Glory beta God,' said Flynn, 'what are yew doin' adin the bush, Major?' By way of response the Major only laid a finger to his lips, admonishing silence. Mum was the word. The Taxman was about.

'The great body of the people were of pastoral habits,' wrote Samuel Lewis. 'A hearty, affectionate, loyal race of men fresh from nature's hand; uncommon masters of the art of overcoming difficulties by contrivances.'

In 1980, on my return from years in London, the Irish population register had shown an increase for the first time since 1841 or just prior to the last (and worst) Famine when the uncommon masters of overcoming difficulties were reduced to eating not only their own dogs but their own dead, with gallows-meat cut down after a public hanging, of which there was no scarcity. This had become their ordinary, as testified by Lecky the historian and poet Spenser, no friend of Ireland. The Irish were actually living in Ireland again; the outflow of immigration had ceased, for the time being.

But best of all was to climb the high demesne wall and drop silently down into Killadoon wood with the Keegans and their dogs and follow the path by the pond to the river, trespassing through Clements's land and now forninst us a private very Protestant river owndid by those unseen damnably peculiar ones; a brown stream dangerously deep-swirling by with treacherous currents in which poor Catholics like us, none of whom could swim a stroke, would surely drown. Aroo in din? Aroo dare?

It was a thoroughly Protestant stretch of river there by the bend with the disused cemetery hidden under weeds and the back lodge with suspicious Proddy lodge-keepers ever alert and ready to expel Catholic trespassers from these hallowed precincts; as once a haggish virago had erupted from the lodge, screeching, 'Git outa death gordon dis

minute!' at us innocently gathering walnuts under the great
walnut tree.

The river became if possible even more Protestant as it
progressed, flowing by Mulligan's house opposite Castletown
gates by Christ Church on the site of the old kennels for
Tom Conolly's pack of hounds brought over from England.
The 'silly tiresome boy' had been the son of the Earl of
Stafford, and had contrived to keep the 1798 insurrection
out of Celbridge, as he might have kept out the plague,
prevented it from spreading.

Hereabouts the river poured in a red flood most purpose-
fully through the Anglo-Saxon lands, flowing dark brown
with its sunken weeds streaming bold as battle standards,
while along the peaceful banks the pheasants still strutted,
while the black rabbits of unique breed scuttled into their
burrows; until emerging again as a Catholic river on the far
side of St Wolstan's in Dongan's land once more, full of
abandoned things bloated by long submersion, bicycle
frames and water-logged boxes for Irel coffee and parts of
beds, a sorry-looking horse skull and a broken sofa; to flow
on towards Lucan and the Strawberry Beds and Harold's
Cross greyhound track at Chapelizod and then Guinness's
brewery with a line of barges tied up on the quayside with
wooden barrels being stowed on deck by strong men in
their short-sleeves; and then under all the bridges, to go out
stinking horribly of diarrhoea past the Customs House and
Ringsend, to empty itself copiously into the bay, a drunkard
running to vomit up intemperance.

I'd watched it start out at Straffan, before the dams at
Golden Falls and Poulaphuca stopped the flooding, as a
shallow narrow but clean Catholic stream flowing sedately
through the Pale with its pinkeen and small pollock and
gudgeon and trout, flowing through Protestant lands and
changing colour as it went, entering the confiscated estates
and flushing darkly as if thoroughly embarrassed as it
advanced with a rush of blood to the face but still all swelling

with pomposity as it (no longer 'she') rounded a bend shat into by cattle, until it flowed between the embankments beyond Kingsbridge Station, now Heuston, to emerge again as an unclean Catholic river, to go and discharge itself – now dark as cascara or porter – most frothily into the choppy waters of the bay.

From the yew tree the Dote and I watched the comings and goings in the garden from our high platform of barn doors lashed together as a raft and provisioned Crusoewise with Rolos and apples and armed with Daisy air-rifles, repeaters. To unwelcome callers (i.e., all callers) we were simply Not at Home.

With us in our treehouse we had a cat to devour the kill; the poor missel thrush dropped at point-blank range. We were dead-eye-dicks like 'Red' Connors, legendary rifleman of the Bar B-Q ranch with Hopalong Cassidy and Mesquite Jenkins, roisterers of the bunkhouse and the corral, relishing our grits and side-meats and beans and coffee around a camp-fire out on the prairie or the range under the stars, hearing coyotes.

Strangers walked about the deserted garden and orchard, passed into the rockery, sampling pears and plums, mystified as to our whereabouts. My father was that strange hop-o'-my-thumb or how-do-you-do; an absentee landlord *permanently in residence.*

I myself never wished to leave the big garden with its interleading paths under the rustic arbours and rustling palm trees, passing the cracked sundial and tennis-court with wormcasts on wet days (of which there were so many) and the hedgehogs in summer, those strange slow-moving creatures with the faces of bats creeping out of hibernation in the beech hedge; never wished to leave the walled rockery where the monogamous starlings returned to their wall-nest every summer. A place of teeming bees and wasps and the aromatic odours of the tomato plants in the greenhouse; all of that never-to-be-relinquished world.

But how futile now to affect to be that other gormless imbecile that was me once, younger than my own grand-children (Paris, Yanika, Oscar Santi) today; or to pretend that the hand which writes so confidently in its late sixties can be the selfsame hand that wrote with such uncertainty at six.

I am a different person now. The me then and the me now, co-existent in two such entirely different worlds, are two entirely different beings.

Deans Grange Cemetery
Blackrock, Co. Dublin

Grave No: 53–V3, St Brigid
Lillian Higgins, age 74, 5 Haigh Terrace, Dun Laoghaire
died 16th January 1966.
Bartholomew Higgins, age 74, 11 Springhill Park, Killiney
died 28th September 1969.

These are the only two interments in this grave.